Pan-Arabism
and Arab Nationalism

About the Book and Editor

This text focuses on the history of and prospects for Arab unity—an issue of critical importance to students and scholars of Middle East politics and culture. Dr. Farah combines analysis of valuable survey research with historical and theoretical works by leading Arab and Western scholars that interpret the current debate on the status of Pan-Arabism and its future role in the Arab world.

The contributors discuss the relationship between Pan-Arabism and individual state nationalism and explore the impact close ties between Arab nationalism and Islam have had on Arab unification efforts. Opposing views of Palestinian nationalism as both a unifying and disruptive force in the Arab world are also presented. Additional chapters discuss the importance of Arab identity among states struggling with the double challenges of internal division and external pressures and examine the waning of Pan-Arabism in the face of emerging "Western-style" states.

This study of the Arab nationalist movement will be useful in courses on the Middle East and North Africa. It will also be of value to scholars, general readers, and specialists in their efforts to understand the sources and nature of conflict in the modern Arab world.

Tawfic E. Farah is the editor of the *Journal of Arab Affairs* and president of the Middle East Research Group, Inc. He edited *Political Behavior in the Arab States* (Westview, 1983) and coauthored *Survey Research in the Arab World* (Westview, 1985).

For Arne J. Nixon,
a friend who never blinks

Pan-Arabism
and Arab Nationalism
The Continuing Debate

edited by Tawfic E. Farah

Foreword by James A. Bill

Westview Press / Boulder and London

Copyright © 1987 by Westview Press, Inc.

Published in 1987 in the United States of America by Westview Press, Inc.; Frederick A. Praeger, Publisher; 5500 Central Avenue, Boulder, Colorado 80301

Library of Congress Cataloging-in-Publication Data
Pan-Arabism and Arab nationalism.
   Bibliography: p.
   Includes index.
   1. Panarabism.   2. Nationalism—Arab countries.
3. Arab countries—Politics and government—1945–
I. Farah, Tawfic.
DS63.6.P36 1987   320.5′4′09174927   86-22366
ISBN 0-8133-0378-8 (alk. paper)
ISBN 0-8133-0377-X (pbk.: alk. paper)

Printed and bound in the United States of America

The paper used in this publication meets the requirements of the American National Standard for Permanence of Paper for Printed Library Materials Z39.48-1984.

10   9   8   7   6   5   4   3   2   1

Contents

Foreword

The Arab world today slowly explodes from within while the super-powers with their technological superiority apply relentless pressure, thereby fueling and feeding the centrifugal social forces that lay imbedded in the Arab experience. The internal divisions that crisscross the Arab world divide along religious, regional, class, and ideological lines. The traditional conflict and tension that have historically resulted in an uneasy balance today threaten to shred the Arab social and political fabric. The resultant suffering and pain, accompanied by desperate and violent political acts, indicate the deepening seriousness of the situation. The experiences of Lebanon and the Palestinians are two cases very much in point.

In the face of a bombardment that includes Israeli preemptive military attacks, Soviet and American political intervention, Western cultural imperialism, and international economic pressures, Arab society, already divided against itself, seeks to return to the two primordial pillars that buttress a tenuous survival: the family and Islam. As the flood of Western technology inexorably pours into the Arab world, it is accompanied by such social and cultural by-products as the breakup of the family, urban impersonalism and anomic conflict, pornography and crime, and rampant materialism. Although by no means dominant or even generally accepted, these social illnesses are present throughout the industrialized world and are extremely contagious.

Beleaguered and besieged, the Arabs increasingly respond by retreating to their familial and religious roots. Former ideological recipes such as Marxism, Western capitalism, Arab socialism, Pan-Arabism, and secular materialism clearly have declining appeal in the Arab world. A revived and reassertive Islam—a civilization and way of life that stresses primordial units and beliefs—is evident not only in Arab climes but throughout much of the Third World. While Islam has always been very much alive, it is now a surging force with deep and direct political significance. As such, it has inundated forces such as Pan-Arabism and, to a lesser degree, Arab nationalism. In the face of this revival, the traditional Pan-Arab/Arab nationalist dialectic has faded in importance.

In all of Tawfic Farah's scientific surveys of the attitudes and orientations of young Arabs (described in his Introduction), whether carried
out in the Middle East or in California, he finds an increasing preoccupation with and commitment to Islam. This important conclusion,
which is reinforced by the research results of Faisal al-Salem, occurs at
a time when there is little security and political trust among Arab young
people. Despite the power and prevalence of the Islamic movement,
however, the ideational candles of Arab nationalism and Pan-Arabism
continue to flicker.

Saad Eddin Ibrahim reminds us that there is an overlap between
Islamic univeralism and Pan-Arabism. One need not necessarily preclude
the other. Islam in fact could again act as an aggregating and integrating
force that might in the end promote Pan-Arabism. Alternatively, according
to the argument of Fouad Ajami, Pan-Arabism may be near death and
Islam could be the force that applies the *coup de grace*.

This collection of essays examines all facets of the Pan-Arab issue.
It has the valuable advantage of combining modern social science survey
research and sensitive, introspective self-analysis by Arabs themselves.
With three exceptions, all the contributions are the work of Arab scholars.
Although they do not all agree in their analyses, they share a deep
concern about the malaise that affects their lives and the lives of their
people. Will a powerful populist Islam help heal the internal wounds
or will it only exacerbate such social and political ulcers? Will this
revived and reviving Islam shield the Arab world effectively from the
interventionary incursions of the superpowers? What will be the relationship between resurgent Islam and Pan-Arabism? These and other
fundamental questions are raised in this volume.

The future of the Arab world promises to be a painful one. Yet, the
Arab people have a proven capacity to overcome adversity and to survive
the deepest of challenges. The modern world carries with it a new,
special, and frightening complex of challenges. This volume is printed
proof that the best Arab minds are once again at work searching for
the best methodology of survival. In so doing, they herein begin the
indispensable exercise of self-assessment and self-criticism. By examining
their own attitudes and orientations, they show that they have been
able to take the first and most difficult step. The reader is privileged
to be able to accompany them as they begin this personal, professional,
and political journey, a journey that concerns the survival and well-
being of a people.

James A. Bill
The University of Texas
Austin, Texas
October 22, 1985

Preface

Now that the oil era has come to a very unceremonious end in the Arab *Mashreq*, it is time for a sober and somber assessment—a self-criticism—of the Arab body politic. Indeed, this effort at self-criticism is already underway, led by the many symposiums sponsored by the Center for Arab Unity Studies and the Arab Intellectual Forum.

Undoubtedly there is a generalized feeling of anger, rage, and wrath in the Arab world. Petrodollars are not as readily available to anesthetize and depoliticize those in the younger generation, many of whom did not benefit from the oil era and the "freer" economy of the *infitah*. They are chafing against the status quo: present regimes, establishment intellectuals, and establishment Islam. They demonstrate a high potential for volatile and violent political action. They heed the call not of Pan-Arabism or establishment Islam but of popular Islam in its many varieties.

A few words about Pan-Arabism are in order. Pan-Arabism is a romantic concept that has been a ritualistic but obligatory doctrine in most Arab states. As Jacques Berque reflects:

> [It] is a mode of being . . . a symbol that forces itself upon geographers and historians alike. . . . It conceals an almost incantatory force, a prestige so out of proportion to any material basis that the causes of this transcendence must be sought elsewhere than in stark objectivity. They, doubtless, lie in a past which marries to the glory of its conquests the classicism of its language and the integrity of its creed. In keeping with Mediterranean symmetry that the Arabs do not repudiate, their contribution, their genius, and their being are one of the most authentic and enduring components of the Old World.[1]

In Europe, for example, epochs succeed each other, the new drives the old, the earth periodically cleanses itself of its past so that people in our century have trouble understanding their ancestors.[2] But in the Arab world, the past is as alive as the present. Both eras live in the same individual.

The heritage of Pan-Arabism is borne by peoples still largely underdeveloped who have suffered the degradations of half a millennium. A disproportion continually appears between past glories and present misfortunes—or problems, at any rate. The result is a superabundance of affectivity; perpetual oscillation between enthusiasm and pessimism; a sort of whirlwind, sweeping up and blending bitterness and hope, calculation and passion. The past century, in particular, has brought a profound ambiguity.[3]

Pan-Arabism as a dream, a romantic idea, an obligatory rhetoric is alive and well; but experience and reality are different. Accepting a doctrine and actually living by its principles are, of course, two different matters. The Arab reality is very different from the Arab dream. Is this now an exhausted idea? Has it spent itself?[4]

Pan-Arabism has been a useful concept for a number of reasons. Firstly, it served the secularly educated elites well. It helped them build bridges to the traditional and religious masses—no small accomplishment. On the populist level, the Arab nationalist produced an effective message of compromise between the world of the masses and secular modernity. Arab nationalist intellectuals tried to find points of agreement between Arab nationalism and Islam. Even Christians could view the prophet Muhammad as the historic father of Arabism and Islamic history as the core of Arab history. Nationalist and social reformers made a practice of assuring the masses that their actions and programs were anchored by the principles of the Qur'an.[5]

Secondly, the elites in the religiously and ethnically segmented Arab states have had to place considerable emphasis on Pan-Arabism as a means of decreasing the salience of internal divisions. In this manner, Arab nationalism brought together Islam and secularism. As Malcolm Kerr remarked, "nationalism nationalized religious sentiments and symbols, and reconditioned them in the service of what was at least nominally a secular ideal. It had come to serve as a new civic religion, without actually displacing or even challenging the old one."[6] Arab nationalism, it might be argued, has rendered important services to the elites. But are Islamic and secular ways of life really compatible? Is Arab nationalism spent?

Arab nationalism appears to be spent because its priests have been depoliticized, distracted, and anesthetized by the petrodollar boom. The petrodollar boom involved buying, selling, contracting, brokering, trading. It is a nonpolitical era. Ideology is boring. The role model in the petrodollar era is the well-dressed businessman concluding a deal, not the crusading revolutionary.

Development became the "in" word in the political lexicon. And development needed technocrats. Technocrats belong to a different world. Their ethos is one of productivity, organization, innovation, efficiency; in short, the antithesis of the world of political strife. A technocrat seeks technical solutions. As Elbaki Hermassi aptly remarked, "synthetic ammonia cannot be manufactured by enthusiastic peasants."[7]

While the majority of the elites became depoliticized and anesthetized, other elites, and many in the masses, seemed to be moving in an opposite direction. They revolted against Westernism, consumptive and secular attitudes. A milder version of this view postulates reservations about Western ways and Westernized elites, and an insistent reassertion of the indigenous politicized Islamic culture. A more extreme view stipulates that popular Islam is the sole legitimate source of identity for the elites as well as for the masses. This view calls for a cultural declaration of war against the West and against Westernized indigenous elites. The civic religion of Pan-Arabism lost the day to a new political religion. Symbiosis is out of the question.

Furthermore, ample evidence suggests that individual Arab states are gaining an edge over the Arab nation. In fact, many symbols of the Arab nation are inimical to the interests of the Arab states. Consider, for example, the Arab League—an expression of Pan-Arabism that has become obsolete. New forms of state-to-state relations are emerging, such as the Gulf Cooperation Council, which coordinates economic and security matters in the Gulf.

This collection of readings is a contribution to the ongoing debate. It includes survey-research studies testing attitudes in the Arab world on many issues related to Pan-Arabism. Elie Chalala's review of the writings of noted proponents of Arab nationalism provides insight into the history and development of that movement. Saad Eddin Ibrahim stresses the importance of the religious factor in Arab nationalism, particularly among the Arab masses, and points out the common ground between the Islamic revolution and the nationalist movement. Faisal Al-Salem's study of group identity among high-school students in the Arab Gulf states suggests that Pan-Arabism has little concrete meaning for Arab youth. In Stewart Reiser's study, the question of Islam's role in the Arab world is explored, and the effect of religious conviction, both Christian and Muslim, on attitudes toward a violent solution to the Palestine question is tested. Fouad Ajami frankly announces the demise of Pan-Arabism as a political force and in a second reading explores future possibilities for a settlement of the Arab/Israeli conflict on other terms. Hassan Nafaa contends that Pan-Arabism, as an ideology, is alive and well, whatever its current state as a political movement. William Brown relates U.S. mideast policy to the continuation of a dying Arab nationalist movement. Abdul-Monem Al-Mashat examines changing patterns of interaction among the Arab states in terms of the "international interactions" approach. Paul Starr tests the psychological effects of violent conflict on the self-image of Arab students. Fouad Ajami concludes the series of readings with a look at the Arab world today (and its need to reconcile tradition and modernity) through the eyes of two of its noted poets, going on to describe three successors to the "defeated" Arab nationalist movement, two that have also failed, and a third that has not yet run its course but shows little chance of success.

Is Pan-Arabism dead? The readings do not answer that question. But they do raise questions, uncomfortable questions, that many in the Arab world cannot ask and are not anxious to find the answers to.

Finally, a word of appreciation is due to my friends and colleagues who serve on the International Editorial Board of the *Journal of Arab Affairs*:

Baha Abu-Laban
University of Alberta

Fouad Ajami
School of Advanced
International Studies—
Johns Hopkins University

Lisa Anderson
Harvard University

Ralph Braibanti
Duke University

Juhaina Al Easa
Qatar University

Hassan Al-Ebraheem
Kuwait University

Rasha Al-Sabah
Kuwait University

Faisal Al-Salem
UNESCO

Mohamad Beshir
Khartoum University

James Bill
University of Texas, Austin

Abdul Wahab Bouhdeiba
Tunis University

Mohamad Bouzidi
Mohamad the V University
Rabat, Morocco

Michel Chatelus
Institut d'Etudes Politiques
Grenoble, France

Nazli Choucri
Massachusetts Institute of
Technology

Akram Diranieh
King Abdulaziz University

Hazem El-Beblawi
Egypt's Export Bank

Ali Ghandour
Alia Royal Jordanian Airlines

Iliya Harik
Indiana University

Michael Hudson
Georgetown University

Adnan Iskander
American University of Beirut

Ali D. Johany
University of Petroleum
and Minerals

Ahmad Khalifa
Center for Criminological and
Social Research, Cairo

Yasumassa Kuroda
University of Hawaii

Giacomo Luciana
Instituto Affari Internazionali
Rome

Masahiro Sasagawa
Bunkyo University

Ali Shembesh
University of Garyuonis,
Benghazi

Thomas Sorensen
Capital Group, Inc.

Michael Suleiman
Kansas State University

Udo Steinbach
Deutsches Orient Institut
Hamburg

Mohamad Zabarah
San'aa University

Edward Szymanski
Center for Studies on Non-
European Countries of the
Polish Academy of Sciences

Thanks, too, go to my colleagues and friends at MERG Research Services: Suhayl Bathish, Fowzi Farah, Hassan Bissat, and Carol Smith; to Beverly Plank who made sense of my manuscript; to my mother, Itaf Fahim Farah; to my friends who never blink: Arne Nixon, Munif Abu Rish, Edward Eggleston; to Richard Stevens of Kuwait and Georgetown Universities; Monte Palmer of Florida State University; and Mark Tessler of the University of Wisconsin at Milwaukee. And to my wife, Linda, my son, Omar, and daughter, Aliya, who are forever patient and understanding.

Tawfic E. Farah
Fresno, California

Notes

1. Jacques Berque, *Arab Rebirth: Pain and Ecstasy* (Al Saqi Books, London, 1983), p. 1.
2. Ryszard Kapuscinski, *Shah of Shahs* (New York: Harcourt Brace Jovanovich, 1985), p. 98.
3. Jacques Berque, *Arab Rebirth*, p. 1.

4. The literature on Pan-Arabism is vast. Among the most recent works are Bassam Tibi, *Arab Nationalism: A Critical Inquiry* (New York: St. Martin's Press, 1981); Fouad Ajami, "The End of Pan-Arabism," *Foreign Affairs*, vol. 57, no. 2 (Winter 1978–1979), pp. 355–373 (reprinted as Chapter 5 in this book); Hassan Nafaa, "Arab Nationalism: A Response to Ajami's Thesis on the End of Pan-Arabism," *Journal of Arab Affairs*, vol. 2, no. 2 (1983), pp. 173–199 (reprinted as Chapter 7); William Brown, "The Dying Arab Nation," *Foreign Policy*, vol. 54 (Spring 1984) pp. 27–43 (reprinted as Chapter 8); Jamil Matar, "Studies In Arab Nationalism and Unity: A Review Essay," *Al Mustaqbal Al Arabi*, vol. 76 (June 1985), pp. 149–160; Saud Al Faisal, "Arab Unity: A General Look," *Al Mustaqbal Al Arabi*, vol. 79 (September 1985), pp. 130–133; and the comments of Hassan Al-Ebraheem and Souad Al-Sabah on Al Faisal's paper in the same issue of *Al Mustaqbal Al Arabi*, pp. 134–138.

5. Malcolm H. Kerr, "Arab Society and the West," manuscript, p. 11.

6. Ibid.

7. Elbaki Hermassi, *Leadership and Development in North Africa* (Berkeley and Los Angeles: University of California Press, 1972), p. 207.

Introduction

A New Arab Man: Transformation and Change in the Arab World

Tawfic E. Farah

There is a dearth of reliable attitudinal data and information in the Arab states, even though sociological studies are numerous.[1] Why? The reasons are many, but primarily they are part and parcel of the general intellectual malaise in the Arab states.[2] Intellectuals are either scared off or "bought off." Intellectuals, in the words of Halim Barakat, are "intellectual civil servants." Civil servants do not delve into sensitive issues. Civil servants play it safe. They write textbooks and essays, attend symposiums. It is easier and safer. Attitudinal studies are a hassle. It is more profitable to publish textbooks.

There are, however, a number of attitudinal studies that deal with the concepts of Pan-Arabism and Pan-Islamism. A representative selection of what is available will be discussed, some focusing directly on the question of Pan-Arabism and others not so directly relevant. Some caveats, however, are in order.

First, it should be stressed that attitudes are simple orientations toward political objectives and concepts. Although in some cases they might indicate a predisposition to act, a precondition for behavior, they should not be confused with behavior itself. It is plausible that most attitudes identified in political-culture studies may be ultimately linked with behavior. However, I suspect that these links are very complex, even though some of the literature points to the existence of a linear relationship between certain attitudes and various forms of political behavior.[3]

Secondly, caution is needed in interpreting and generalizing "national" data. Besides the enormous differences among the twenty-two heterogeneous Arab states, these societies are differentiated and contain subcultures within cultures. Where do we draw the line between dominant culture and subcultures? Attitudinal studies have dealt with this problem

1

cavalierly at best, indicating simply that subcultures of various kinds may exist, without dealing with the fact that individuals may be members of different subcultures, i.e., a Shi'a merchant in Kuwait or a Coptic woman who is a university professor in Egypt.

Thirdly, the attitudinal studies reviewed here are studies of alert elites or of concerned citizenry. They are not studies of mass attitudes.

Fourthly, these studies are not really comparable, even though a few of them are replicative (i.e., Melikian and Diab, Farah). It would be very helpful if we were able to compare attitudes about Pan-Arabism before and after such events as the Camp David Accords, the Israeli invasion of Lebanon, etc. To do so, however, would require precise characterization of the attitudes in particular age groups at various points in time, or co-hort analysis. Lacking such analysis, we have to resort to descriptive data when we attempt to answer questions such as: Is Pan-Arabism on the wane? Is there an Islamic revival? These phenomena are not easily assessed. Many of these developments occur beyond the horizon, in the hearts and minds of the masses. And as social scientists, we are not in touch with the masses. We tend to underestimate, overestimate, and always pontificate about what the masses want. But we really do not know. The masses are just beyond our view. They do not attend symposiums and are not so easily accessible to social scientists as are university freshmen, engineers, doctors, etc.

Any consideration of the attitudes toward Pan-Arabism, identity, and affiliation has to begin with the trailblazing work of Levon Melikian and Lutfy Diab, who conducted their studies among undergraduates at the American University of Beirut. It is followed by another study done at the American University of Beirut, the Kuwait University studies, the Northeastern University study, the Center for Arab Unity study, the California State University study, and the Central California study.

The American University of Beirut Studies

Melikian and Diab's takeoff points for their "Group Affiliations of University Students in the Arab Middle East"[4] are the individual's identification and affiliations. The strength and permanence of such affiliations depend on the needs that they satisfy in the individual and on the status that they confer upon him. The authors assume that a hierarchy of group affiliation exists and that the groups that rank lower on this hierarchy will be more readily relinquished than the higher ranking groups. In the Arab Middle East, where family, religion, and ethnic affiliations are the traditional backbones of the social structure, Melikian and Diab sought to determine the hierarchy of group affiliations of university students.

They administered a 42-item questionnaire to 138 undergraduates in May 1957 and to 69 in May 1958. Over 75 percent of the respondents in both samples came from Lebanon, Jordan, and Syria; the remainder came from Iraq, Saudi Arabia, and Bahrain, and the average age was about 21 years. No significant differences existed in the religion, sex, and political affiliation of the two samples. Seventy-three percent were politically oriented (members of organized political parties such as the Ba'th or *parti populair syrien*) and subscribed to a political ideology such as Arab Nationalism, Arab Unity, and Democracy. A sample of the questions follows:

1. If to show your loyalty to your nation: (a) you were forced to give up your religion permanently, both in private and in public, or (b) you were forced to give up your family and never see them again. Which would you choose? (a) _____ (b) _____
2. If in order to join a certain political party: (a) you were forced to give up your religion permanently, both in private and in public, or (b) you were forced to become a permanent exile from the country to which you belonged. Which would you choose? (a) _____ (b) _____

Their findings indicate that the hierarchy for both samples was similar— family ranked first, followed by ethnic group (Arab, Kurd, Armenian, etc.), religion, citizenship, and political party (most of the parties favored some form of Arab unity), respectively. No relationship was found between the order of the hierarchy and the variables of sex, religion, and political orientation. A strong cultural core was suggested as determining the hierarchy. In "Stability and Change in Group Affiliations of University Students in the Arab Middle East,"[5] the same questionnaire was administered to a matched sample of 114 American University of Beirut undergraduates in the 1970–1971 academic year. Approximately 70 percent of the subjects came from Lebanon, Jordan, and Syria; the remainder came from Bahrain and Kuwait. No significant differences were found between the 1957–58 and the 1970–71 studies in the relative importance given to family, national (ethnic) origin, and citizenship, irrespective of sex, religion, and political orientation. Family still ranked first, followed by national (ethnic) affiliation, and third by citizenship (which, however, was given a significantly higher ranking by males in the 1970–71 study). Significant within-sample differences found in 1957 were also found in 1970–71 among the politically oriented subjects, who gave significantly higher rankings to political party affiliation than did nonpolitically oriented subjects.

Interestingly though, Melikian and Diab found that in the 1970–71 study political party affiliation became significantly more important and religious affiliation became significantly less important. Politically oriented Palestinians were the only subgroup who ranked national (ethnic) origin, rather than family, first, and they also ranked political party affiliation significantly higher than did even the politically oriented other Arabs. Noting that citizenship appeared to be the least important group, Melikian and Diab concluded in the earlier study that the growing importance of ethnic affiliation through Arab Nationalism made the students less interested in identifying themselves as Syrians or Jordanians and more inclined to consider themselves first as Arabs, and they found nothing to contradict this conclusion in the later study.

Paul Starr in "The October War and Arab Students' Self Conceptions"[6] used the "Who am I" method, also called the twenty statements test, to collect data from American University of Beirut undergraduates at three points in time: late April 1973, October 23, 1973 (18 days after the 1973 Arab/Israeli war began), and May 29, 1974 (three days before the Syrian/Israeli disengagement agreement). All three groups were very similar with regard to age, sex, religion, nationality, and academic major. The mean age of the respondents was 19.4 years. Sixty-six percent were Lebanese, 14 percent Palestinian, 8 percent Syrian, 3 percent Egyptian, and the remaining 9 percent were from Jordan, Kuwait, Saudi Arabia, and other Arab states. Males made up 69 percent of the respondents and females 31 percent.

Starr's data indicate that the immediate effect of the war was to bring about a significant increase in the proportion of those who gave positive statements about themselves, those who saw themselves in political terms, in religious or existential terms, or in terms of holding a negative attitude toward Zionism, Israel, or the United States, and those who viewed themselves in terms relating to war or peace. Although the differences were not statistically significant, a greater proportion of the respondents also described themselves as Arabs (24.2 percent in April 1973; 28.2 percent in October 1973; 14.9 percent in May 1974). There was also a slight decrease in the proportion who described themselves in negative terms and in terms of nationality. Of most interest is the fact that all the differences between prewar and wartime designations are in the direction predicted.

Seven months later, however, the pattern of responses was much closer to those expressed in the first test; only one measure was significantly different from the prewar results: there was a decrease in the proportion of respondents who identified themselves in terms of their nationality.

Starr's data suggest that the respondents' self-concepts were positively influenced by the war, but that the positive effects appear to have been short-lived. He speculates that the psychological "rewards" of serious conflicts in the Middle East and other areas may also have been exaggerated and are similarly short-lived.

Unexpectedly, the data showed no pattern of significant difference between respondents from combatant nations and those from noncombatant nations. This indicates that the respondents may have been expressing "Arab" sentiments, and were little influenced by association with a nation state.

Kuwait University Studies

In his "Group Affiliations of University Students in the Arab Middle East (Kuwait),"[7] Tawfic Farah administered a 36-item forced-choice questionnaire to 420 Arab undergraduates, representing 13 Arab countries as well as Palestinians, at Kuwait University in October 1977. Mean age of the respondents was 21.48. Ninety-nine percent were Muslim.

The students, regardless of sex, ranked religion first in their hierarchy of group affiliations, followed by family, citizenship, national origin, and political ideology.

Islam was paramount in the lives of these students. It did not seem to make any difference whether the student was from Saudi Arabia or Lebanon, man or woman. (However, if the student happened to be a politically oriented Palestinian, Bahraini, or South Yemeni, religion was not as salient in his life.) Furthermore, very few of the respondents immediately referred to themselves as Arabs. An Egyptian student, for example, considered himself a Muslim first, an Egyptian second, and an Arab third. The same held true for all other respondents.

Faisal Al-Salem, in "The Issue of Identity in Selected Arab Gulf States,"[8] administered a questionnaire to 1,393 subjects in Saudi Arabia, Kuwait, Bahrain, Qatar, and the United Arab Emirates, in the early 1980s. The mean age of the respondents was 17.009 years; 71.1 percent were female and 28.1 percent were male.

Again, the responses showed that the Arab identity of the respondents was not strong. In response to the question "Who are you?" only 7.1 percent identified themselves as Arabs. Another 3.5 percent identified themselves as Arab Muslims, and 47.2 percent identified themselves as Muslims. The most deeply religious students were from the United Arab Emirates, followed by those from Saudi Arabia, Qatar, Bahrain, and Kuwait.

When asked, "How do you define your country?" only 22 percent chose the response option of "an Arab land"; 20 percent chose "the star of the Gulf," 35 percent chose "the beloved land," and the rest opted for "rich," "beautiful," and "other."

In response to the question "What makes the Gulf states 'Arab'?" the Arabic language was the reason chosen by 33.2 percent of those who answered, 24.9 percent said that the reason lies in the historical existence of Arab tribes in the area, 24.1 percent chose geographic location, and 15.1 percent chose Islam as the reason. Only 36 percent of the respondents agreed with the statement that "the Arab world extends from the Atlantic Ocean to the Gulf," while 64 percent disagreed. This is surprising considering the fact that this is what students are taught in school and hear repeatedly in the media. It is consistent, though, with the students' general tendency to reject the idea of Pan-Arabism. The Arab world is seen not as one nation but as a collection of nations. Students from the United Arab Emirates were at the top of the scale in holding this view, followed by Qataris, Bahrainis, Saudis, and finally Kuwaitis. Yet, in response to a question about the borders between the Arab states, some 49 percent of the respondents said that there are borders, while fully 51 percent said that there are none. The highest percentage in the latter category were Saudis, followed by Emirate students, Bahrainis, Kuwaitis, and finally Qataris. Al-Salem suggests that the Gulf students' opinions on this question are a reflection of their own privileged situation. Their countries are the richest in the Arab world, and they are welcome visitors in most Arab states; so they do not have the problems that other Arabs meet when traveling in the Arab world. Furthermore, as citizens of the Gulf states, they can travel freely in those states, while Arabs from non-Gulf states require an entry visa.

Only 42 of the 1,393 students (3 percent of the total sample) answered when asked why the Arab world constituted one nation; 15 percent of those answering chose similar language and 12.5 percent chose Islam as the unifying factor.

The Northeastern University Study

Stewart Reiser, in "Islam, Pan-Arabism and Palestine: An Attitudinal Survey,"[9] administered a 36-item questionnaire to 595 Arab students from 12 Arab states as well as Palestinians from Israel and other countries. The study was conducted in three parts in the years 1979, 1980, and 1981.

More than half (53.1 percent) of the respondents gave Arab nationalism as their primary association. Two affiliations that had predominated in Farah's Kuwait study, religion and citizenship, were chosen by 38.7 percent of respondents (14.4 percent and 24.3 percent, respectively).

The reasons for choosing to associate themselves with the Arab community, and in many cases advocating the merging of individual Arab states into a larger Arab nation, varied, but several themes emerged: "the desire for a stronger, more rational economy," "greater political and economic independence from the Superpowers," and "increased military power against regional enemies."

Reiser advanced some possible reasons for the difference between the political opinions found in the Northeastern study and those found in the Kuwait University studies. One is that although living abroad, away from the influence of one's own political system, may allow students more freedom to make different choices, there was a good deal of suspicion, as evidenced by the fact that 84.9 percent of the students chose to remain anonymous. The desire for anonymity could indicate a wish to speak one's mind while minimizing the risk of allowing any government to trace political positions to individuals. But in Reiser's opinion the most relevant reason for the strength of Arabism among the respondents was their professional and career orientations. Nearly 74 percent of the aggregate were majoring in engineering and related technical fields. For them, a larger regional area in which to apply their skills may have been important. In fact, 70.4 percent of those majoring in scientific and technical disciplines, compared to 58.1 percent of the aggregate of Arab students, chose Arab nationalism or regional integration as their community orientation.

Another interesting issue addressed by Reiser was Islamic militancy. The historic militancy of Islam has characterized many analyses of the Arab-Israeli conflict as well as other intercultural/religious conflicts in which Muslims have participated. Because a large percentage of Lebanese were involved in the Northeastern survey, a good portion of the Arab aggregate (approximately 40 percent) were Christian. This enabled Reiser to compare Muslim and Christian Arab attitudes toward Israel. To this was added a second independent variable: the degree of religious conviction held by each respondent. Furthermore, Reiser controlled for the respondents' religion and degree of religious conviction in analyzing the respondents' attitude toward the state of Israel. He found that 35.8 percent of the Muslim Arab aggregate and 24.6 percent of the Christian Arab aggregate were willing to recognize Israel; 35.8 percent of the religious Muslims and 35.7 percent of the nonreligious Muslims were willing to recognize Israel; 36.7 percent of the religious Christians and 13 percent of the nonreligious Christians were willing to recognize Israel.

Reiser points out that these results are in sharp contrast to the conventional assumptions of a "militant Islam." Muslim Arabs appear more willing to accept the state of Israel than do their Christian counterparts by 11.2 percent. Within the total Muslim sample, there was no statistical difference between religious and nonreligious Muslim students in their willingness to recognize Israel, a fact which should, according to Reiser, lead at least to a questioning of some notions about Islam's effect on the attitudes toward Israel in the more deeply religious circles. There was considerable difference, however, in the attitudes of those Christian Arabs who described themselves as religious and those who did not. Some 36.7 percent of the religious Christians showed a willingness to recognize Israel, making them, by a very narrow margin, the most accommodating group. But only 13.9 percent of the nonreligious Christian respondents were willing to make peace with Israel, making them by far the most militant of the four groups. Information derived from the written survey and many follow-up interviews indicated that most of the nonreligious Christians were Arab or Syrian nationalists from Lebanon, opposed to the Maronite-dominated phalangist organization and its connections with Israel.

On the whole, Muslim Arabs were somewhat more willing to use military means against Israel than were their Christian Arab counterparts (77 percent, compared to 71 percent). Within the Muslim aggregate, the nonreligious were more inclined to do so than were their religious counterparts (82.8 percent as compared to 75.8 percent). The most interesting finding was the comparison within the Christian aggregate. Nonreligious Christians were significantly more inclined than their religious counterparts to use military means (91.7 percent as compared to 48.5 percent) and, once again, were by far the most militant group of the four.

Center for Arab Unity Study

Saad Eddin Ibrahim and associates, under the auspices of the Center for Arab Unity, conducted the most comprehensive study to date on Pan-Arabism. The study, conducted in 1977, 1978, and 1979, involved ten Arab states: Morocco, Tunisia, Egypt, Sudan, Jordan, Lebanon, Kuwait, Qatar, and Yemen, and included Palestinians in Kuwait. The findings were published in a book entitled *Itajabhat al-Rai al-Am al-Arabi Nahwa Masa'lat al-Wihda* (Trends of Arab Public Opinion Toward the Issue of Unity).[10]

The lengthy questionnaire was made up of 82 questions (14 open-ended and 68 closed). Nineteen questions on attitudes involved the usual socioeconomic data. There were 13 questions on attitudes about general problems, 26 questions on the general Arab environment and the question of unity, 10 questions on social psychological distance, 8 questions on Arab-Israeli conflict, and 4 questions on major powers and the Arab homeland. The respondents (5,557) were not chosen randomly (the majority were convenient target samples); hence, the findings have to be handled very cautiously. If the findings are not representative of Arab public opinion in the ten Arab states, they are nevertheless indicative.

The majority of the respondents, regardless of socioeconomic status, age, and level of education, were aware of the many proposals for Arab political integration. They were not happy with the present level of Arab cooperation, i.e., the Arab League of States, and they demanded a higher level of cooperation, either in the form of a union or a federation among the Arab states. This form of federal government in which every state retains its independence, while a central government handles defense, foreign policy, and national planning, was the ideal kind of unity for the majority of respondents, regardless of social class, age, and level of education.

The majority of the respondents, according to Ibrahim, were political realists. They did not object to forms of constitutional and gradual unity that begin with political, military and economic coordination. Furthermore, most respondents did not take the claims of ideological differences among the Arab regimes seriously. Political and social compatibility among these regimes is not seen as a prerequisite for political unity.

Among the respondents, the Tunisians were the most enthusiastic, while Palestinians and Egyptians had mixed feelings about Arab unity. Peasants, laborers, and students were more enthusiastic about unity than were university professors and the intellectual elites.

Sixty percent of the respondents believed in the centrality of Islam as one of the pillars of Arab nationalism, while one-third saw Arab unity along Islamic lines as a first step for a larger Pan-Arab state. Secularism, according to this study, seems to be losing the day while Pan-Arabism is alive and well.

The California State University Study

In his study, "Group Affiliations of Arab University Students in the United States,"[11] Farah readministered the Kuwait University questionnaire in September 1981 to a random sample of 100 Arab undergraduates attending California State University, Fresno (CSUF). All of the respondents had spent at least two years in the United States and their mean age was 21.68. Ninety-seven percent were Muslims and 15 percent were women.

These students, representing six Arab states in addition to Palestine, ranked religion first in their hierarchy of group affiliations, followed by political ideology, citizenship, national origin, and family.

After a minimum of two years in the United States, the vast majority of Arab undergraduates attending CSUF still considered Islam paramount in their lives, some stating that they had become more devout Muslims in the United States than they were in their own home countries. They attended the mosque in the city of Fresno regularly (their social lives, in fact, revolved around the Mosque), socialized with other Muslims, and read Muslim periodicals. Islam, for these students, however, was not necessarily a reaction against modernity, as it is at times described; it did not preclude getting a scientific and technical education. This was true for both politically oriented and nonpolitically oriented students. In the sixties and early seventies the politically oriented Arab students in the United States were followers of secular Pan-Arabism, i.e., members of the Arab nationalist movement or the Ba'th party, or supporters of the different Palestinian guerrilla groups. But this was not the case among the Arab undergraduates attending CSUF in 1981. Political orientation in September 1981 meant that the student subscribed to a Muslim ideology, was a sympathizer or a member of one of many "Islamic political organizations" (such as, for example, Muslim Brothers Association, Jamat Al-Tafkir w'al-Hijra, Shabab Muhamad, Jund Allah, and al-Jama al-Islamiya), and it did not seem to make any difference what country the student was from.

Very few among the respondents considered themselves Arabs first. In fact, they mentioned being Muslim first, followed by a political ideology. Citizenship was third, followed by loyalty to one's national origin and family.

One cannot say that Islam was experiencing a revival among these students because it really was never moribund. But the students seemed to be experiencing increased politicization along Islamic lines. Their language of politics was increasingly peppered with religious symbolism.

The Central California Study

Farah administered a 35-item questionnaire to a sample made up of 400 Arab undergraduates from Palestine (N-39), Lebanon (N-99), Syria (N-50), Kuwait (N-46), United Arab Emirates (N-42), Bahrain (N-40), Saudi Arabia (N-34). Of the total sample, 57.25 percent were female and 42.75 percent were male. Mean age was 21.78 and 96 percent of the respondents were Muslims. The studies reviewed above provided the point of departure. The findings, which parallel the findings in the Kuwait University and the California State University studies, are elaborated elsewhere. Here, however, an attempt is made to delve into the respondents' systems of political beliefs, expectations, and aspirations, or their "cognitive," "affective," and "evaluative" orientations. It is hoped that we might be able to understand the phenomenon of Islamic militancy through an understanding of the respondents' relationship to other individuals (Arabs) and the respondents' relationship to their governments. The alienation measure used here was adopted from the Streuning and Richardson's scale of alienation.[12] The items were as follows:

1. Most people do not realize how much their lives are controlled by plots hatched in secret by others.
2. These days a person does not really know whom he can count on.
3. It's really hard to figure out whom you can trust nowadays.
4. Things are changing so fast that a person does not know what to expect from day to day.
5. It does not do any good to contact government officials because they are not interested in my problems.
6. Promotion in a job depends more on an influential friend than on qualifications or length of service.
7. The government of my country is working hard to develop our country.
8. In spite of what some people say, the situation of the average man is getting worse all the time.

Surprisingly, most students were not found to be alienated on the personal level. The majority were deeply religious Muslims who trust fellow Muslims. However, the students, regardless of sex or nationality, were alienated from their governments. This alienated relationship warrants further exploration, a look into the respondents' feelings of political efficacy and political trust.

Political efficacy is the feeling that individual political action does have, or can have, an impact upon the political process, i.e., that it is worthwhile to perform one's civic duties. It is the feeling that political and social change is possible, and that the individual citizen can play a part in bringing about this change.[13] This concept was first developed to explain variations in electoral participation. Researchers found a positive correlation between their hypothesized measures of efficacy and participation in the political process. Since then, this finding has been duplicated frequently. A low sense of political efficacy has been viewed as part of the syndrome of attitudes of the politically apathetic. A high sense of political efficacy has been considered a prerequisite for political participation. In addition, one who has internalized this norm is presumably less likely to engage in political acts that challenge the regime. This finding has also been duplicated frequently.

In summary, a sense of political efficacy is said to have important consequences for the continuity of the political system.

Political trust, on the other hand, is said to be conducive to system stability in that it provides discretionary power for political elites. There are obvious ramifications for political life, to the extent that political trust is associated with social trust. Much of political life depends upon agreements that cut across group cleavages, a process requiring a minimum level of trust among the groups. When trust deteriorates, existing political arrangements may become fragile or fail. Though interpersonal trust may not be a necessary, or sometimes even a sufficient, condition for social cooperation among those with similar feelings, it seems clear that social trust facilitates collective action and probably also increases the likelihood of that action becoming routine over time.

The literature on political trust and political efficacy is extensive but the interrelation between the concepts is not yet clear.[14] Using Gamson's theoretical treatment of the subject as a basis, we can postulate a number of behavioral consequences that result from the interplay of political trust and political efficacy:[15]

1. An apathetic citizen might be described as having a low level of trust and a limited sense of political efficacy.
2. A second type might feel a strong allegiance to the political system but still have a low sense of political efficacy.
3. A third type combines political efficacy and trust in government. This individual meets the civic ideal; he is politically active but stays within the bounds of social conventions.
4. The fourth type has a high sense of political efficacy and a low level of political trust. This individual is said to have the potential for volatile political action.[16]

The majority of respondents in the Central California Study were of the fourth type.

In the analysis of the data, we looked at four variables: interpersonal trust; political trust; political efficacy; and two measures of orientation to political activity.[17]

Interpersonal trust. Whether a respondent's trust in government is a reflection of a broader trust in people was determined by the SRC adaptation of the Rosenberg faith-in-people scale. The scale consisted of three items—forced-choice formats (scores combine into a simple additive index). These items were:

1. Generally speaking, would you say that most people can be trusted, or that you cannot be too careful in dealing with people?

2. Would you say that most of the time people try to be helpful, or that they are mostly looking out for themselves?
3. Do you think that most people would try to take advantage of you if they had a chance, or would they try to be fair?

Political trust. Trust in government was measured by an item adopted from SRC, worded as follows: "How much of the time do you think you can trust your government to do what is right—just about always, most of the time, some of the time, or almost never?" The items were scored one through four, with the lowest value assigned to respondents answering "just about always" (high trust) and the highest value assigned to respondents answering "almost never" (lowest trust).

Political efficacy. People's belief in their ability to influence government was measured by a question adopted from Almond and Verba. It was worded as follows: "Now suppose that a law was being considered by your government which you considered to be very harmful or unjust. If you made an effort to block passage of this law, how likely is it that you would succeed? Very likely; somewhat likely; or not very likely?"

Orientation to action.[18] To measure the respondents' orientation to political action, we determined each respondents' ability to specify a plan or a strategy for influencing government. We referred to this as an "engagement index." The mode of action was referred to as "engagement direction." The question we posed was adopted from Almond and Verba: "What methods would you be most likely to use in trying to persuade the government that the law it was considering was harmful or unjust?"

1. *Engagement index.* The responses were separated into those who responded to the question and those who did not. In addition, a follow-up question was asked: "Let's say that the method or methods of persuasion that you use don't prove successful. Then what would you be most likely to do?"
2. *Engagement direction.* It was hypothesized that the efficacious person would tend to take part in political activity, but the particular method of action would likely be a function of the beliefs about the type of behavior required to bring it about.

Accordingly, the responses were coded into "violent" and "nonviolent" political strategy. Only 18 percent of the respondents indicated that they would use nonviolent methods. The answers to the follow-up question, "What would you do if the initial strategy failed?" did not indicate any change in their feelings.

These students appear to have a high degree of political efficacy along with a very low level of political trust. They mistrust the present governments, establishment intellectuals, and establishment religion. As one respondent remarked to the interviewer, "we cannot do any worse than your generation did." These individuals have the potential for volatile and violent political action.

Notes

A version of this chapter was presented at the International Political Science Association meeting in Paris, July 15–20, 1985, and the conference on State and Integration in the Arab States held in Corfu, September 2–9, 1985. I am grateful for the comments received about the paper at both conferences.

1. See Saad Eddin Ibrahim, "Towards an Arab Sociology," *Al Mustaqbal Al Arabi*, vol. 75 (May 1985), pp. 129–139.

2. Judith Miller, "The Embattled Arab Intellectual," *The New York Times Magazine*, 9 June 1985, pp. 56–57.

3. J. McGuire, "The Nature of Attitudes and Attitude Change," in Gardner Lindzey (ed.), *Handbook in Social Psychology* (Reading, Mass.: Addison-Wesley, 1968), vol. 3, pp. 136–272; Solomon E. Asch, *Social Psychology* (Englewood Cliffs, N.J.: Prentice-Hall, 1952), pp. 580 ff; Steven Gross and C. Michael Niman, "Attitude Behavior Consistency: A Review," *Public Opinion Quarterly*, vol. 39 (Fall 1975), pp. 358–368; Norman H. Nie, G. Bingham Powell, Jr., and Kenneth Prewitt, "Social Structure and Political Participation: Developmental Relationships," *American Political Science Review*, vol. 63 (June and September 1969), pp. 361–378 and 808–832; and Sidney Verba, Norman H. Nie, and Jac-on Kim, "The Modes of Democratic Participation: A Cross-National Comparison," in Harry Eckstein and Ted Robert Gurr (eds.), *Comparative Politics Series 2* (Beverly Hills, Calif.: Sage Publications, 1971), Publication no. 01-013.

4. Levon H. Melikian and Lutfy Diab, "Group Affiliations of University Students in the Arab Middle East," *Journal of Social Psychology*, vol. 49 (1959), pp. 145–159.

5. Levon H. Melikian and Lufty N. Diab, "Stability and Change in Group Affiliations of University Students in the Arab Middle East," *Journal of Social Psychology*, vol. 93 (1974), pp. 13–21.

6. Paul Starr, "The October War and Arab Students' Self Conceptions," *The Middle East Journal*, vol. 32, no. 4 (1978), pp. 444–456.

7. Tawfic E. Farah, "Group Affiliations of University Students in the Arab Middle East (Kuwait)," *Journal of Social Psychology*, vol. 106 (1978), pp. 161–165.

8. Faisal Al-Salem, "The Issue of Identity in Selected Arab Gulf States," *Journal of South Asian and Middle Eastern Studies*, vol. 4 (Summer 1981), pp. 21–32.

9. Stewart Reiser, "Islam, Pan Arabism and Palestine: An Attitudinal Survey," *Journal of Arab Affairs*, vol. 3, no. 2 (Fall 1984), pp. 189–204.

10. Saad Eddin Ibrahim, *Itajabhat al-Rai al-Am al-Arabi Nahwa Masa'lat al-Wihda* (Trends of Arab Public Opinion Toward the Issue of Unity) (Beirut: Center for Arab Unity Studies, 1980).

11. Tawfic E. Farah, "Group Affiliations of Arab University Students in the United States," in Tawfic E. Farah, (ed.), *Political Behavior in the Arab States* (Boulder, Colo.: Westview Press, 1983), pp. 33–36.

12. A compendium of such measures is available in J. Robinson et al., *Measures of Social Psychological Attitudes* (Ann Arbor, Mich.: Institution of Social Research Publications, 1968). Also see Robert Cunningham, "Perception of Institutions and Individuals: A Look at Alienation in the Middle East," *Comparative Political Studies*, vol. 4, no. 1 (April 1971), pp. 91–100.

13. Research on political efficacy is enormous. Easton and Dennis, for example, list more than forty studies, and this number could easily be doubled. See David Easton and Jack Dennis, "The Child's Acquisition of Regime Norm: Political Efficacy," *American Political Science Review*, vol. 61 (March 1967), pp. 25–38.

14. Among the many works on political trust, see Martin D. Abravnel and Ronald J. Bush, "Political Competence, Political Trust, and Action Orientations of University Students," *Journal of Politics*, vol. 37 (February 1975), pp. 57–82; Yogendra K. Malik and Jesse F. Marquette, "Democracy and Alienation in North India," *Journal of Politics*, vol. 37 (Feb. 1975), pp. 35–55; Joel D. Aberbach, "Alienation and Political Behavior," *American Political Science Review*, vol. 63, no. 1 (March 1969), pp. 86–99; Joel D. Aberbach and Jack L. Walker, "Political Trust and Racial Ideology," *American Political Science Review*, vol. 64, no. 4 (December 1970), pp. 1119–1219; George I. Balch, "Political Trust and Styles of Political Involvement among American College Students," paper presented at the annual meeting of the Mid-West Political Science Association, Chicago, Ill., April 29–May 1, 1971; Richard L. Cole, "On the Causes and Consequences of Political Trust: A Causal Analysis," paper presented at the annual meeting of the Mid-West Political Science Association, Chicago, Ill., April 28, 1972; John Fraser, "The Mistrustful-Efficacious Hypothesis and Political Participation," *Journal of Politics*, vol. 32 (May 1970), pp. 444–449; Martin Kraus, Kevin Houlihan, Mark I. Oberlander, and Lawrence Carson, "Some Motivational Correlates of Attitudes toward Political Participation," *Midwest Journal of Political Science*, vol. 14 (Aug. 1970), pp. 383–391; Edger Litt, "Political Cynicism and Political Futility," *Journal of Politics*, vol. 25 (May 1963), pp. 312–323; Edward L. McDill and Jean Claire Ridley, "Status, Anomia, Political Alienation and Political Participation," *American Journal of Sociology*, vol. 68 (Sept. 1968), pp. 205–213; Edward N. Muller, "The Representation of Citizens by Political Authorities: Consequences for Regime Support," *American Political Science Review*, vol. 64, no. 4 (December 1970), pp. 1149–1166; Harrell R. Rodgers, Jr., and George Taylor, "Pre-Adult Attitudes toward Legal Compliance: Notes toward a Theory," in Dan Nimmo and Charles Bonjean (eds.), *Political Attitudes and Public Opinion* (New York: David McKay, 1972), pp. 215–227; Donald E. Stokes, "Popular Evaluations of Government: An Empirical Assessment," in Harland Cleveland and Harold D. Lasswell (eds.), *Ethics and Bigness: Scientific, Academic, Religious, Political and*

Military (New York: Harper & Row, 1962), pp. 61–73; Meredith W. Watts, "Efficacy, Trust and Orientation toward Socio-Political Authority: Students' Support for the University," *American Journal of Political Science*, vol. 17 (May 1973), pp. 282–301.

15. William Gamson, "Political Trust and Its Ramifications," in Gilbert Abcarian and John W. Soule (eds.), *Social Psychology and Political Behavior: Problems and Prospects* (Columbus, Ohio: Charles F. Merill, 1971), pp. 40–55; and *Power and Discontent* (Homewood, Ill.: Dorsey Press, 1968), pp. 42–52.

16. In his discussion of the relationship between political trust and political efficacy, Gamson reports data collected by Jeffery Paige as evidence for his typology. In his study of black residents of Newark, New Jersey, in the aftermath of the 1967 riots in the city, Paige found that low trusters were no more apt than others to have engaged in riots. When political efficacy (measured by a political information item) and trust are examined together, however, he reports these findings: persons with high efficacy and low political trust constitute the group most apt to have engaged in riots; persons with a medium level of trust and high efficacy are those who are most apt to have engaged in conventional civil rights activities; but those with both a high level of trust and a high sense of efficacy constituted the group most likely to have limited their activity to the ballot box (Gamson, "Political Trust and Its Ramifications," pp. 40–55). Cole conducted a secondary analysis of the 1970 national sample. He tested for causal linkages in a political trust model that incorporated nontraditional modes of political behavior. He found a very strong relationship between political efficacy and political trust (Gamma = .55). However, when the combined impact of efficacy, trust, and other variables were considered, the model failed to account for as handsome percentages of the "nonconventional"-tactic sympathy as one would have expected (Cole, "On the Causes and Consequences of Political Trust," p. 19). Aberbach and Walker report moderately strong correlation coefficients between trust and three indexes of political expectations—among them, political competence (Gamma = .40 for blacks; Gamma = .32 for whites) ("Political Trust and Racial Ideology," pp. 1205–1207).

17. Obviously the significance of political efficacy to the regime varies with the value placed on the role of the citizen in public affairs. For an interesting interpretation of the role of the citizen in the Soviet political system, see Frederick C. Barghoorn, *Politics in the USSR* (Boston: Little Brown, 1966) and James H. Oliver, "Citizen Demands and the Soviet Political System," *American Political Science Review*, vol. 63 (June 1969), pp. 465–475.

18. It is important to say something here about the scales utilized in this study, especially those that deal with the concept of political efficacy. Studies such as this one, which deal with the concept of political efficacy, tend to assume functional equivalence as long as the measures employed are nearly identical. This obviously leaves much to be desired. As Przeworski and Teune state: "It is often found that measurement equivalence cannot be assumed even between subgroups of a single population, but rather must be treated as an

empirical question subject always to testing." A. Przeworski and H. Teune, *The Logic of Comparative Social Inquiry* (New York: John Wiley, 1970), p. 119. See also Balch, "Multiple Indicators"; and James D. Wright, "Does Acquiescence Bias the 'Index of Political Efficacy'?" *Public Opinion Quarterly,* vol. 39, no. 2 (Summer 1975), pp. 219–226.

1

Arab Nationalism: A Bibliographic Essay

Elie Chalala

I

During the 1940s and the 1950s, the predominant discourse in the Arab world focused on Arab nationalism. This discourse continued into the late 1960s, but with the addition of a new generation of Arab intellectuals, who, while remaining loyal to Arab nationalism, called for a radical reformulation of nationalist ideology, particularly in its goals and in the policies pursued to implement them. With the death of Egyptian president Gamal Abd al-Nasir in September 1970, the cause of Arab nationalism suffered a serious setback. Nasir, because of his charisma and the strategic and political importance of Egypt in the Arab world, was an exceptional force in mobilizing support for the Arab nationalist cause. His death put the debate on Arab nationalism into eclipse. The 1970s witnessed a new dialogue that stressed realism: the goals of Arab nationalism were impractical and the status quo in the Arab world, i.e., the state of disunity, was a fact of life. The nationalist cause suffered again with the emergence of militant Islamic fundamentalist movements in various Arab countries beginning in the late 1970s. This put the Arab nationalists on the defensive: they would have to explain why religious solidarity had emerged as a stronger force than nationalism in mobilizing people for action.

These are not the only causes behind the retreat in the talk about Arab nationalism. Sadoun Hamadi offers three other reasons for this retreat: (1) the psychological impact of the failure of the unity attempts, particularly that between Egypt and Syria (1958–1961); (2) the social and economic concerns that took precedence over the nationalist ones; (3) the contemporary view that emphasizes socialism and democracy

18

rather than nationalism, as it did in the nineteenth and early twentieth centuries.[1]

Despite the credibility of these explanations, it would be false to say that Arab nationalism has ceased to be a potential force in Arab politics. Even though Egypt's separate peace with Israel was a setback for Arab nationalism, the rejection of Sadat's peace efforts by a clear majority of the Arab states illustrated that Arab nationalism remains an influential political force. Obviously, Arab nationalism has not become the powerful mobilizing force its early intellectual and political advocates predicted. But the conclusion that Arab nationalism as an idea, with its potential and actual power, is dead can hardly be substantiated. The constraints that Arab nationalism places on Arab policies are discernible in many cases, foremost among them the Palestinian question. This fact in itself justifies further study of Arab nationalism, and this chapter is a contribution to that study.

In the following pages, I will offer a review of some of the literature on Arab nationalism, both the classic and the modern. First, I will provide some definitions relevant to the study of Arab nationalism. Second, I will offer a discussion of the intellectual and political origins of Arab nationalism: its intellectual advocates, its aims, components, and its relationship with Islam (an issue that has been historically an inseparable part of the discourse), and the criticisms levelled at this ideology and its proponents. Third, I will review those parts of the literature that argue that Arab nationalism has ceased to exist as an important force in Arab politics, as well as those that wage a defense on its behalf.

In my review of the literature on Arab nationalism, I note three important stages of nationalist discourse. The first stage, characteristic of the nineteenth century, showed the lack of any clearly developed theory of Arab nationalism. Though there were efforts in this direction, Islamic ideology, or, to be specific, religious solidarity, took precedence over nationality. The development of an elaborate theory of Arab nationalism marks the second stage, typical of nationalist thought in the periods following W.W. I and W.W. II. But the existence of such a theory did not end the debate on Arab nationalism. The components of this theory—language, history, geography, and particularly Islam— were being challenged by many scholars, Arab and non-Arab. Also central to the debate was the major goal of Arab nationalism: Arab unity. The reformulation of Arab nationalist theory is the third critical stage, characteristic of the period from the mid-1950s to the early 1970s. Even after the radical reformulation of Arab nationalist theory, there were political parties and intellectual critics who asked for more revisions, and in demanding this, they pointed to the military defeats the Arabs suffered at the hands of Israel in 1948 and 1967 and to the failures by Arab governments who ruled in the name of Arab nationalism. The criticism centered on the methods used to implement unionist goals. The emergence of a group of scholars who mourn the death of Arab nationalism cannot be explained without considering both the intellectual crises of ideological debate and the actual policies of the regimes or movements that have advocated the cause of Arab nationalism.

II

The term "Arab world" is frequently used in both English and Arabic literature. Fayez Sayegh defines this term to mean

> The area known . . . from the Atlantic Coast in North Africa to the Persian Gulf in Asia—stretching continuously and without break along the southern shores of the Mediterranean in Africa and the eastern Mediterranean shorelands in Asia, and bulging in the latter sector to embrace all Mesopotamia as well as the peninsular subcontinent enclosed between the Red Sea, the Indian Ocean and the Persian Gulf.[2]

A problem in the discourse on Arab nationalism is deciding who can be considered an "Arab." There are different definitions of this term. One definition is given by George Antonius in his classic work, *The Arab Awakening*:

> The connotation of the word *Arab* changed accordingly. It is no longer used solely to denote a member of the nomad tribes who peopled the Arabian Peninsula. It gradually came to mean a citizen of that extensive Arab world—not any inhabitant of it, but that great majority whose racial descent, even when it was not of pure Arab lineage, had become submerged in the tide of Arabisation; whose manners and traditions had been shaped in an Arab mould; and, most decisive of all, whose mother tongue is Arabic. The term applies to Christians as well as to Moslems, and to the off-shoots of each of those creeds, the criterion being not Islamisation but the degree of Arabisation.[3]

Another definition, which does not differ much from that given by Antonius, is offered by Sati al-Husri, one of the preeminent theorists of Arab nationalism:

> Every person who speaks Arabic is an Arab. Everyone who is affiliated with these people is an Arab. If he does not know this or if he does not cherish his Arabism, then we must study the reasons for his position. It may be a result of ignorance—then we must teach him the truth. It may

be because he is unaware or deceived—then we must awaken him and reassure him. It may be a result of selfishness—then we must work to limit his selfishness.[4]

According to Richard Plaff, in an article entitled "The Function of Arab Nationalism," the Prophet Muhammad asserted that "whosoever speaks Arabic is an Arab."[5] A third definition of who is an Arab is given by Charles Malik. His definition, though similar to those of Antonius and al-Husri, remains cautious in concluding that the peoples who speak Arabic constitute an Arab nation:

The word "Arab" denotes neither a race nor a religion. For the most part, its connotation today is "Arabic-speaking." The overwhelming majority of the Arabic-speaking peoples (or Arabs) are Moslem, just as the overwhelming majority of the Moslems are non-Arab; so the two terms do not coincide. Although there are vast diversities of culture among them, the Arabs have certain cultural traits in common. They also have common aspirations. Whether all Arabic-speaking peoples constitute a single nation depends first on the meaning of the term "constitute" and second on the "Arab" adaptation of the European concept of "nation." All this, of course, is independent of the question whether they *should* constitute a nation.[6]

III

There are three periods according to which we can distinguish different types of discourse on Arab nationalism: pre–W.W. I, post–W.W. I, and after the 1948 Arab-Israeli war. This division, however, is by no means agreed upon among students of Arab nationalism. Much of the literature in the West accepts the existence of Arab nationalism as a widely discussed ideology only by the 1930s. But as will be shown later in this chapter, there are many scholars who disagree and trace Arab nationalism to the nineteenth century and even to earlier times, such as the pre-Islamic era.

Majid Khadduri writes that

Before World War I, while the Arab idea of nationalism was mingled with the idea of Islamic unity, Arab nationalism scarcely aimed beyond the rehabilitation of the Arab race in a multinational empire. Some thinkers called for a restoration of the Arab empire, presumably implying that Arab political leadership should be separated from that of the Turks, but most Arabs were content to remain within the frame of the Ottoman unity, as long as their proper place was recognized by the Turkish rulers.[7]

The beginnings of Arab nationalism and the identity of its earliest advocates remain an unsettled debate. Some would trace it to the teachings of Muhammad Ibn Abd al-Wahhab (1703–91), the originator of the Wahhabi movement in Nejd towards the eighteenth century; others to Muhammad Ali (1769–1849) and his son Ibrahim Pasha's attempt to found a Near Eastern empire based on Egypt and the territories of the Levant. Several scholars and theorists of Arab nationalism trace its origins to the writings of important thinkers such as Rifa'a al-Tahtawi (1801–1873), an Egyptian student sent by Muhammad Ali to study in France; the Persian thinker Jamal al-Din al-Afghani (1839–97); his pupil Muhammad Abduh (1849–1905); Rashid Rida (1865–1935); Abd al-Rahman al-Kawakibi (1849–1902); Negib Azoury (d.1916), and to the revolution of the Sherif Hussein of Mecca in 1915. All of the aforementioned scholars and advocates of Arab nationalism fall within the first period of the discourse.

Zaki al-Arsuzi, one of the lesser known founders of the Ba'th party, unlike his Ba'thist rival Michel Aflaq, is not well known for involvement in Arab nationalist polemics. Nevertheless, in discussing Arab nationalism, al-Arsuzi traces it to ancient times, to the *al-Jahilia*, to the pre-Islamic era, when, according to him, a national feeling prevailed.[8]

According to Bassam Tibi, Rifa'a al-Tahtawi can be considered as the first Arab nationalist thinker. Tibi writes that in al-Tahtawi's thought

> the social takes precedence over the religious, and here, for the first time, an Arab is using the word "nation" in a secular sense . . . al-Tahtawi stresses that love of a country is one of the prime virtues of civilisation. Where there is no *hubb al-watan* [love of country] civilisation must be condemned to perish. The word *watan* does exist in classical Arabic, but only in the sense of the country from which one originates, or in which one lives. Al-Tahtawi also uses *watan* in that sense, as in his reminiscences of his home village Tahta. But it is Egypt, and not Tahta, that is his *patrie*, which is why he must be considered the first Arab nationalist thinker.[9]

Antonius, among others, asserts that the beginnings of Arab nationalism can be traced to the Wahhabi movement and Muhammad Ali. The Wahhabi movement called for the revitalization of Islam; its followers "were purists and wished to restore Islam to what they took to be its original purity." On the views of the spiritual leader of the Wahhabis, Muhammad Ibn Abd al-Wahhab, Tibi writes that he "did not object to the despotic autocracy of Ottoman rule as such, but to the corruption and debauchery into which it had fallen. He believed that only the Arabs could bring Islam back to its original pristine purity, and he considered it his life's purpose to mobilize the Muslims for the achievement of this backward-looking utopia."[10]

Were the Wahhabis Arab nationalists; did they advocate nationalism? Sylvia Haim finds no compelling evidence for the claim that they were nationalists. She writes that "such views [those of Antonius] . . . lack historical evidence. The Wahhabis were not nationalists by any acceptable definition of the term. . . . Their concern was with Islam, not with the Arabs, and they directed their zeal against lax, backsliding, or heretical Muslims rather than toward the creation of an Arab national state."[11]

Antonius also considers Muhammad Ali and his son Ibrahim Pasha to be advocates of Arab nationalism. Ibrahim Pasha's nationalist leanings are evident from some of his policies during his rule over Syria, as well as some of the statements he made and the reaction he received from the Arab Christians during that rule. Albert Hourani quotes Ibrahim Pasha as having said: "I am not a Turk. I came to Egypt when I was a child, and since that time, the sun of Egypt has changed my blood and made it all Arab." This statement to a French visitor has often been quoted, as has the visitor's comment that Ibrahim's aim was to found an entirely Arab state and "give back to the Arab race its nationalist and political existence."[12] As for the Christians' reaction, Tibi writes that

> The devotion [of Syrian Christians toward Ibrahim Pasha] can be explained by the fact that Ibrahim Pasha had not attempted to justify his campaign against the Ottomans in religious terms, but claimed to be fighting for the Arabs against the Turks. He considered that the unification of Egypt and Syria would be the beginning of the foundation of a great Arab state, thus presenting the Arab Christians with the possibility of social emancipation, because in a specifically Arab state they would be full citizens, while under the Islamic Ottoman theocracy they were not members of the *umma* and therefore had the status of subjects.[13]

According to Tibi, this support for Ibrahim Pasha is attributable to the French influence on the Christians. The French wished to block the British with an Arab state, and France "encouraged the Maronite authorities, who were loyal to her, to support him [Ibrahim Pasha]."[14]

Haim challenges the argument that Muhammad Ali is an Arab nationalist. Muhammad Ali, according to her,

> was a dynast and an opportunist who tried to take advantage of the enfeeblement of his Ottoman masters and of the Anglo-French rivalry in the Levant in order to enlarge the domain which luck, circumstance, and his own considerable ability had enabled him to seize and retain. . . . he would have been skeptical of the use or value of ideology as a tool of

political power, and it is safe to say that had he attempted to use it in the Levant he would have found it useless, since it is generally agreed that in his times political passions in the Middle East were stirred by religion, not nationality.[15]

On the relationship of Muhammad Ali to Arab nationalism, Albert Hourani concurs with Haim: "Did Muhammad Ali aim at creating an Arab kingdom? Nothing in his words and policy seems to show it, although there are signs of it in the words of his son and chief helper, Ibrahim Pasha."[16]

Though not an Arab, Jamal al-Din al-Afghani has been considered one of the early intellectual precursors of Arab nationalism. The writings of this Persian scholar are contradictory, especially regarding his preference for either religious or national solidarity. In one of his articles, he seems to show preference for national solidarity, as being more efficacious than any other type of solidarity in gaining and establishing political power: ". . . Al-Afghani argued that a 'national' unity based on a common language was both more powerful and more durable than one based on a common religion." Sati al-Husri mentions that al-Afghani had prefaced one of his articles with a few lines in Arabic that read: "There is no happiness except through nationality [*al-jinsiya*] and no nationality except through language."[17] In another article, al-Afghani said that the religious tie among the Muslims is the only bond that "has made the Muslims shy away from the consideration of nationality and refuse any kind of solidarity [*assabiyya*] except Islamic solidarity."[18]

Muhammad Abduh, who coedited a journal, *Al-'Urwa Al-Wuthqa*, with al-Afghani in Paris, held views similar to his teacher's. "But he went a step further in showing his allegiance to the idea of an Islamic caliphate. He makes it in an article of faith. . . . For it (the Ottoman state) alone protects the authority of religion . . . and religion would have no authority without it."[19]

Was al-Afghani a precursor of Arab nationalism? Haim questions the role al-Afghani played in encouraging Arab nationalism, claiming he was mainly concerned with pan-Islamism. His support of a union of Muslim states was the factor that made Abdul Hamid, "who was himself interested in Pan-Islamism, welcome him [al-Afghani] to Istanbul." Haim adds that "What al-Afghani did was to make Islam into the mainspring of solidarity, and thus he placed it on the same footing as other solidarity-producing beliefs. His political activity and teaching combined to spread among the intellectual and official classes of Middle Eastern Islam a secularist, meliorist, and activist attitude toward politics, an attitude the presence of which was essential, before ideologies such as Arab nationalism could be accepted in any degree."[20]

Muhammad Abduh, a pupil of al-Afgani, is also considered a precursor of Arab nationalism. Again, Haim is skeptical, claiming Muhammad Abduh simply exemplified and made popular a hopeful attitude toward politics, a belief that human action, based on rational and scientific principles, could ameliorate the human condition. She adds that "if both al-Afghani and Muhammad Abduh are essential to the understanding of a phenomenon such as Arab nationalism, it is as well to emphasize that they nevertheless cannot be considered as its initiators. To do so would be to run the risk of confusion by dissolving the lineaments of a clear-cut ideology and a specific history into amorphous speculation and loose generalization."[21]

Tibi appears to have a different assessment of al-Afghani and Abduh's contribution to Arab nationalism. Even though he establishes a clear distinction between Wahhabism and Islamic modernism, he concludes that the two movements remain an "inherent part of the national movement in the Middle East." Considering the time in which al-Afghani and his pupil Muhammad Abduh lived, their modernism can be considered revolutionary. "They had to face Europe as a colonial power, and their attitudes were hence uncompromising. In their writings, Islam becomes an anti-colonialist ideology." Thus a relationship exists, though indirect, between these three Muslim scholars—Ibn Abd al-Wahhab, al-Afghani, and Abduh—and Arab nationalism, premised on opposition to foreign domination, whether Ottoman or European, and on emphasis on the Arab origins of Islam. In Tibi's opinion, they had contributed to the nationalist cause, although in their minds "they were not nationalist but Muslim."[22]

Tibi's assessment of al-Afghani and Abduh is shared by William Cleveland. By recognizing the threat from Western Europe, and by not accepting the long-term superiority of European civilization, both Abduh and al-Afghani "attracted young Muslims and gave to Islamic religious sentiment a politically-charged coloring. This Islamic activism played a significant part in the early formulations of Arab nationalism and, as recent events in the Middle East have shown, continues to be a reservoir from which all classes of Muslims draw strength in times of uncertainty."[23] Al-Afghani's writings, which showed the Arabs the importance of reviving their own religious, social, and national life if they were to overcome European superiority, had made "evolution and revolution" to be "recognized for the first time by the Arabs as a vital necessity for their states, nations, and communities."[24]

Another scholar considered to have contributed to Arab nationalism is the Syrian Rashid Rida, who settled in Egypt. He said that the Arabs had a special place within the Islamic nations, and that "other Muslims were pupils of the Arabs." Despite this and his opposition to the

Ottoman rule, Rida "rejected any tendency toward establishing separate Arab states based on non-Islamic solidarity in the Islamic world."[25]

But in the opinion of Haim, one can trace more roots of Arab nationalism in Rida's writings than in al-Afghani and Abduh. This is mainly due to Haim's classification of Rida as a *salafi*. She writes that "it is in the arguments of the *salafiyya* that we may trace the first intellectual burgeoning of Arab nationalism." The term *salafiyya* means "a return to the ways of the Prophet, his Companions, and the Muslims of the early centuries, when Islam was in its pure state and the Arab caliphate in the heyday of its glory. . . . Thus implicit in the arguments of the *salafiyya* is a glorification of Arab Islam and a depreciation of the Ottoman Islam."[26]

More specifically, Rida's association with nationalism is supported by his use of the term *umma*, meaning nation in Arabic. Haim writes that "traditionally, the word [*umma*] meant the body of all Muslims, and made no distinction based on race, language, or habitation. But Rashid Rida here seems to be saying that the Turks, Muslims as they were, were not really part of the *umma*, that the *umma* consisted only of Arab Muslims."[27]

But according to both Haim and Khadduri, Rida falls short of being considered an advocate of Arab nationalism. Though he clearly shows his partiality for the Arabs, Haim says that this was really a defense of Islam which, so Rashid Rida thought, had been best insured by the Arabs. It was only after the "Young Turks deposed Abdul Hamid, [and] . . . they manifested indifference to Islam . . . that Rashid Rida felt able wholeheartedly to support Arab nationalism."[28] To this, Khadduri adds that in the "latter part of his life," Rida "turned to reassert primary loyalty to Islam in its puritanical Wahhabi form in Arab lands that remained in his eyes immune from foreign influence."[29]

Abd al-Rahman al-Kawakibi, another Syrian who left Aleppo for Egypt in 1898, is considered to have gone further than al-Afghani, Abduh, and Rida in presenting the Arabs' case against the Turks. He wrote two important books which are widely referred to by students of Arab nationalism, *Taba'i al-Istibdad* (The characteristics of tyranny), and *Umm al-Qura*, the name with which Mecca was known. In *Taba'i al-Istibdad*, al-Kawakibi clearly advocates an Arab unity based on the separation of religion and politics:[30] "Here are the nations of Austria and America who have been guided by science to find a variety of paths and deep-rooted foundations for national unity and harmony, but not administrative unity, for national harmony, but not sectarian unity. Why is it that we cannot follow one of these paths?"[31] This line of nationalist thinking in al-Kawakibi's thought lies in his emphasis on language and race. He claimed that the Muslims "are now a dead people with no corporate being or feelings. Their stagnation is the result of tyranny, of the decline of Islamic culture, and of the absence of racial and linguistic bonds among Muslims, and partly for this reason the Ottoman Empire is not fit to preserve Islam."[32]

But what appears to be clear nationalist thinking disappears in his second book, *Umm al-Qura*. In this work, al-Kawakibi becomes "more concerned with wresting Islam from the Turks and restoring it to the Arabs. Arab hegemony is seen as the only way to salvage Islam from decay."[33] For al-Kawakibi, the Arabs "are of all nations the most suitable to be an authority in religion and an example to the Muslims."[34]

Despite his contradictory position on religion and nationalism, al-Kawakibi, according to Haim, "may be considered as the first true intellectual precursor of modern secular Pan-Arabism. . . . For all his preoccupation with the state of Islam, al-Kawakibi, once he introduced the idea of a spiritual caliph, was led to consider politics as an autonomous activity divorced from divine prescription, and fully subject to the will of men. Such an idea is an essential prerequisite of nationalism."[35]

Negib Azoury (d. 1916), an Ottoman Christian who studied in Paris and worked as an official in the provincial government of Jerusalem, advocated views similar to those of al-Kawakibi. In 1905, he published *Le réveil de la nation arabe*. According to Azoury, the separation of civil and religious powers was in the interest of both Islam and the Arab nation. Also, he suggested something that al-Kawakibi did not: "He desired to have an Arab empire set up; its 'natural' frontiers would be the valley of the Euphrates and the Tigris, the Suez Canal, the Mediterranean, and the Indian Ocean."[36]

Haim correctly observes certain significance in Azoury's views. First, his program "constitutes the first open demand for the secession of the Arab lands from the Ottoman Empire," and second, this demand came from a Christian and not a Muslim since, according to Haim, the Muslims "were chary of any move that might disrupt the Ottoman Empire, the only great Muslim power in the world." However, Azoury's importance as an intellectual figure has been downplayed. "The Ligue de la Partie Arabe [which was established by Azoury] was probably a one-man business, since no Arab, so far as it is known, was associated with it, and Azoury seems to have been a shady character who may have been a French agent actually taking money from French sources. At any rate, it is certain that he went so far as to ask for it."[37]

Other Arab Christians are considered as precursors of Arab nationalism; some even predate Azoury. Several Lebanese and Syrian Christian scholars called for Arab nationalism in the nineteenth century, among them Nasif Yazeji, born in 1800, a man of letters whose concern was classical Arabic literature. On Yazeji, Antonius writes that "the beauty of the buried literature had awakened the Arab in him and bound him as by a spell. He became the apostle of its resurrection. . . . The novelty of his preaching was all the more striking as it addressed itself to Arabs of all creeds, to Christians as much as to Moslems, and urged them, at a time when religious fanaticism was still violent, to remember the inheritance they had in common and build up a fraternal future on its foundations."[38]

Though the Arab nationalist credentials of the Hashemites—an Arab family which is descended from the Quraysh tribe to which the Prophet belongs and which after W.W. I briefly ruled over Syria and Iraq (until 1958) and still rule in Jordan—remain questionable in a sizable part of the Arabic-language literature, many scholars, Arab and non-Arab, consider the 1916 revolution of the Sherif Hussein of Mecca as nationalist in character. Ahmad Sudqi al-Dajani, for example, says that Arab nationalism as a political term was used first in 1916 by Sherif Hussein.[39] The Hashemites' relationship to Arab nationalism has also been stressed by propagandists hired by the Iraqi regime prior to the 1958 revolution that overthrew the Hashemite monarchy, and by the present Jordanian regime. Making a case for the Hashemites' advocacy of Arab nationalism helped these two regimes maintain legitimacy, especially when under attack by the preeminent Arab nationalist leader of the time, Gamal Abd al-Nasir of Egypt.

The Arab nationalist character of the 1916 revolt is disputed by both William Cleveland and Sylvia Haim. Cleveland writes that while the revolt "provided a more specific focus for those intent on gaining an independent Arab state," it nevertheless "was proclaimed in the name of preserving Islam, not in the name of Arabism or the Arab nation."[40] Haim writes that the Sherif Hussein did not justify his rebellion by "an appeal to Arab nationalism; he appealed rather, to traditonalist sentiments, calling the Young Turks impious innovators who had put Islam in danger, and representing himself as rising against them in the interests of the Faith."[41]

Ibn Abd al-Wahhab, al-Tahtawi, al-Afghani, Abduh, Rida, al-Kawakibi, and Azoury all belong to the eighteenth and nineteenth centuries. Before moving on to review some of the twentieth-century works on Arab nationalism, two important questions must be answered: When did Arab nationalism emerge as a political force? Do the writings of the eighteenth and nineteenth centuries' scholars constitute a theory of nationalism, namely Arab nationalism?

Sylvia Haim does not see any basis for the claim that Arab nationalism as a political theory emerged prior to the 1930s: "The absence of a specific ideology of Arab nationalism until the end of the First World War is indeed noteworthy. It was not until the 1930's that a serious attempt was made to define the meaning of Arab nationalism and what constitutes the Arab nation. These attempts became more frequent in the 1940's, and in the period since then they became a flood; hardly a month passes which does not see the publication of one or more books on this subject."[42]

Zeine Zeine, a well-known Arab historian, traces "the seeds of the Arab separatist movement" to the emergence of "Turkish nationalism from 1909 onwards."[43] But Hourani's account is quite different: "It is true, nevertheless, that explicit Arab nationalism, as a movement with political aims and importance, did not emerge until towards the end of the nineteenth century."[44]

Ahmad Sudqi al-Dajani attempts to explain the confusion as to whether nationalist thought predates the nineteenth century, even going so far back as to predate Islam. Al-Dajani says that such confusion stems from mixing up the national existence with its expression in political terms and ideology.[45] What then explains these divergent views about when Arab nationalism emerged? A careful reading of the literature reveals that the ideological presuppositions of the different writers influence their different interpretations of when nationalism emerged and also of whether or not the nineteenth-century writings constituted a theory of nationalism.

Haim's view is motivated by a certain philosophical approach that emphasizes the role of religion as an important factor in shaping people's attitudes and loyalties. Prior to the twentieth century, religion was the predominant force, and thus it was unlikely that people would be influenced by nationalism, a concept alien at the time to the Arabs and the Muslims in general. Other scholars, the majority of which are Arabs, are similarly influenced by ideological premises that stress the role of nationalist ideology.

A third group of scholars is influenced by Marxist and class assumptions. Though theoretically differing with Haim, they end up reaching the same conclusion: there was no nationalist thought in the nineteenth century. Among these scholars are Faysal Daraj and Walid Qaziha. Faysal Daraj, who wrote an article titled "The Form of Arab Nationalist Thought in the Nineteenth Century," argues that if one scientifically studied the works of al-Afghani, al-Kawakibi, and Rida, one would have to conclude that they do not constitute a consistent nationalist ideology. Among the several propositions is the claim he advances that Arab thought in the nineteenth century did not reflect nationalist consciousness of its own and an awareness of certain historical tasks; instead, it reflects an organic crisis that affected all Arab peoples. Thus, this thought is historically defined.[46]

Qaziha attempts to prove the social and economic basis of nineteenth century Arab nationalism. He says that al-Kawakibi and Rida belonged to social and political elites, to a class of landowners who lived in the cities. Qaziha focuses attention on the significance of two major points emphasized by al-Kawakibi: the first is administrative decentralization of the Ottoman state. Here, Qaziha argues, al-Kawakibi reflects the interests of the landowners (*al-a'yan*). The second point centers on limiting the powers of the Turks in the Arab region and delegating those powers to traditional Arab social leaders, who belonged to the big families.[47]

Samir Amin, born in Egypt and educated in France, is better known for his work on economic issues than on Arab nationalism. He becomes relevant here, however, because of a book published originally in French and later translated into English, *The Arab Nation*, in which he attempts to provide a class analysis of Arab nationalism. Arab unity, one major goal of all the theories of Arab nationalism, is explained in economic terms. Amin writes that "we maintain that Arab unity was the initial product of the mercantile integration of the Arab world, as carried out by a class of merchant-warriors."[48]

In discussing the social forces that made Arab civilization, Amin singles out the ruling class. This class, according to him, was urban, a world of courtiers, clerics, artisans, and clerks. "The ruling class was the cement which held things together: everywhere it had adopted the same language, the same orthodox Sunni Islamic culture. . . . This was the class which made the Arab civilisation." Arab unity declined due to the "decline of trade." Because of this, "the Arab world had become no more than a heterogeneous conglomerate, under a foreign power, the Ottoman Empire." As to whether Arab nationhood exists or not, Amin's answer is consistent with his class approach. The basis of the nation is "a social class which controls the central state apparatus and ensures economic unity in the life of the community." The "phenomenon of nationhood" rises or falls "according to whether the social class in question reinforces its unificatory power or loses it together."[49]

Amin's explanation of Arab nationalism and Arab unity is criticized by Bassam Tibi:

Amin attempts a Marxist analysis, and he interprets the history of the Arab nation in terms of economic and social history. While many authors have been primarily concerned to write the intellectual history of Arab nationalism, Amin confines himself to the socio-economic sphere. It seems to me that neither of these approaches should exclude the other; expertise on the ideology of Arab nationalism must be complemented by an analysis of the social structures in which this ideology has emerged and now exists.

Amin has not thought it necessary to concern himself with the literary products of Arab nationalism, and has confined himself to a class analysis, which I consider to be a serious weakness in an otherwise stimulating approach.[50]

Tibi is also critical of arguments that say that the capitalist class constituted the social base of Arab nationalism. One of the advocates of this argument is C. E. Dawn, who claims that the Arab national movement was supported not only by Western-educated men of letters and officers from petty bourgeois backgrounds, but also, and particularly after 1914, by large landowners and *grand bourgeois* forces. But this is disputed by Tibi, who says:

> The secularism of the Arab national writers, based on the acculturation of Western bourgeois ideas, could hardly have found a social base in the upper reaches of Syrian society. . . . Syria was by no means a bourgeois society. It was more a semi-feudal society with some incipient bourgeois features. It is therefore not surprising that the undeveloped Syrian bourgeoisie, and the petty bourgeois writers, were unable to lead a revolt against the Ottoman Empire by themselves. They allied with the feudal masters of the Arabian peninsula, the Hashemite dynasty, and left it to them to lead the rising.[51]

The discourse on Arab nationalism in the nineteenth century is characterized by the difficulty of producing compelling evidence that nationalist consciousness and even a consistent nationalist theory did exist. There are two main interpretations of the last century's writings on nationalism: first, that what has been interpreted to be an Arab nationalist theory was nothing but an attempt to salvage Islam. Second, that what appeared as nationalist thinking had nothing to do with nationalist consciousness; instead, it was an attempt by the wealthy classes to protect their interests. But most important of all is the absence of a coherent theory of Arab nationalism.

Yet clearly such a theory existed by the first quarter of this century. No one can claim that there were no thinkers or politicians then who unambiguously advocated Arab nationalism. The development of such a theory marks the beginning of the second period. On this period, Khadduri writes that "the new circumstances introduced by World War I greatly affected the course of Arab nationalism and called for the reformulation of Arab aims. . . . British support for Arab claims against the Turks brought to the fore those revolutionary leaders who made their imprint on Arab nationalism and transformed it from a slow and peaceful movement into a revolutionary and a separatist one. From that point onward, Arab nationalism demanded complete independence, whether from Turkish or some other foreign rule."[52]

Though problematic, secularism is another feature that marked the second period. Arab nationalism, according to Hourani, had a secular character:

> Explicitly, Arab nationalism was a secular movement. The leaders wished to deprive the French of their most powerful weapon, the existence of Christian and dissident-Muslim minorities who looked to them for protection; they wished to state their opposition to Zionism in national terms, in terms of the threat to the interests of the Christian and Muslim Palestinians alike, rather than of religious hostility; and they needed the help of what was still by and large the best educated part of the population and the one with most experience of Europe.[53]

Faysal, Sherif Hussein's son, is considered to be an Arab nationalist even in the modern secular sense. Faysal, an ally of the British, ruled Syria for a period of three years after the end of World War I before being expelled by the French. During this brief rule, Faysal made many statements that indicate what can be considered in Haim's words a "rudimentary theory of Arab nationalism." About the Arabs, Faysal said that they are "one people," who live "in the region which is bounded by the sea to the east, the south, and the west, and by the Taurus mountains to the north."[54] Identifying himself as an Arab, Faysal said: "We are Arabs . . . before being Muslims, and Muhammad is an Arab before being a prophet."[55] He also said, in a speech in Aleppo in June 1919: ". . . there is neither minority nor majority among us, nothing to divide us. We are one body, we were Arabs even before the time of Moses, Muhammad, Jesus, and Abraham."[56]

But the development of a consistent theory of Arab nationalism is attributed to the writings of theorists like Sati al-Husri, Michel Aflaq, Abd al-Rahman al-Bazzaz, Edmond Rabbath, and Constantine Zurayq.

Unquestionably, with the end of World War I, when all the Arab parts had seceded from the Ottoman Empire with the exception of the Alexedretta Province, there was a need for an ideology that could gain support from European powers and move toward holding all Arab regions together, uniting them into one state. The articulation of an elaborate nationalist ideology, therefore, was a necessity. That ideology is Arab nationalism.

One attempt to develop an Arab nationalist theory was that of Edmond Rabbath, a Christian from Aleppo, a lawyer and once a member of the Syrian parliament. In 1937, he wrote a study in French entitled *Unité Syrienne et Devenir Arabe*. According to Rabbath, the Arabs formed a distinct racial group, and the history of the region, though labeled as Babylonian, Assyrian, or Phoenician, is Arab. The Arabs, Rabbath continues, are united by a common civilization. What is called Islamic, and here Rabbath means the history of the Arabs, is wrong. For him, Islam is the Arab national religion which has served to make the Arabs into a cohesive group. Language also played its part in bringing the Arabs together as did geography.[57]

Another early writer on Arab nationalism is Abdullah al-Alayili. According to al-Alayili, what contributes to nationalist feeling are factors like language, interest, the geographical environment, ancestry, history, and customs.[58]

Haim correctly observes that "the man who did most to popularize the idea of nationalism among the literate classes of the Arab Middle East was the writer Sati al-Husri whose large output began in the 1940s and still continues." Al-Husri was a native of Aleppo, brought up in Constantinople, and educated more as a Turk than an Arab. Before World War I, he had been an Ottoman official of some standing in the Ministry of Education. When Faysal ruled in Damascus at the end of the war, al-Husri joined his movement and became Minister of Education; he followed Faysal in his exile from Syria, and then went to Iraq, where he became, and remained for many years, the Director General of Education.[59]

In Sati al-Husri's view, there are three sentiments that could create a political community: "nationalism, territorial patriotism, and loyalty to the state." Al-Husri's definition of a nation is not liberal by any standard. In his opinion, a nation is "something really existing: a man is, or is not, an Arab whether he wants to be or not."[60]

Al-Husri concentrated his energy on making three main points: no freedom for the individual outside the nation, Egypt is a part of the Arab nation (Tibi mentions that al-Husri was the only one to extend the term Arab nation to include North Africa), and Pan-Arabism neither contradicts nor is inimical to Islam.[61]

History for al-Husri, however, is not as important as language. "A common history is important but only secondary. It can strengthen, it cannot create, the national bond; and it can only strengthen if it is deliberately used to do so. We are not the prisoners of our past unless we want to be; every nation must forget part of its history, and only remember what helps it."[62]

Michel Aflaq adopted extensively from al-Husri's theory of Arab nationalism. On Arab nationalism, Aflaq said that it is "racial in the sense that we hold sacred this Arab race which has, since the earliest historical epochs, carried within itself a vitality and a nobility which have enabled it to go on renewing and perfecting itself, taking advantage of triumphs and defeats alike."[63]

Although Aflaq is known for his mystic and ambiguous style, Khadduri's reading of the Ba'thist leader's view of nationalism lends clarity: "Arab nationalism, in Michel 'Aflaq's view, is the embodiment of the Arab spirit. Language, history, and traditions, important as they are, are only external bonds. Nationalism means a striving toward the national goal and a will to progress which awakens whenever the nation's course of progress is retarded or existing conditions deteriorate and the nation lags behind the progress of the world. Arab nationalism is thus the 'procession' of the Arab nation toward the realization of its needs and aspirations."[64]

Haim assesses Aflaq's impact by saying that "he, at the end of half a century of searchings and gropings, shows himself as the writer who, however small his output, provides a doctrine which contains all the necessary and classic features of nationalism."[65]

Abd al-Rahman al-Bazzaz, a young Iraqi teacher, said that the Arabic language is the "soul of the Arab nation." In *Islam and Arab Nationalism*, al-Bazzaz states that Arab nationalism is based not on a "racial appeal but on linguistic, historical, cultural, and spiritual ties, and on fundamental vital interests."[66]

Writing in 1958, in the heyday of Arab nationalism, Fayez Sayegh, a Palestinian political scientist, put the determinants of this ideology as follows: "There was unanimous agreement that community of language, culture, and history among Arabs had contributed to the formation of the Arab nation, and now marked the Arabs and distinguished them as a nation from others." Sayegh adds that "the awareness of Arabs that they were Arabs, and their determination to be identified as such," was also a determinant of Arab nationhood according to the nationalists, as was "the geographical continuity of the Arab homeland."[67]

A recent defense of Arab nationalism has been offered by Walid Khalidi in the context of the Palestinian question. Khalidi hoped to convince Western intellectuals and politicians that it is difficult for the Arab states to dissociate themselves from the Palestinians. He wrote that the Arab system is "first and foremost a 'Pan' system. It postulates the existence of a single Arab Nation behind the facade of a multiplicity of sovereign states. In pan-Arab ideology, this nation is actual, not potential. . . . From this perspective, the individual Arab states are deviant and transient entities; their frontiers illusory; their rulers interim caretakers or obstacles to be removed."[68] Advancing a similar argument, though not so strongly as Khalidi, is Michael Hudson. In an important work, *Arab Politics: The Search For Legitimacy*, Hudson writes that "Arab nationalism remains a formidable legitimizing resource for kings and presidents alike, and the considerable potential power of a revolutionary like George Habash derives in no small measure from his impeccable Arab nationalist credentials."[69]

The Arab nationalist theory articulated by the aforementioned scholars is questioned in a sizable body of literature. The underlying premise of most criticism is that there is no single Arab nation, but several: Egyptian, Iraqi, Lebanese, Tunisian, etc. This may not be often stated explicitly, but it is evident in the questioning of the various components that are argued to constitute Arab nationalism. What is also criticized is Arab nationalist thought itself, particularly in the second period, namely during the 1930s, 1940s, and 1950s. This thought is understood by some to be fascist, fanatic, and radically different from the liberalism that characterized nationalism in the nineteenth and early twentieth centuries.

History as a component of Arab nationalism is not only questioned by Westerners but by Arab scholars as well. Muhammad Izzat Hejazzi says that the historical experience of Saudi Arabia and Kuwait with imperialism is not necessarily similar to that of Egypt. As for heritage as a unifying factor, Hejazzi does not see the Saudi heritage to be identical with either the Yemeni or the Syrian.[70]

The Arabic language, which in al-Husri's thought is the most important component of Arab nationalism, is also contested. Carl Leiden is one critic of the emphasis al-Husri places on language: "The most obvious common feature in the Arab world is its language, but it is also fair to say not all Arabs speak precisely the same Arabic and, like fragments of the English-speaking world, they do not always take each others' quarrels to heart merely because of the language."[71]

Richard Plaff is also skeptical of the role of the Arabic language. He writes that "the division of Arabic language between the classical form used in writing and the many colloquial variations used in daily speech adds a further complication for the Arab nationalist. With less than twenty percent of the total population within the Arab world capable of reading classical Arabic, or even 'journalistic' Arabic, the language is a limited tool for spreading the message of nationalism through the printed word."[72] Some Arab scholars also are reexamining the unifying role of language. Hejazzi questions the Arabic language as a common characteristic of all the Arabs, saying that classical Arabic is in fact confined to formal settings like symposiums.[73]

Arab nationalist thought is further criticized as being elitist and insensitive to both the socioeconomic dimension of nationalism and to regional nationalisms. Al-Husri's elitism has been noted by many scholars of Arab nationalism, including William Cleveland, whose work, *The Making of an Arab Nationalist*, is a study of Sati al-Husri's thought.

Al-Husri pays little attention to the notion of class or economic factors. Cleveland adds that al-Husri seeks no inspiration from the people or the masses for his ideology.[74]

In evaluating the theoretical contributions of al-Husri, Khadduri writes that he "ignores the strength of local or regional forces that cannot be dismissed as merely parochial feeling [*iqlimi*] just because they run contrary to Arab unity—the cherished objective of his nationalist ideal."[75]

Arab unity is a major goal of Arab nationalism. Until the 1960s, unity took precedence over everything else, over socialism, freedom, or any other goal. Arab unity for al-Husri is paramount. It is more important than Islamic unity. This unity, al-Husri says, is a natural idea that stems from the Arabic language, the history of the Arab nation and from the connections between the Arab countries.[76] In Arab unity, Aflaq finds strength, a factor which in his opinion is crucial in the Arab nation's strategy for struggling against colonialism.[77]

Arab Unity, the title of a book by Sayegh, is equivalent to "the natural condition of health," while its absence, meaning disunity, is the "the state of sickness." Though the concept of unity is not under attack, what is questioned is the approach and the means used to achieve Arab unity, based on critiques of the 1958–1961 Egyptian-Syrian union and other unity attempts. One such critic is Muhammad Helmi. He says that one of the chief barriers to Arab unity is the unscientific, unrealistic means used to accomplish the goal. This nonscientific approach differentiates the Arab experiences with unity from those of the European countries. The latter adopted a gradual approach whereby they started their unity attempts in transitional economic unities, then moved to the European Common Market and finally toward political unity. In other words, political unity, which usually comes first in the Arab world, in Europe will come last. Hejazzi adds that the difference between the Arab and the European approach towards unity can be explained by the difference between a society developed by every standard and one backward by every standard. Thus, he says, it is not surprising that all attempts to achieve Arab unity have failed.[78]

Another major criticism of Arab nationalist thought is that it is marked by some fascist features, which distinguish nationalists of the post–World War I period from those of the nineteenth century. In *Arab Nationalism: A Critical Inquiry*, Bassam Tibi draws a clear distinction between the two generations of nationalists. He accounts for a significant transition from francophilia and anglophilia into what he calls germanophilia. According to him, this change "can be considered simply as the substitution of one set of ideas for another." Tibi sees this germanophilia as narrow, one-sided, and influenced by German nationalist ideas current during the Napoleonic Wars and marked by romantic irrationalism and a hatred of the French. "They were particularly attracted by the notion of the 'People,' as defined by German Romanticism, which they proceeded to apply to the 'Arab Nation,'" while philosophers such as Kant, Hegel, and others were excluded due to their "universalism." "For the nineteenth-century nationalists, such as Adib Ishaq, the liberal national state was simply a means of emancipation; its democratic constitutional character was always taken for granted. The germanophiles of the World War I period, however, saw the national state as the apogee of the 'Arab Nation'—in other words, as an end in itself." Tibi considers Sati al-Husri as an ideal representative of the germanophile school: "It was Sati' al-Husri who began this tradition of populist germanophile Arab nationalism. His nationalism was not mystificatory, fanatic, or fascist, but he laid the foundations for the kind of fanatical nationalism formulated by his disciple Michel Aflaq, which has found expression in the semi-fascist military dictatorship in Iraq and Syria under the aegis of the Ba'th Party."[79]

Regarding the Nazi influence on Aflaq, Eric Rouleau quotes the following from a letter he received from a companion of Aflaq who had taught at the University of Damascus: "He [Aflaq] came back to Syria full of admiration for the works of Alfred Rosenberg, the theorist of Nazi racism, and in particular for the *Myth of the Twentieth Century*, which he had read in Grosclaude's translation. He thought at the time that Hitler's Germany, by contrast with the communist countries, had succeeded in achieving the perfect synthesis of nationalism and socialism." Furthermore, included in Aflaq's polemics is a statement in which he says that the Arab nation is endowed with an "immortal mission," a statement which Gordon Torrey explains in terms of Aflaq's acquaintance with nineteenth century German philosophy.[80]

This lack of distinction between the different theorists of nationalism is one of Tibi's criticisms of William Cleveland, the author of *The Making of an Arab Nationalist*. According to Tibi, Cleveland's "insistence on the notion of 'the transition from Ottomanism to Arabism' makes him overlook the fundamental change of direction within Arab nationalism from francophilia to germanophilia."[81]

If language, history, ancestry, and interests are some of the components that make up the Arab nation, another component, perhaps the most important of all, is Islam. The significance of religion rests on the claim that those who consider Islam a basic component of Arab nationalism are not secular, while those who accept the affinity between Islam and nationalism are likely to be accused of weakening the Arab nation by excluding non-Muslim groups. Is this the only factor that makes the relationship between Islam and Arab nationalism significant? Not at all. There is another factor, a strategic one: how to mobilize support for the

Arab nationalist cause without using Islam as a means. In other words, would there be an Arab nationalism without Islam?

The problematic relationship between Islam and Arab nationalism and how this relationship is reflected in the development of a nationalist theory is expressed by Sylvia Haim:

> The idea that the Arabs by themselves constitute a true political entity could not be a familiar one in the Middle East. Hitherto, Muslim historiography had been based on and had taken its bearings from the fact of the Revelation given to Muhammad and the prodigious consequences which followed it. It had not previously occurred to a writer to claim historical continuity with pagans and idolaters, to seek glorification in their exploits, or to put on a par Hammurabi and Harun al-Rashid, Sargon and al-Ma'mun, Christians and Jews with Muslims, on the score that all these constituted original manifestations of the same original Arab genius. Yet such a revolutionary theory was necessary if the Arab nation were to be defined and endowed with an ancestry and entity. For it would not do to identify Arabs and Islam completely, since Islam comprised many more people than the Arabs, and since it would also make nonsense of the claim that the Arabs were different from the Turks and therefore had the right to secede from them.[82]

The complexity of the following debate may provide the reader with an idea of the relative success of this secular theory.

Abd al-Rahman al-Bazzaz tries to reconcile Islam and Arab nationalism. Aware of the importance of the universal character of Islamic religion, al-Bazzaz stresses its revelation to the Arabs and not to others. Al-Bazzaz implies that the Arabs should be proud that the Prophet is one of them and the Koran was written in their language. Realizing that what preceded Islam was an era referred to as *al-Jahilia*, meaning ignorance, he does his best to deny any discontinuity in the history of the Arabs. This becomes clear when al-Bazzaz says that Islam retained many of the pre-Islamic Arab customs and that because the pre-Islamic Arabs were civilized a genius like Muhammad could arise from among them.[83]

The works of Christian theorists of Arab nationalism illustrates that reconciliation with Islam remains a prerequisite for popular support. Constantine Zurayq, a Christian and a distinguished professor of Arab history at the American University of Beirut, said that "Arab nationalists should fall back on the sources of their religion and derive from it inspiration and spiritual guidance." In the life of the Prophet, he "found the basis of a new civilization."[84] Rabbath, like Zurayq a Syrian Christian, "carried the idea of the religious basis of Arab nationalism a step further by arguing that Islam is in essence a national religion. True, he analyzed

Arab nationalism essentially in terms of culture and language, but he attributed to Islam the basis of political unity."[85]

Michel Aflaq, also a Christian and one of the founders of the Ba'th Party, went to extremes in a lecture delivered in 1943, which commemorated Prophet Muhammad's birthday. In it, Aflaq "shows a conscious and total departure from orthodox religious attitudes and explicitly represents Islam not as a divine revelation but in part as a response to Arab needs at the time of Muhammad and in part as a foundation of Arabism."[86]

Aflaq not only considers Islam as the beginning of Arabism, but he also tries to reassure non-Muslims that there is no need to fear the natural affinity between Islam and Arab nationalism:

> The Arabs are unique among the other nations in that their national awakening coincides with the birth of a religious message, or rather that this message was an expression of the national awakening. . . . They did not expand for the sake of expansion . . . but to perform a religious duty which is all truth, guidance, mercy, justice and generosity . . . as long as the affinity between Arabism and Islam is strong and as long as we see Arabism as a body with Islam as its soul, there is no room for fear of the Arabs going to extremes in their nationality.[87]

Despite crises such as the Lebanese Civil War, which have affected the communal coexistence of different religious and ethnic groups in the Arab world, there are still those ready to view Arab nationalism as a solution to the sectarian problem. In a recent article entitled "Arab Christians and the Future," Zurayq still defends the way Islam treated the Christians. He writes that the Europeans in the Middle Ages did not treat Islam better than Islam treated the Christians and Christianity. While considering sectarianism to have emerged under the Ottomans and their Millet system, he believes that the basic conflict about the future of Arab Christians is not between Christianity and Islam or between Christians and Muslims. Rather, it is a conflict between the reactionaries and those believing in liberation on both sides. This problem becomes more complicated, and the future becomes darker, whenever reactionary forces grow stronger on either side. On the contrary, the problem becomes easier whenever the forces of liberation become strengthened.[88]

Advocating a similar view on this subject is Victor Sahab. Though he acknowledges that Muslims and others had persecuted Arab Christians throughout history, the Muslims, he says, had been more lenient than others. He does not see the solution in either the establishment of separate religious states or in secularism in its Western definition. Sahab downplays the impact of the Lebanese Civil War on Arab nationalism and on the relations between the Christians and the Muslims. As a solution, he suggests the establishment of an Arab state hostile to the West like Nasir's Egypt. His example is Nasir's position in support of the Christian Cypriots against the Muslim Turks.[89]

Sahab is not the only one who argues that Arab nationalism has a place for non-Muslims, and uses the Arab nationalist regime of Nasir as an example. In a study of the speeches and statements made by Nasir, Marilyn Nasr found the Egyptian president to have been more secular than the Christian Michel Aflaq, who organically mixes religion and nationalism so that nationalism includes Islam and Islam includes nationalism. Nasr's study of the relationship between religion and Islam in Nasir's thought reveals interesting findings. She writes that the early usage of the Arab nation can be traced to the term nation, that refers to Egypt and not to the nation of Islam. But later on, there was a change in the usage of the term: there was a shift from Egypt as the nation to that of the Arab nation, and this was evident in Nasir's speeches in 1953, 1954, and 1955. As to what relationship Nasir saw between the Egyptian or the Arab people on one hand and the Muslim world on the other, such relationship was found to be that of "cooperation" and "solidarity." As for the relationship between Egypt and the Arab world, that relationship was one of "belonging," "integration," and "organic." How Nasir used the term Arab nationalism is also revealing: it lacked religious connotations and meanings. He referred to it as "movement," "ideology," "race," and "nationality." Similarly, Nasir's referrence to Arab unity turns out also to be secular. Nasr writes that in talking about Arab unity, the religious factor is absent from Nasir's speeches as a basic component of nationalism. The basic components, for Nasir, are the unity of language, the unity of history, and the unity of hope.[90] This makes Nasir's views consistent with al-Husri's definition of the basic components of Arab nationalism.

Again Najm Bezirgan has a slightly different assessment of the place of Islam and Arab nationalism in Nasir's thought: ". . . it is difficult to trace, in his writings and speeches, a sustained theory of Arab nationalism. In practice, however, he wavered between emphasizing a secular and an Islamic approach to nationalism according to the dictates of the political realities in the Egypt of his day."[91]

All the theoretical attempts to reconcile Islam and Arab nationalism and all the arguments that religious conflicts do not harm the cause of Arab nationalism are questioned. Critics challenge both the logic of the synthesis and the motives of these scholars making reconciliation attempts.

Bezirgan observes some inconsistency in Aflaq's definition of the relationship between Islam and Arab nationalism. On one hand, the Ba'thist leader gives a definition similar to that of al-Husri, yet he seemed uncomfortable with it: "Islam is universal and eternal, but its universality does not mean that it cannot accommodate, at the same time, different meanings and different trends . . . its eternity does not mean that it does not change . . . but despite its continuous change, its roots will remain the same . . . [Islam] is relative to a specific time and space and absolute in meaning and action within the limits of this time and space." But in 1950, Aflaq is quoted to have said that the state he conceived for the Arabs was a secular institution, founded on a social base, or nationalism, and a moral base, or freedom.[92]

Was there a successful attempt to develop a secular theory of Arab nationalism, a theory in which Islam is not a pivotal factor? Bezirgan's answer appears to be in the negative. Islam and Arab nationalism, as they relate to each other, are still interwined: "As is clear from this survey of the literature on the relation between Arab nationalism and Islam, religion has always been the idiom in which the overwhelming majority of the nationalist intellectuals have expressed themselves. Recent Arabic thought has not known any militant attack on religion, although religious institutions and the clergy have been attacked, particularly by the Arab Marxists and the leftists."[93]

Today, secularism remains an open issue among Arab intellectuals. One of the themes raised in a recent symposium on Arab nationalism and Islam, organized by the journal *Mustaqbal Al 'Arabi*, was that secularism is now seen as a means to address the division in Arab nationalist thought. Some of the participants saw secularism as a means to end the division while others saw it as impractical and inconsistent with the natural affinity between Islam and Arab nationalism.[94]

Another important factor in the debate is the phenomenon of the zealousness with which some Christian Arabs advocated an intimacy between Islam and Arab nationalism. What are the motivations behind such zeal? Haim answers this question by showing how the considerations that motivate Muslim writers on Arab nationalism are different from those of the Christians: "When Muslim writers argue that Islam and Arab nationalism are not incompatible, and even that each is implicit in the other, we can see that they are studying a vital problem which concerns them intimately." Such writers used to "encounter traditionalist objections" as well as "convince themselves that in being Arab nationalists they are also good Muslims." The Christian writers who advocate Arab nationalism, according to Haim, are often reacting to the breakdown of the Millet system without which "the younger generations [of Christians] no longer found communal ties satisfying, and some of them transferred their affections to an Arab nation of which they claimed to be fellow members, along with the Muslims."[95]

It can be argued that al-Husri's writings belong to the interwar period, though most of his works started to be published in the 1950s. This argument is based on his themes and concerns which were peculiar to the historical period in which he lived. Though his works have continued to inspire many Arab nationalists since the 1948 Palestine War, al-Husri would almost totally disagree with injecting the Arab nationalist theory with such notions as the class struggle, as the Neo-Ba'thists did in 1963, and he would have also disagreed with placing socialism and freedom, two of the three slogans of the Ba'th party, on the same footing as unity. He would have rejected all these revisions even had he lived until 1968.

The discourse on Arab nationalism underwent some changes following the 1948 Palestine War. "Radical Arab nationalism" is what characterized the post-1948 period. The 1948 Arab defeat is described by Tareq Ismael to have been

> so traumatic to the Arab masses . . . that it fostered a transformation of Arab nationalism from the glories of the past to the failures—particularly the failure in Palestine—of the present. . . . Palestine symbolized the failure of Arab nationalism to meet the supreme challenge: the challenge of national survival. Liberal Arab nationalism had fed on the euphoria of Arab heritage; such euphoria appeared bankrupt indeed in the reality of Arab ineptitude in Palestine. Thus, a profound reappraisal of Arab society had ensued. Every aspect of Arab society has come under fire—social, political, economic, religious. Under the threat of extinction as symbolized by Palestine, Arab nationalism has reasserted itself, not in the glorification of the past but in the reform of the present.[96]

Three important forces took an active role in the radical reformulation of Arab nationalism: Nasserites, Ba'thists, and Arab nationalists. Though these three groups joined forces in the 1950s and part of the 1960s, they parted company at a later stage. Nasir's Arab nationalism assumed the more moderate role later in the third period, namely in the 1960s, while radicalism marked the nationalism of the Ba'thists and the Arab nationalists.

Nasir, Egypt's strongman from 1952 to 1970 and the most charismatic Arab leader since the Prophet Muhammad, was the most important force in popularizing the idea of Arab nationalism. He made this contribution even though he did not develop an elaborate theory of Arab nationalism as did al-Husri and Aflaq. Regarding the conditions that made Arab nationalism a powerful force, Leiden highlights the establishment of the state of Israel in May 1948, but equally attributes the powerful emergence of Arab nationalism to the leadership of Nasir himself: ". . . Arab nationalism required able Arab leadership. . . . It was only in the aftermath of this war [1948–1949 war] that the leader emerged; Gamal Abdel Nasser of Egypt. In short, Nasser and Israel were the symbiotic catalysts for the Arab nationalism that bloomed with fervor and excitement in the 1950s and 1960s and which still exists although in diminished form."[97]

Egypt's size and strategic importance in the Arab world were two important factors that contributed to the powerful emergence of Arab nationalism in the 1950s and the 1960s. Nasir defied all Western objections and concluded a significant arms deal with the Communist bloc in 1955, nationalized the Suez Canal in July 1956, and fought against the British, French, and Israeli forces that attacked Egypt in October 1956. He also fought against all Western defense arrangements in the region, foremost among them the Baghdad Pact. And most important of all, he achieved a long-cherished Arab nationalist goal, unity (the 1958 Egyptian-Syrian unity). Nasir, unlike al-Husri and the early Aflaq, talked about socialism and carried out different types of reforms that appealed to large segments of the Arab population. In calling for this, he also differed from the classical theorists of nationalism, for they succeeded only in reaching the literate members of the middle class while Nasir appealed to the peasants and workers.

The Ba'th party was a second factor that contributed to the powerful emergence of Arab nationalism in the 1950s and 1960s. Though it was overshadowed by Nasir, due both to his incumbency and his articulation of the same Arab nationalist values advocated by the Ba'thists, the Ba'th party gradually evolved and appealed to significant groups in Syria, Lebanon, Jordan, and Iraq. The Ba'th party started to play an important role in Arab politics in 1954, especially when it distanced itself from Aflaq's racial nationalism and after it was united with Akram Haurani's Arab Socialist party, the membership of which was mostly of poor peasant origins. This unification resulted in breaking down the domination of the urban petty bourgeoisie which made up Aflaq's party, and also in adding the term "socialism" to the party's name. As a result of these developments, the Ba'th party emerged as an effective force in Syrian politics, for it was then appealing both to the rural strata and to the middle class which was politically conscious and sincerely nationalistic. This effectiveness was manifest in the 1954 elections when the Ba'th party emerged as the third most numerous party in the parliament with sixteen deputies. The 1958–1961 unity between Egypt and Syria, which was initiated by the Ba'th party leadership, was a major accomplishment for the party. Though it resulted in the dissolution of the Ba'th as a separate party, the party leadership had translated its Arab nationalist commitment to unity into practice.[98]

Though the cause of Arab nationalism suffered a setback after Syria's secession from Egypt in 1961, as did the Ba'th party itself as a result of its endorsement of the secession, in 1963 a Ba'thist regime overthrew the Syrian regime that had dissolved the union with Egypt. This rejuvenated interest in Arab nationalism, an interest further reinforced by a Ba'thist military coup in Iraq. The result was serious attempts to establish a new unity, between Syria, Iraq and Egypt. But these attempts between the Ba'thist leaders and the Egyptian president failed, resulting in serious divisions within the Ba'thist leadership, divisions that brought forth a new young generation of Ba'thists who can be called "radical Arab nationalists."

What the new generation challenged was not only the classical formulation of the nationalist theory by people like al-Husri, but also the revised Arab nationalism as advocated by both Nasir and the traditional leadership of their own party, namely Aflaq and Salah al-Bitar who were referred to as the Old Guard.

This new generation of Ba'thists, known as the Neo-Ba'thists, and other Arab nationalist groups such as the Arab Nationalist Movement (ANM), began to move in a radical-leftist direction. This move was due to historical events, such as the failure of the Arab "progressive" regimes, Syria's secession from Egypt in 1961, the reorganization of the Ba'th party after the secession, and the victory of the Algerian revolutionaries. Later on, this radical trend was reinforced further by the Arab defeat of 1967, and the increase in U.S. support for Israel which followed. Though most of the Arab nationalist movements, including the ANM and the Ba'th party, supported Nasir during the 1950s, they became disenchanted with his policies. Their disenchantment was due to the unwillingness, or the inability, of the Arab liberation movement, as represented by the 1952 Egyptian revolution and the traditional leadership of the Ba'th party, to carry out the initial goals they had set for themselves: equality for all the deprived social groups, political democracy, ending Western influence in the Arab world, liberating Palestine, and waging a struggle to overthrow Arab conservative regimes.

These radical Arab nationalists, the Neo-Ba'thists and the ANM, which later converted itself into several military organizations acting within the PLO framework, advocated a radical approach to liberate Palestine (the popular war of liberation strategy), and to carry out an all-Arab revolution. By adopting this approach, they refused any compromise with the ruling Arab classes, whose interests, they claimed, are linked with those of the West. Thus, their solution was the destruction of the political and economic power of that group. The Neo-Ba'thists, the only then-ruling radical group (1966–1970), clearly showed their rejection of policies influenced by traditional Arab nationalist considerations. They passed radical propositions such as "scientific socialism" in the Sixth Regional Congress of the Ba'th party held in 1963 in Syria. They showed no interest in the various Arab unity schemes that were suggested by statesmen and political movements alike. They dissociated themselves from many policies collectively adopted by a majority of the Arab countries. They also violated many of the decisions reached by Arab Summit Conferences held during the 1964–1970 period. Unlike early nationalists, including even Nasir and the more traditional leaders, their main emphasis was that social transformation within Arab societies must precede any unity plans. One of the main objections they had against Nasir was that he wanted to establish unity at the state level, referred to as unity from "above," while they believed in establishing a unity from "below," at the level of the masses.

After the Neo-Ba'thists' tenure ended in November 1970 and the ANM became preoccupied with Palestinian politics, the critics of traditional Arab nationalist thought confined themselves to intellectual circles. Many of these critics can be still considered radical Arab nationalists, and several have leftist or Marxist leanings. Some of them started writing in the 1960s and continue today.

One of these critics was the late Marxist Arab nationalist thinker Yasin al-Hafiz. Critical of the Arab revolutionary and progressive intellectuals who refrained from addressing the issue of sectarianism and the minorities in the Arab world, he called for a renewal in Arab national thought. One of his arguments was that Arab society lives in a prenationalist stage, or without nationalism and citizenship. The people still live isolated into parochial loyalties: family, tribe, religion, and village.[99]

Another important critic of Arab national thought, also coming from the left, is Nadim al-Bitar. He starts his article, "Towards a New Unionist Thought," by making important methodological observations. He says that when we study the phenomenon of suicide, we study the cases of suicide. When we study the revolutionary phenomenon, we study the revolutions in history. Arab unionist thought, according to al-Bitar, was studying the revolutionary phenomenon without studying revolutions in history. What unionist thought provided to the study of unity approximates journalistic articles rather than scientific thought. He concludes by saying that unionist thought is not just a political necessity; it is a science, and science is based on facts, incidents, and tendencies.[100]

One more critic is George Taribishi. His main criticism is that Arab traditional thought paid no serious attention to the regional state, to the *Qitriyya*, seeing those states as cartoons. The *Qitriyya*, according to Taribishi, is one of the foremost dangers posed to Arab unity.[101]

This by no means exhausts the literature published in Arabic since the 1960s, a literature generally critical of traditional nationalist thought. But these intellectual efforts have been limited to a small, yet daring, circle of intellectuals. Their voice was heard and carefully listened to in the 1960s, but with the emergence of a new era in Arab politics, commonly called the Saudi or oil era, their influence has diminished.

However, there is another group that goes to extremes and mourns the death of Arab nationalism. The views of this group will be explored next.

IV

Some contemporary scholars proclaim the death of Arab nationalism, or what is often referred to as Pan-Arabism. This thesis was advanced earlier, but it gained considerable importance when it was made by an Arab scholar, Fouad Ajami, in a celebrated article in *Foreign Affairs* in 1978, as well as in other publications. The title of his 1978 article spells out his argument: "The End of Pan-Arabism." Ajami writes that "an idea that has dominated the political consciousness of modern Arabs is nearing its end, if it is not already a thing of the past. It is the myth of pan-Arabism, of the *Umma Arabiyya Wahida Dhat Risala Khalida*, 'the one Arab nation with an immortal mission,'" and he adds: "Now, however, *raison d'etat*, once an alien and illegitimate doctrine, is gaining ground. Slowly and grimly, with a great deal of anguish and violence, a 'normal' state system is becoming a fact of life." This thesis is eloquently developed throughout the article. In another article, "The Struggle For Egypt's Soul," published in *Foreign Policy*, Ajami demonstrates how Egypt's policy toward the Arab-Israeli conflict confirms that both Arab unity and Pan-Arabism are a myth. Between Egypt and the Arab world, Ajami writes, there is a gap, not simply created by a leader like Sadat, but with psychological and cultural foundations.[102]

The death of Pan-Arabism, or the end of utopian ideologies and the dreams of a new and united Arab world, is vividly pictured in Ajami's book *The Arab Predicament*:

> Thus the movement from the era of nationalism and ideology to the era of commissions and the middlemen. In the former, the Arabs had subsisted on Nasser's grandeur; some (unfortunately for them) were taken by the metaphysics of Michel Aflaq, the theorist of the Ba'th Party, and his abstractions about Arab unity, love, and the primacy of the nation. A decade later, they were being treated to the theatrics of the middlemen, to the great achievements of Adnan Khashoggi [a successful Saudi businessman]; they were told about the 'regional packages'—large deals in-

volving Saudi capital, Egyptian labor, and Sudanese land that would achieve, without political struggles and disagreements, the unity that had eluded the pan-Arabists.[103]

Stressing a similar theme is William Brown. A distinctive difference between Brown and Ajami is that the former highlights the implications of the 1982 war for the importance of Pan-Arabism as a force in Arab politics. Writing in *Foreign Policy*, Brown says that

the 1982 Israeli invasion of Lebanon showed how wide the gulf between nation and state in the Arab world has grown. For the first time, Israeli troops invaded an Arab capital far from the territory that Jews could claim through divine promise. And the attack was directed specifically against the Palestinians, symbols of the Arab nation. Yet no Arab leader responded to Arafat's appeals. Moreover, most Arab governments initially refused to provide haven for the PLO fighters. Algeria, Iraq, Jordan, and Tunisia provided limited hospitality. The Sudan, Syria, and the two Yemens also opened their doors. But in every case, the Palestinian guests have been isolated and carefully watched. Everyone uses them, but no one trusts them. As symbols of the Arab nation, they are inimical to the interests of an Arab state.[104]

While Ajami may find many scholars in the West agreeing with his thesis that Arab nationalism has ceased to exist, a sizable proportion of Arab intellectuals disagree. Hassan Nafaa, an Egyptian scholar, expressed the displeasure of these intellectuals in a lengthy study devoted to criticizing Ajami's views. According to Nafaa, "the fact of Arab nationalism cannot be argued away. It is a major political and social phenomenon, as well as a mobilizing ideology that has shaken the whole region since the last years of the nineteenth century." Nafaa argues that Ajami confuses "the idea and its implementation, the ideology and the political movement. The idea of 'one Arab nation with an immortal mission' has never been translated into a viable political project. It is still a slogan, like that of the Communist Manifesto: 'Workers of the world unite!' To say that pan-Arabism has died because it failed to achieve the one Arab nation is like saying Marxism does not exist anymore because it failed to unify the workers of the world!" As for Ajami's argument that a state-system logic has replaced that of the Pan-Arabist one, Nafaa says the following: "In such conditions, a 'workable pan-Arab system of states' based on the concept of *raison d'Etat* is hardly conceivable. Because in the states where institutions are dead and the mechanism process of consensus formation is blocked, the *raison d'Etat* may be the *raison de la famille royale* or that of a dictator. Such a system will constantly be under the pressure of centrifugal forces which are unable to express themselves through adequate legitimate channels; and, after his emergence, a powerful Arab leader could be tempted to manipulate them."[105]

One of the scholars Nafaa cites to support his attack on Ajami is Carl Leiden. Nafaa's reading of Leiden is selective. Though Leiden believes the idea of Arab nationalism is not dead, his analysis of the Arab world leads him to conclude that Arab nationalism is unlikely to survive as a significant force: "But the Arab world today is so complex and fragmented, with such a maldistribution of population and resources (with a result that exploitation is also skewed in its local intensities) that it seems unlikely that Arab *qawmiyya* nationalism will survive as a major formative force." He also says: "But the old nationalism that reached the peak of its intensity under Nasser in the late 1950s and early 1960s is not likely to again be so formidable within the foreseeable future."[106]

But still Leiden makes a defense of nationalism in general, and of Arab nationalism in particular: "Yet, the idea is not dead; it still possesses force and it is possible that it can be resurrected at some later time." As to its future, he says that "nationalism will always exist where one group feels exploited by another. This of course will happen in the Arab lands as often as it will happen elsewhere. But its total demise is equally unlikely; those who articulate its virtues will be around for a long time. But other *wataniyya* nationalisms will arise as well as 'regional' agglutinative nationalism."[107]

Essential to the arguments that question the basic components of Arab nationalism, and to those announcing its demise, is the lack of loyalty to nationalist ideology felt by many religious minorities in the Arab world, such as the Iraqi Shiites, groups assumed by many Arab nationalist theorists to be Arab, and even by a country like Egypt, which is considered by many to be the center of Arabism. These assumptions are challenged by many scholars in the Arab world who still defend the Arabism of Egypt and the Iraqi Shiites. Muhammad Rida Muharam writes that Egypt's affiliation with Arabism is firm and anthropologically proven, and true historically and geographically regardless of the varying degrees of the Egyptians' perceptions. Arabism, he adds, is evident in the names of the people as well in those of the streets.[108]

Wamid Jamal Nazmi, in "The Iraqi Shiites and the Question of Arab Nationalism," writes that there are three reasons for Shiite Arab nationalist feelings and solidarity with the Sunnis, whose Arab nationalist credentials are not in question: (1) the emergence of the constitutional movements in Turkey and Iran, (2) the fear of increasing Western imperialist penetration, and (3) the impact of Islamic reformist thought. He adds that the Iraqi Shiites were among the foremost who embraced ideas calling for reforms and Arab nationalism.[109]

Another defender of Arab nationalism is Clovis Maksoud, the permanent United Nations representative of the Arab League, perhaps one of the most important Pan-Arabist organizations. When asked if Pan-Arabism has become a myth, Maksoud's answer was a qualified no. Despite several challenges, mainly because of the Camp David agreement and Sadat's 1977 visit to Jerusalem, which were in violation of an Arab consensus of not negotiating with Israel separately, Arab nationalism, in Maksoud's opinion, remains a reality. Maksoud added that Egypt's separate peace with Israel proved Arab nationalism to be a reality because negotiating with Israel did not become a precedent to be followed but rather an aberration. Arab nationalism in its classical emphasis on language and culture, however, must be recast in a new light, Maksoud said. What should be emphasized today are the functional aspects of Arab nationalism. These, according to Maksoud, lie in improving the economic relations among the Arab states, efforts which should culminate in monetary unity. One further proof cited by Maksoud of the continuing viability of Arab nationalism is the perception of the Arabs by both friendly and unfriendly nations: they consider the Arabs as one bloc, and this is due to the constant interaction between the Arab states and also due to the fact that events in one Arab country are bound to affect other Arab countries.[110]

There are several problems with those arguments announcing the death of Arab nationalism. What specifically is dead? Is it the ideology that aims at unifying all the Arab states into one? Or is it any pragmatic definition of Arab nationalism that may provide a consensus of common denominators from which Arab policymakers are expected not to deviate? Some examples of these common denominators are the Rabat Summit Conference's decision to recognize the PLO as the sole representative of the Palestinian people, the Baghdad Summit Conference's decision to sever diplomatic relations with Egypt, and the overall Arab consensus of not making separate peace with Israel.

Whichever definition Ajami refers to, the evidence so far proves Arab nationalism to be wounded, but not yet dead. The "death" thesis is problematic for two reasons. First, Arab nationalism, as has been discussed, embodies religious, cultural, linguistic, and historical factors. Though the ideology of Arab nationalism in the present time is not effective as a means to generate legitimacy and mobilize people for action, this cannot be diagnosed as "death." Like any ideology, Arab nationalism has been a response to certain historical conditions. When this ideology, as well as its advocates, carried the day in the 1950s and 1960s, it was because of the 1948 loss of Palestine by several Arab constitutional and liberal regimes. This historical factor can also explain the popular support the Islamic fundamentalist movements enjoy today in many Arab countries, in turn attributable to the failure of the Arab nationalist regimes in implementing the goals they set for themselves, foremost among them the liberation of Palestine. Yet, if the religious groups fail to gain sufficient support to seize power and implement their own programs, nationalist ideology may reappear. Such a possibility exists because the components of the Arab nationalist ideology are living values, such as religion, culture, and language. Thus, it cannot be categorically stated that Arab nationalism as an ideology is dead.

A second flaw in the "death" prognosis lies in overlooking the still important role of the middle class in Arab politics. Most advocates of Arab nationalism since the early 1950s have come from the ranks of this class, whose interests are less linked with foreign powers than those of the upper classes. Thus, any power struggle between these two classes is likely to result in the middle class resorting to Arab nationalist ideology as a means to mobilize support. The argument that Arab nationalism is dead, therefore, is hardly tenable as long as the middle class remains a formidable force in Arab politics.

Brown's argument appears oversimplified. There is apparent misinterpretation of why the Palestinians, who are "symbols of Arab nationalism," were not welcomed in many Arab countries. Simply, they were not welcomed because any "welcome" during the war would have constituted an acquiescence of Ariel Sharon, Israel's then–Defense Minister. Furthermore, the Arab states' refusal to accept the Palestinian fighters is not due to a lack of nationalist commitment or Arab solidarity, but rather to a fear of bringing the Arab defeat in Lebanon home, and thus showing their peoples their own ineptness.

V

It cannot be predicted that future developments in the Arab world will not recreate the momentum Arab nationalism had in the 1950s and the 1960s, when one speech by the late Gamal Abd al-Nasir could push millions of Arabs into the streets of Beirut, Damascus, and Cairo. Yet, this ideology, whose aim has been to unify the whole Arab world, has suffered several setbacks, and some are irreversible. In today's Arab world, the classical definitions of Arab nationalism are a thing of the past. Yet, many scholars, in their efforts to understand the role of nationalism in the Arab world, cling to these very definitions. The danger is that in recognizing the failure of Arab nationalism, the very real political role of this ideology may be discounted. Therefore, I suggest a rudimentary strategy for future research on Arab nationalism. One important element of this strategy is a new definition of Arab nationalism, one which reflects the current state of Arab politics.

It is a mistake to think that what links one Arab state with another could be similar to the link between France and Nigeria. While the existing relationships between the Arab states fall short of meeting the expectations of many Arab nationalists, these ties maintain certain nationalist characteristics. What else explains the tens of billions of dollars given by the Arab oil-producing states to Egypt, Syria, Jordan, and the PLO in their struggle against Israel? What else explains an almost equal amount given by the same states to Iraq in its war against Iran? What else explains a consensus in adopting certain policies on a wide range of issues by a consistent majority of the Arab states? A second element of the future research strategy, therefore, should center on studying all forms of relationships between the Arab states in comparison with relations among other states, especially states belonging to a particular region, such as Africa or Latin America. This study might yield significant results, particularly regarding whether what links one Arab state with another is similar to what links Mexico with Guatemala, especially when these two countries share both religion and language. If the results show dissimilarity in the links, as I believe likely, the research then must focus on the components of the relationships between the Arab states. Thus new components could emerge to replace the classical ones of Arab nationalism. Such a study would also contribute to a new theory of Arab nationalism, more realistic and more reflective of the effects of the partition of the Arab world early in this century.

Notes

1. Sadoun Hamadi, "Tajdeed al-Hadeeth 'An al-Qawmiyya al-Arabiyya" [Renewing the discourse on Arab nationalism], *Mustaqbal Al 'Arabi* (January 1984), pp. 6–7.

2. Fayez Sayegh, *Arab Unity* (New York: The Devin-Adair Company, 1958), p. 11.

3. George Antonius, *The Arab Awakening* (New York: Capricorn Books, 1965), p. 18.

4. William Cleveland, *The Making of An Arab Nationalist* (Princeton: Princeton University Press, 1971), p. 127.

5. Richard Plaff, "The Function of Arab Nationalism," *Comparative Politics*, vol. 2, no. 2 (January 1970), p. 154.

6. Charles Malik, "The Near East: The Search for Truth," *Foreign Affairs*, vol. 30, no. 2 (January 1952), p. 232.

7. Majid Khadduri, *Political Trends In The Arab World* (Baltimore and London: The Johns Hopkins Press, 1970), p. 19.

8. Zaki al-Arsuzi, *Al-Mu'alafat al-Kamila* [The complete works], Vol. 4 (Damascus: The Political Administration Press of the Army and Armed Forces, 1974), pp. 215, 346. On al-Arsuzi's background and his relationship with the Ba'th party, see Eric Rouleau, "The Syrian Enigma: What is the Ba'th?" in Irene Gendzier, ed., *A Middle East Reader* (New York: Pegasus, 1969).

9. Bassam Tibi, *Arab Nationalism: A Critical Inquiry*, trans. by Marion Farouk-Sluglett and Peter Sluglett (London and Basingstoke: The Macmillan Press, 1981), p. 61.

10. Ibid., pp. 62–64. See also Sylvia Haim, ed., *Arab Nationalism: An Anthology* (Berkeley & Los Angeles: University of California Press, 1962), pp. 3–4, and Antonius, pp. 21–34.

11. Haim, pp. 3–4.

12. Albert Hourani, *Arabic Thought In The Liberal Age: 1798–1939* (London: Oxford University Press, 1970), p. 261.

13. Tibi, p. 72.

14. Ibid., p. 73.

15. Haim, pp. 3–4.

16. Hourani, p. 261.

17. Quoted in Haim, p. 14.

18. Muhammad Amara, ed., *Al-Afghani, Complete Works* (Cairo), p. 349, quoted in Najm Bezirgan, "Islam and Arab Nationalism," *Middle East Review*, vol. 11, no. 2 (Winter 1978–1979), p. 38.

19. Ibid., p. 38.

20. Haim, pp. 9, 14–15.

21. Ibid., pp. 18–19.

22. Tibi, pp. 64, 68.

23. William Cleveland, "Sources of Arab Nationalism: An Overview," *Middle East Review*, vol. 11, no. 3 (Spring 1979), p. 26.

24. Arnold Hottinger, *The Arabs: Their History, Culture and Place in the Modern World* (Berkeley and Los Angeles: University of California Press, 1963), p. 193.

25. Bezirgan, p. 38.

26. Haim, p. 21.

27. Ibid.

28. Ibid., pp. 23–24.

29. Khadduri, p. 181.

30. Bezirgan, p. 39.

31. Muhammad Amara, ed., *Al-Kawakibi, Complete Works* (Cairo: 1970), p. 417, quoted in Bezirgan, p. 39. See also Hourani, pp. 271–273.

32. Haim, p. 26.

33. Bezirgan, p. 39.

34. Ibid., p. 39.

35. Haim, p. 27.

36. Ibid., pp. 29–30.

37. Ibid., p. 30. See also As'aad Razouq's article, "Negib Azoury, Al-Wahdawee al-Majhul" [The unknown unionist], *Mustaqbal Al 'Arabi* (November 1978), pp. 86–95.

38. Antonius, p. 47. See also p. 48 on Butrus al-Bustani and other Syrian and Lebanese Christians' contributions to Arab nationalism.

39. Ahmad Sudqi al-Dajani, "Mulaahazat Hawla Nash'at al-Fiqr al-Qawmi al-'Arabi wa Tatawruhu" [Notes on the origins of Arab nationalist thought and its development], *Mustaqbal Al 'Arabi* (August 1980), p. 129.

40. Cleveland, p. 28.

41. Haim, p. 34.

42. Ibid., p. 35.

43. Zeine Zeine, *Arab-Turkish Relations And The Emergence Of Arab Nationalism* (Beirut: Khayat's, 1958), p. 77.

44. Hourani, p. 262.

45. Al-Dajani, p. 129.

46. Faysal Daraj, "Shaql al-Fiqr al-Qawmi Fi al-Qarn al-Ataasi' 'Ashar" [The form of Arab nationalist thought in the nineteenth century] *Mustaqbal Al 'Arabi* (September 1978), pp. 94, 97.

47. Walid Qaziha, "Fikraat al-Wahdaa al-Arabiyya Fi Matla' al-Qarn al-'Ishreen" [The idea of Arab unity in the beginning of the twentieth century], *Mustaqbal Al 'Arabi* (November 1978), pp. 15, 16–17.

48. Samir Amin, *The Arab Nation*, trans. by Michael Pollis (London: Zed Press, 1978), p. 7.

49. Ibid., pp. 21, 81.

50. Tibi, pp. xi–xii. For a critical review of Amin's work, particularly from an Arab nationalist perspective, see Victor Sahab's review "Al-Umma al-Arabiyya wa Siraa' al-Tabaqaat" [The Arab nation and class struggle], *Mustaqbal Al 'Arabi* (January 1979). The reviewer finds Amin's book (the Arabic translation) to include factual errors.

51. Tibi, pp. 87–88.

52. Khadduri, p. 20.

53. Hourani, pp. 295–296.

54. A speech reproduced by Sati al-Husri in *Yaum Maisalun* [The battle of Maisalun] (Beirut: 1948), p. 207, quoted in Haim, p. 35.

55. Quoted in *Faysal ibn al-Hussein fi aqwalihi wa khitabatihi* [Faysal ibn al-Hussein in his sayings and speeches] (Baghdad: 1945), p. 175, cited in Haim, p. 35.

56. See Haim, p. 35.

57. See Ibid., pp. 37–38.

58. Abdullah al-Alayili, "What Is Arab Nationalism," in Haim, pp. 121–123, 124, 125, 126, 127.

59. Haim, pp. 42–43. On al-Husri's life and thought, see studies of him by Tibi and Cleveland. See also Hourani, p. 312.

60. Hourani, pp. 312–313.

61. Haim, p. 44. On Egypt in the writings of al-Husri, see the interesting work by Khayrieh Qasimieh, "Misr Fi Kitaabat Sati al-Husri" [Egypt in the writings of Sati al-Husri], *Mustaqbal Al 'Arabi* (May 1979), esp. pp. 131, 139. In defense of Egypt's Arabism, see Muhammad Rida Muharam, "Al-'Awdaa Ilaa Urubaa" [The return to Arabism], *Mustaqbal Al 'Arabi* (June 1981).

62. Quoted in Hourani, pp. 313–314.

63. Michel Aflaq, "Nationalism and Revolution," in Haim, p. 243.

64. Khadduri, p. 195.

65. Haim, p. 72.

66. Abd al-Rahman al-Bazzaz, "Islam and Arab Nationalism," in Haim, p. 174. He is also quoted in Hourani, p. 309.

67. Sayegh, pp. 73–74.

68. Walid Khalidi, "Thinking the Unthinkable: A Sovereign Palestinian State," *Foreign Affairs*, vol. 56, no. 4 (July 1978), pp. 695–696.

69. Michael Hudson, *Arab Politics: The Search For Legitimacy* (New Haven: Yale University Press, 1977), p. 6.

70. "Nadwaat Al-Mustaqbal Al-'Arabi: Al-Wahdaa al-Arabiyya bayna al-Waaqi' wa al-'Amal" [Mustaqbal Al 'Arabi's Symposium on Arab Unity Between Reality and Hope], *Mustaqbal Al 'Arabi* (September 1979), p. 138.

71. Carl Leiden, "Arab Nationalism Today," *Middle East Review*, vol. 11, no. 2 (Winter 1978–1979), p. 45.

72. Plaff, p. 154.

73. "Nadwaat Al-Mustaqbal Al-'Arabi: Al-Wahdaa al-Arabiyya bayna al-Waqqi' wa al-'Amal," p. 138.

74. *The Making Of An Arab Nationalist*, pp. 180, 181–182.

75. Khadduri, pp. 209–210.

76. Sati al-Husri, *Araa' wa 'Ahaadeeth fi al-Wataniyya wa al-Qawmiyya* [Views and addresses on patriotism and nationalism] (Beirut: Center for Arab Unity Studies, 1984), pp. 107, 109–110.

77. Itamar Rabinovitch, *Syria Under the Ba'th, 1963–1966* (Jerusalem: Israel Universities Press, 1972), pp. 9–10.

78. "Nadwaat Al-Mustaqbal Al-'Arabi: Al-Wada al-Arabiyya bayna al-Waqqi' wa al-'Amal," pp. 139–140. See Sayegh, p. 77. There were several attempts toward unifying two or more Arab states: in 1963, there was an attempt between Egypt, Syria, and Iraq; in 1971, between Egypt, Syria, and Libya; in 1978, between Iraq and Syria; in 1981, between Syria and Libya; in recent times there was an attempt to unify Libya with Tunisia; and presently there is a similar effort to unify Morocco and Libya.

79. Tibi, pp. 91–92. On the racial dimension of Aflaq's thought, see Rouleau, pp. 161–162, and Gordon Torrey, "The Ba'th—Ideology and Practice," *The Middle East Journal*, vol. 23, no. 4 (Autumn 1969).

80. Rouleau, p. 161; see also Rabinovitch, p. 447.

81. Tibi, p. xi.

82. Haim, p. 37.

83. Ibid., pp. 55–56.

84. Constantine Zurayq, *al-Wa'i al-Qawmi* [The nationalist consciousness] (Beirut: 1939), pp. 112–113, 117, quoted in Khadduri, p. 184.

85. Khadduri, p. 184.

86. Haim, p. 62 and p. 58; see also Bezirgan, p. 42.

87. Michel Aflaq, *Fi sabil al-Ba'th* [Toward the Ba'th] (Beirut: 1975), p. 128, quoted in Bezirgan, p. 42.

88. Constantine Zurayq, "Al-Maseeheehun Al-'Arab wa al-Mustaqbal" [Arab Christians and the future], *Mustaqbal Al 'Arabi* (May 1981), pp. 28, 30.

89. Victor Sahab, "Al-Maseeheeun Al-'Arab wa al-Qawmiyya al-Arabiyya: Min Yahmee al-Maseeheeun al-'Arab?" [Arab Christians and Arab nationalism: who defends Arab Christians?], *Mustaqbal Al 'Arabi* (August 1981), pp. 129, 131, 132, 136. On the question of Arab nationalism and Christians, particularly the Christian Copts in Egypt, see "Hawla al-'Aqbaat wa al-Qawmiyya al-Araabiyya" [The Copts and Arab nationalism], *Mustaqbal Al 'Arabi* (March 1982).

90. Marilyn Nasr, "Al-Qawmiyya wa al-Deen fi Fiqr Abd al-Nasir" [Nationalism and religion in the thought of Abd al-Nasir] *Mustaqbal Al 'Arabi* (February 1981), pp. 98–100.

91. Bezirgan, p. 42.

92. *Fi sabil al-Ba'th*, p. 131, quoted in Ibid., pp. 42–43.

93. Ibid., p. 43. Bezirgan's statement is not quite correct. Sadeq al-Azem is an Arab intellectual who wrote a book that severely criticizes religion, *Naqd al-Fiqr al-Deenee* [A criticism of religious thought] (Beirut: Dar al-Tali'ah, 1969).

94. Adel Hussein, "Nadwaat al-Qawmiyya al-'Arabiyya wa al-Islam" [A symposium on Arab nationalism and Islam] *Mustaqbal Al 'Arabi* (February 1981), p. 137.

95. Haim, pp. 57–58. On this question, see Hisham Sharabi, *Arab Intellectuals And The West: The Formative Years, 1875–1914* (Baltimore: The Johns Hopkins Press, 1970), pp. 64.

96. Tareq Ismael, *The Arab Left* (Syracuse: Syracuse University Press, 1976), pp. 12–13.

97. Leiden, pp. 47, 45.

98. See Kamel Abu Jaber, *The Arab Ba'th Socialist Party* (Syracuse: Syracuse University Press, 1966); John Devlin, *The Ba'th Party: A History From Its Origins to 1966* (Stanford: Hoover Institution Press, 1976); see also Rouleau.

99. Ghasan Istefan, "Hawla al-Ulmaniyya 'And Yasin al-Hafiz" [Secularism in Yasin al-Hafiz's thought], *Mustaqbal Al 'Arabi* (January 1979), p. 177, 172. See 'Asad Ghandour, "Yasin al-Hafiz wa Qadayaa al-Thawra al-Arabiyya" [Yasin al-Hafiz and the questions of Arab revolution], *Mustaqbal Al 'Arabi* (January 1979), p. 180. See also, *Fi al-Mas'alat al-Qawmiyya al-Deemuqraatiyya* [On the question of democracy and nationalism] (Beirut: Dar al-Tali'ah, 1981). This work includes a critique of the traditional nationalist and unionist thought.

100. Nadim al-Bitar, "Nahwa Fiqr Wahdawee Jadeed" [Towards a new unionist thought], *Mustaqbal Al 'Arabi* (May 1979), pp. 6–7.

101. George Tarabishi, *Al-Dawlah al-Qutriyya wa al-Nazareeyah al-Qawmiyya* [The regional state and the nationalist theory] (Beirut: Dar al-Tali'ah, 1982), pp. 8, 10.

102. Fouad Ajami, "The End Of Pan-Arabism," *Foreign Affairs*, vol. 57, no. 2 (Winter 1978–1979), p. 355 (see also pp. 357, 360–361, 365–368); and "The Struggle For Egypt's Soul," *Foreign Policy*, no. 35 (Summer 1979), p. 20.

103. Ajami, *The Arab Predicament: Arab Political Thought and Practice Since 1967* (London: Cambridge University Press, 1981), p. 156.

104. William Brown, "The Dying Arab Nation," *Foreign Policy*, no. 54 (Spring 1984), p. 34.

105. Hassan Nafaa, "Arab Nationalism: A Response To Ajami's Thesis On The 'End of Pan-Arabism,'" *Journal Of Arab Affairs*, vol. 2, no. 2 (Spring 1983), pp. 173–174, 182, 196.

106. Leiden, p. 50.

107. Ibid., pp. 48, 50.

108. Muhammad Rida Muharam, "Al-Awdaa Ilaa al-Urubaa" [The Return to Arabism], pp. 24–25.

109. Wamid Jamal Nazmi, "Shee'aat al-Iraq wa Qadeeyyat al-Qawmiyya al-'Arabiyya: al-Dawr al-Taareekhee Qabl al-Istiqlaal" [The Iraqi Shiites and the question of Arab nationalism: their historical role before independence], *Mustaqbal Al 'Arabi* (August–October 1982), pp. 78, 90.

110. Clovis Maksoud, interview conducted by Diane James, Los Angeles, California, May 7, 1985. I am thankful to Ms. James for making the interview available as well as for other help.

2

The Concerns and the Challenges

Saad Eddin Ibrahim

This chapter is the conclusion of a lengthy quantitative study on Arab nationalism that was conducted by Saad Eddin Ibrahim and associates in 1977, 1978, and 1979. The study was entitled Itajabhat al-Rai al-Am al-Arabi Nahwa Masa'lat al-Wihda *(Trends of Arab public opinion toward the issue of unity) and was published in 1980 under the auspices of the Center for Arab Unity Studies. The study involved ten Arab states—Morocco, Tunisia, Egypt, Sudan, Jordan, Lebanon, Kuwait, Qatar, and Yemen—and included Palestinians living in Kuwait. In their research, Ibrahim and associates used 82 lengthy questions, 14 of which are open-ended and the remaining 68 closed. The respondents, who were not chosen randomly (the majority were convenient target samples), totaled 5,557. The findings of this study cannot be considered as representative of Arab public opinion.*

—ED.

. . . We have tried to present a topography of the psychological and political realities of the Arab world as documented through a series of field studies. Each chapter expanded and detailed one aspect of these realities, with its high and low points, ambiguities and clarities, and rights and wrongs. The findings were presented just as they were recorded by our researchers in ten different Arab countries, and in the way we translated them into numbers, charts, coefficient relationships, and demonstrative statements. These voluminous details may have gotten in the way of revealing a comprehensive view of Arab realities, just as an enormous trees would obscure a view of the whole forest.

More important than gathering data and interpreting them is discerning the factors that constitute the general map of Arab reality in the present time. In order to construct the map in a way that would reveal a sense

From Saad Eddin Ibrahim, *Itajabhat al-Rai al-Am al-Arabi Nahwa Masa'lat al-Wihda* (Trends of Arab public opinion toward the issue of unity) (Beirut: Center for Arab Unity Studies, 1980). Reprinted with permission. Translated by Elie Chalala.

of the future, we have to be able to separate the basic trends from the
ancillary ones. The sociologist who subscribes to an objective method
may be content with using statistics and measures in a way that would
allow the facts to speak for themselves and would protect the derived
conclusions from being influenced by his own preferences. We have
tried to adhere to this scientific tradition as much as possible in presenting
the data collected by our field workers and if, on occasion, we did
provide some explanations or attempt to elucidate a point, it was always
at the end of a chapter and was brief. But the sociologist who lives
with his research for three years—as we did, who gathers an enormous
amount of data; who interacts with the subjects of his research, lives
with them, and interacts with the opinions they had expressed; who
continues to interact with new data as he gathers it, organizes it, examines
it, takes a census of it, analyzes it, presents it, and scientifically comments
on it, that researcher will end up with a holisitc view of the subject
he is examining. This holistic view supersedes the parts from which it
is made. The very process of gathering and examining these parts is
bound to have influenced the researcher's reasoning and conscience.
Thus, the holistic view is a complex result of all the parts making up
the field data and the interaction between the data itself and the
researcher's individuality.

Alongside this comprehensive view, perhaps even because of it, the
researcher develops a set of feelings and perceptions, especially if he
is committed both to scientific accuracy and a political cause. This writer
is one such, committed as fervently to the idea of Arab unity as he is
to precision in research. But his commitment to Arab nationalism is
what drove him to apply his scientific training to objectively study the
question of unity. An objective study, if it is accurate, will reveal aspects
about the subject that will disturb and hurt the researcher—precisely
because of his nationalist commitment—or will be a source of joy and
elation for the same reason. Whatever those feelings, we deliberately
chose to keep them out of the heart of the study and reserved them
for the conclusion.

Briefly, in this chapter, we will attempt to tie together the main
findings and weave a full picture of how the Arabs are disposed,
psychologically and politically, to the idea of unity and all that is
connected with it, and also to express some personal feelings that came
about as well as some impressions we developed within the course of
the three-year period during which this research was conducted.

The Nationalist Ideology

The Arab nation came into being at the end of the 8th century A.D.
as a result of the spread of Islamic religion and the Arabic language

by the emigration of many Arab tribes that settled in the region stretching from the Gulf to the Ocean and intermarried and integrated with the people there who adopted Islam. The three centuries that followed laid the foundation for an immense cultural process. Not only was the Arab nation objectively in existence by the 11th century, but it had been developed educationally, sociologically, and intuitively, like any other nation in the full scientific import of the word. And it continued developing and crystallizing for the next ten centuries.

Intellectually speaking, there is a difference between the objective existence of the Arab nation and the call of nationalism. Nationalism means a people's awareness of being culturally different from other peoples, a consciousness of affiliation with a particular entity and a desire to have this consciousness transformed into a political expression embodying the people's hopes for independence, self-determination, and a better life.

According to this definition, Arab nationalism is a new notion that goes back to the 19th century. Prior to that time, it was the religious identity embodied in Islam that predominated. This identity united the Arabs with other non-Arab Muslims and enabled them to live and socialize under the aegis of the Islamic empire. The rise of their own cultural identity, represented by Arabism, can be seen as the result of several interconnecting structural, international, and cultural factors and forces. The Islamic empire, which was started and ruled by the Arabs, was first taken over by the Persians and then by the Turks. When Arab nationalism was propounded in modern times, the reins of government were still in the hands of the Turks, represented by Ottoman Sultans. But by that time, the Arab world in both its western and middle parts had fallen into the hands of the Western imperialists. The severely weakened Ottoman Empire had failed to prevent the Western imperialists from taking those parts of the Arab nation. Although the Arab East remained under Ottoman rule until the beginning of the century, suffering harsh treatment, oppression, maladministration, and Turkish corruption, it nevertheless was affected by new cultural and intellectual trends that were sweeping the Arab world throughout the 19th century, trends that carried within them new liberal ideas about democracy, freedom, progress, science, and "nationhood."

The weakness and crumbling of the Ottoman Empire, imperialist aggression, Turkish despotism, modern intellectual currents, all these factors interacted to create the right climate for the call of Arab nationalism. This nationalist idea centered around two aims: the independence of the Arab world and the unification of all its parts into one state. The modern history of the Arab nationalist call and that of the political movements that were associated with it for a century are historically documented and available to anyone interested in digging deeper into the question of Arab nationalism.

The nationalist call tends to preach an ideology. In this case, the ideology is an awareness of the existence of a separate Arab world that encompasses a nation whose inhabitants feel and share a sense of belonging and a belief in the legitimate political expression of the nation's hopes of achieving unity, independence, and freedom. And like any new evangelical call, those who believed in it began as small groups and then spread out to the eastern north and then to the rest of the Arab world, south and west. This call received support from the nationalist organizations and parties, and from the late leader Gamal Abd al-Nasir, although the advocacy of this call predated him by a century. These forces moved the discourse on Arab nationalism from the level of political and intellectual elitist circles to that of the masses in the street, from Baghdad to D'ar Al-Ba'daa.

What are the achievements of Arab nationalism after the century and a half since its birth?

As for belief in this idea, we found that around 80 percent of those whom we asked believe in the existence of the Arab world as a separate cultural entity and in the existence of one Arab nation living within the boundaries of that area. We found an intense desire that there be a stronger cooperation between the various parts of the Arab world and that this cooperation should assume the form of political unification. We also found a commonality of feelings and an awareness of the greater problems that face the Arab nation.

As for the political achievements of Arab nationalism, they have been rather modest and have not quite lived up to the great expectations that the people had pinned on their leaders and regimes. Most Arab countries gained independence; the Arab League was founded with its specialized agencies in different fields. The Arabs attempted to forge more than one unity, but all came to nothing. The Arabs also waged several wars against Israel on behalf of the Palestinian people, but in most of these they came away with either political or military defeats.

Arab Unity

If the nationalist ideology gained firm ground throughout the 20th century, this solid base at the level of belief and feeling was accompanied by several setbacks in the area of political achievements, both in unifying the countries of the Arab nation and in battling external enemies.

Despite these setbacks, the hope of realizing Arab unity runs strong amongst most Arabs. But today this call for unity is underlined by a measure of realism and rationalism. Arab public opinion reflects a growing awareness of the obstacles to be overcome if such a unity is to be realized. This realism had manifested itself in many respects among those whom we interviewed.

For example, few people believe that total unity can be brought about in the near future; they regard the possibility of unity as more likely in a distant, if not a far-off, future. Nonetheless, the majority believe in partial unification in the near future, a unity that would include two or more Arab states, the probability of which would depend on whether the states are adjacent and whether their political differences can be surmounted.

The majority of Arab public opinion opted for a federal unity, in which each country preserves its internal independence and deals with its domestic affairs, leaving for a centralized government the power to oversee matters involving defense, foreign policy, and coordination of the various countries' developmental plans in the social and economic realms.

Most Arabs have expressed a preference to see the hoped-for unity accomplished through peaceful and democratic means, whether the unity in question was partial, as between two states or more, or total. They have rejected outright any use of military force to bring about that unity.

A further indication of the realism inherent in Arab public opinion bearing on matters of unity is a deep awareness of the obstacles to accomplishing such a goal. Among these are the foreign powers, headed by the United States, Arab rulers, and a diminishing political consciousness.

To the majority, the idea of Arab unity is no longer the mere expression of a romantic, symbolic, and emotional longing, though these feelings are still present. What is novel is a clear conception that the prospect of unity depends on linking such a hope to practical considerations and interests. Arab public opinion perceives unity not only as a buffer to foreign domination but also as a means to serve each country, bringing prosperity to all its members.

Islam, Nationalism, and Arab Unity

Islam as a religion and a culture was an essential factor in the expansion of the Arab nation, whose population lives in the area stretching from the Gulf to the Ocean. But the definition of who is an Arab today is first a cultural definition, not a religious one. An Arab is anyone who speaks Arabic, adopts the Arab culture, intuitively feels it, and is also conscious of belonging to a particular human group known as the Arab nation. Among the leaders of the Arab nationalist movement are those who are not Muslims. In other words, religion is not a condition either for being an Arab or for Arabism. At its outset, the Arab nationalist movement attempted to stress the cultural and the secular identity of Arab nationalism over every other identity. This emphasis was necessary and functional, for at that time the Arabs were struggling against the Turks, who are Muslims and who were ruling the Arabs in the name of the Islamic Caliphate. Although that period came to an end with the fall of the Caliphate and the secession of the Arabs from the Turkish Empire, the emphasis on the cultural and the secular identity of Arabism continued to be a factor among the second and third generations of the leaders of the Arab nationalist movement and remains important today. But the truth is that none of those leaders denied the essential role Islam played in the creation of the Arab nation; they were not hostile towards Islam nor did they attack it in the name of Arab nationalism. All this confirms another identity pushing to the surface, that is, a stress on Arab culture as a link and a uniting factor between the Muslim and non-Muslim Arabs.

This secular presentation of Arab nationalism, advocated by nationalist thinkers and those supporting Arab unity, was confined to learned elites. But the popular masses, especially the peasants, the workers, and the Bedouins, did not intellectually distinguish between their cultural and religious identity. For them, there is only one identity in which religion, culture, language, and nationalist affiliation mix. Furthermore, these masses see Arabism and Islam as being the same, i.e., they are inseparable. This explains why they respond to the call to Arabism as a call to Islam, and to the call to Islam as a call to Arabism. This phenomenon manifests itself more in the North African countries where all the people are Arab Muslims; and, to a great extent, in Egypt.

That is why we have found that the majority of the people whom we interviewed consider Islam as one of the essential components of the Arab nation. A large group—if not the majority—among those interviewed do not oppose uniting the nation on an Islamic basis. Some would even go as far as to see Arab unity as a first step towards a greater unity, namely the unity of all the Islamic peoples. Those preferring such unity, however, are not a majority, but they seem to represent a minority that is growing.

There are several reasons why we raise the question of religion at the end of this study, an issue that was also referred to in the third section. Firstly, the religious factor kept coming back on more than one occasion while we were conducting our field work, and mainly by those who were interviewed. Secondly, the revivalist Islamic movements have grown considerably in various parts of the Arab world. The Iranian events further confirmed that religion remains a powerful force in Middle

Eastern societies. "The reawakening of Islam," as it is called in the West, grew stronger with the increasing difficulties of the Arab ruling regimes (mostly those of secular orientation) in confronting major problems. In other words, most people take refuge in religion as the road to salvation in the times of trial and overwhelming crisis. It was therefore not surprising that the religious movements had been strengthened in the wake of the 1967 defeat.

What we intend to focus on here are the following:

• There is neither a basic contradiction nor an inconsistency between the Islamic religion and Arab nationalism. Any attempt to create artificial preferences between the religious and the secular identity would lead to a vicious circle. In fact, such attempts would entail waste of effort and energy and would benefit the enemies of Islam and Arabism.

• If Arab nationalism in its recent rebirth stressed the cultural identity, it was to draw a distinction between Arabs and Turks. This was essential, for the Arabs were waging a battle against Ottoman despotism, which claimed to speak in the name of Islam. But this battle was waged and settled a good half-century ago. There is no longer anyone dominating the Arabs in the name of Islam. Those who attack Arab nations in particular and the Islamic ones in general are from outside the region, the foreign powers.

• Like most great heavenly religions, Islam in practice has two faces: the first concentrates on reviving the past and on metaphysics. It resists change and preaches obedience to outdated conventions and thus becomes a power in the hands of despotic regimes and local and international forces, powers known for their hostility towards the people. The other face is revolutionary Islam, which focuses on originality, justice, progress. It spearheads the resistance against internal exploitation, imperialism, and foreign domination and thus becomes a power in the hands of nations. The Algerian revolution is a classical example of this second face of Islam. Everything this Islam calls for coincides and is consistent with the call of modern Arab nationalism. What Arab nations rejected at the end of the last and the beginning of this century was not this type of Islam. Instead, what had been rejected was the metaphysical and the outmoded practice that was preached in the name of Islam and did not protect Islam from foreign domination.

• Metaphysical, despotic, and rigid Islam not only is the enemy of the people but also resists progress, nutures blind dogmatism, and fails to offer basic solutions to the question of citizenship and of the rights of the non-Muslim minorities. Revolutionary Islam, however, is more able to address today's problems and to lay down a basis for equality and justice to all citizens, Muslim and non-Muslim alike.

• Foreign powers are disturbed by any political movement that calls for independence, freedom, and justice—whether the movement is of an Arab or Islamic orientation. The West had encouraged any Islamic movement or alliance that opposed progress. We have witnessed this in the fifties (the Baghdad Pact) and the sixties (the Islamic Alliance). This type of Islam posed no danger to the West. On the contrary, it furthered the West's aims and interests. As for the rise of any revolutionary political Islamic movement, the West would try to crush it in its inception, and the same would be the fate of any Arab coalition. It is the West, represented by Britain, that encouraged the creation of the Arab League in the forties. And it is the West too that tried to seize the first opportunity to break the back of any nationalist Arab revolutionary movement like Nasserism.

• The Islamic revolution and Arab nationalism are complementary, or at least the common ground between them is great. Both oppose imperialism, Zionism, and racism; both call for justice, equality, and liberation. This demands a reevaluation of Islam by leaders of nationalist thought and proponents of Arab unity. These leaders should realize that for the majority of the masses, mainly peasants and workers, religious and national identity are interlocked to the point of being one and the same. It is neither possible nor in the interest of the Arab nation to arbitrarily distinguish between the two identities.

• This same common ground between Islamic revolution and Arab nationalism places a similar responsibility on the shoulders of Muslim intellectuals. They too have to take a second look at Arab nationalism and should become aware that there is no contradiction between religious and national identity. It is neither possible nor in the interest of Islam to arbitrarily separate one identity from the other, and these intellectuals should not encourage their followers to establish illusionary preferences between the two identities. Muslim intellectuals have a further task, which is to extend the common ground so that it becomes complementary. Even more important, they should come out with new formulas regarding citizenship and the non-Muslim minorities. It is insufficient that these minorities live safely in countries where the majorities are Muslims; what is needed is that they should be able to feel and exercise their rights and responsibilities according to the principles of justice and equality.

Lebanon, Sudan, and Morocco

We have seen that the level of national consciousness and enthusiasm for Arab unity is weaker in some Arab countries than in others. In this regard, we mention Lebanon, Sudan, and Morocco. We attempted to explain the reasons for the weak Arab unionist tendencies in these countries. We will not belabor this point except to say that the three countries combine human, social, and ethnic groups more diverse than those of the other seven countries in which we conducted our studies. This means that we cannot underestimate the importance of the lack of homogeneity in education and in ancestry as factors influencing the formation of values and orientations.

Most people in the Arab world speak Arabic and embrace Islam. This unity of religion and language is the basis for a unity of culture and values and for a unity in lifestyle and an overall view on issues. We have mentioned that in each of the three countries there are communities which differ from the majority either in language or in religion, or in both. It is this fact that creates differences in directions, as well as in national affiliation and the desire for achieving Arab unity.

We would like to point out that these differences are in no way metaphysical or permanent. There are structural factors that could create an opportunity for changing these directions in a way that serves the nationalist and unionist ends of the majority. Class and particularist factors have shown throughout history their tremendous power in forging beliefs and nationalist tendencies. This means that the ethnic groups that show little enthusiasm at the present time for Arab unity may be won over to support the nationalist cause if the right conditions become available. Among these conditions are the following:

- Creating Arab unity schemes that include tangible material and economic interests for the ethnic groups' members.
- Ensuring and solidifying their political participation and their perception of citizenship and equality with those of the Arab majority groups.
- Offering these groups the opportunity to protect and develop their own cultural heritage within the framework of the broad Arab culture.

The second point that we raise in this regard is that we completed our study in the Arab countries at one historical period. This means that what appeared to be weak Arab nationalist sentiment or unionist tendencies in Lebanon, Sudan, and Morocco is, firstly, weak in relation to the other seven countries. The majority in these three countries—

over 50 percent—confirmed its nationalist affiliation and unionist tendencies. Thus, what we consider "weakness" is only in comparison with other countries where over 80 percent of the population expressed their Arab nationalist affiliation and unionist tendencies.

Secondly, the present orientations in these three countries—as documented during the 1978–1979 period—tell nothing about past or future orientations.

Most likely the Arab nationalist and unionist consciousness was stronger in Lebanon in an earlier period than it is at the present. No doubt the Lebanese Civil War, the complications of the Palestinian problem, and the overall deteriorating situation in the Arab world during the past ten years had a tremendous impact in defining the political currents in Lebanon at the time we were conducting this study. The Lebanese events polarized the opinions of the major groups that make up Lebanon. This polarization—as we had seen in different parts—assumed the form of feeling strongly either for or against Arab affiliation and unity.

Moreover, we have noticed a reduction in the number of those espousing moderate views, namely those who cautiously support or oppose the idea of Arab unity and nationalism. It is believed that once the political turmoil of Lebanon settles, this polarization will be reduced, especially if the future stability is accompanied by an increase in the size and interdependence of the economic interests between Lebanon and other Arab countries, as it was in the 1950s and the 1960s.

It is most likely that in Morocco and the Sudan, nationalist and unionist tendencies are on a constant rise. In the Sudan, this can be attributed to the end of the civil war in 1973 and also to the growing cultural and economic interaction between the Sudan on one hand and the Arab oil-producing countries on the other.

It is evident in several ways that the nationalist idea is beginning to be influential in Morocco. There is a continuing process of Arabization and an increase in the number of those reading Arabic, a development reflected in an increased circulation of publications from the Arab East in a market that had formerly been monopolized by French-language publications. There has also been a growing interest among Moroccans, rulers and citizens alike, in Arab affairs, especially the Palestinian question. Morocco's participation in the 1973 war, and its hosting of several Arab summit conferences, tallies with the Arab nationalist tide, a phenomenon many observers have noted to be common to all the countries of North Africa. We have already shown the responses given to us by the Tunisian community, whose strong nationalist tendencies turned out to be one of this research's surprises. Morocco appears to be moving in the same direction. That is, we would expect—should we in the perspective of a few more years conduct a similar study—to find nationalist feelings and unionist tendencies in Morocco to be increasing rather than decreasing, especially if the oil-rich countries continue to interact with Morocco.

The Major Problems at the Outset of the Eighties

What this fieldwork explicitly revealed was presented in the preceding chapters. What it implicitly revealed, however, was derived and stated in this concluding chapter. We want to end this research with a word on the important issues that will confront the Arab world in the decade of the eighties.

We should hasten to point out, as we begin, that the social-political history of any society does not follow a chronological order. Instead, it works in a dialectical manner, leaving little room to distinguish a day or a decade from the next. Moreover, human reason tends to perceive matters according to systematic methods, perhaps due to its inability to understand them comprehensively within time and place.

Despite this limitation, the following issues are bound to preoccupy the Arab world throughout the decade that began a few months ago:

- An increase in external threats and the intensification of the struggle between the superpowers over the domination of the Arab world.
- The growing complexity of the relationship between religion and state.
- The struggle between the Arab rich and poor.
- The eruption of internal class struggle within various Arab countries.
- The question of democracy and the revolution against oppressive regimes.
- The sectarian question and the issue of minorities in general.

It suffices to mention those main points without going into their complex implications. This is not the proper place for such a discussion. In various parts of this study, we have already touched upon some of these issues. But the main reason for reiterating these points in this concluding section is to highlight them in order that they may assume top priority on the future agenda of Arab nationalists. It is imperative that thinkers who emphasize Arab unity should research and study these problems and arrive at rational solutions that are highly verifiable and to which the Arab people from the Gulf to the Ocean can relate. To reach a correct theoretical position is no great feat. To turn a theoretical proposition into a viable political program is the challenge.

These are the concerns and these are the challenges.

3

The Issue of Identity
in Selected Arab Gulf States

Faisal Al-Salem

Introduction

Identity has been considered one of the major factors in the formation of a viable political community; it is therefore of primary concern to political behaviorists who study the issue empirically. How do citizens of the Arab Gulf states identify themselves? Why do they identify themselves the way they do? What are the political, social, and economic implications of identity? These are some of the questions we will attempt to address in this paper.

Of all the important social and psychological themes directly related to political behavior, and to nation-building in particular, perhaps none is so pervasive as the concept of identity. One's identity is revealed through his association with a nation, religion, political party, social or ethnic group.[1]

The concept of group identity was addressed by Marx in his work on "class struggle." Marx and Engels suggested that the "history of man is the history of class struggle," in which workers would develop a sense of "consciousness" in *opposition* to the capitalists. Freud, however, used the concept to mean a person's "emotional tie with others" in his explanation of the need of the individual to affiliate, which, according to him, is essential to man's emotional development as a social human being.[2]

An empirical study of the concept of identity would have been practically impossible in Freud's time. With the advent of the behavioral

Revised and reprinted with permission from *Journal of South Asian and Middle Eastern Studies* 4 (Summer 1981). Copyright 1981 by *Journal of South Asian and Middle Eastern Studies*.

approach to the study of politics in the second half of the twentieth century, however, it was found that class, party, religious, and ethnic identifications could be measured relatively, according to occupation, income, education, and the like.

Thus identity was found to be relevant to the study of voting patterns, i.e., why people vote and why they vote the way they do. In Western democracies where politics "function" within the party system, people tend to identify themselves with a political party. American children, for instance, learn to consider themselves Democrats or Republicans through the socialization process that begins in the child's formative years.[3]

In the Gulf states there is a lack of political institutions of the type that exist in the West. Although historically the Arab Gulf states did develop semipolitical institutions, these were restricted to the ruling family,[4] while the economic structure was maintained by other classes. Thus loyalty and identity were always focused on the person of the ruler. It was not until the discovery of oil in the 1930s and its subsequent development that a modern sense of nation-building began to evolve. By studying the responses of Gulf high-school students, we will attempt to define some aspects of their political identification.

Method

The methodology applied in this study consisted of a questionnaire containing open-ended and multiple-choice questions testing the identity issue. Data was processed by SPSS computer programs to obtain chi square, regression, and correlation coefficients and other related statistics.

The Sample

Approximately 500 samples each were collected from Saudi Arabia, Kuwait, Bahrain, Qatar, and the United Arab Emirates (U.A.E.). Collecting data was extremely difficult. Questionnaires involving "personal" items are alien to the culture in general. This caused us to limit our study to the five countries under discussion. Of 2,700 responses, only 1,393 were valid, which further limited the study. The breakdown of respondents by country is shown in Table 3.1.

The mean age of the respondents was 17.009 years; 71.1 percent of the sample were females and 28.1 percent were males. Some 0.8 percent of sample did not indicate gender. It is interesting to note that the number of female respondents was almost triple that of the males. Females were also more conscientious in filling out the questionnaires.

Most of the respondents came from large families, with an average of seven members, as shown in Table 3.2. The socioeconomic status of the respondents, as indicated by the father's occupation, is shown in Table 3.3. It must be noted that some students failed to indicate the precise nature of their father's work. This may have been because they felt ashamed of their father's low-status occupation, and therefore a portion of the "unclassified" category could conceivably fall into the "laborer" category.

Results

The first identity question, "Who are you?" (ID1), consisted of six subvariables from which the respondents could choose: a) family name, b) nationality, c) religious affiliation, d) an Arab, e) an Arab Muslim, f) other. As can be seen in Table 3.4, the majority of the respondents chose the subvariable "other," giving personal answers ranging from calls for revolution to expressions of sexual frustration.

Family name and nationality ranked second after "other," with some 35 percent of the sample identifying themselves by either of these two categories. One may surmise that those who mentioned family names were particularly proud of them. Families are also the main source of income and security, which would prompt students to identify with them.

It was hypothesized that older students would demonstrate greater political awareness. Contrary to this expectation, it appears that younger students relate to issues of nationality, religion, etc., more than do older students. The sample clearly showed that the older the student, the less he is involved in these issues. It can be concluded, therefore, that students gradually lose the sense of political involvement in their self-concept as they get older. Apparently wealth has not created a new "political man" in the Gulf.

The second identity question, "How do you identify yourself?" (ID2), consisted of four subvariables: a) family, b) tribe, c) religion, and d) state. Responses are shown in Table 3.5. All but 69 respondents out of the total sample of 1,393 answered this question. Statistical analysis confirmed the hypothesis that religion plays an important role in the lives of Gulf Arabs (Table 3.6). It was further hypothesized that the younger students would tend toward extremism in terms of their religion. Statistical analysis showed that students between the ages of fifteen and sixteen had proportionally the highest representation among those identifying themselves by their religion, with the numbers dropping off sharply as the age increased.

TABLE 3.1
Respondents by Country

Country	Number of Respondents	Percent of Sample
Bahrain	469	33.7
Saudi Arabia	111	8.0
Qatar	232	16.7
U.A.E.	235	16.7
Kuwait	287	20.6
Other	59	4.3
Total	1393	100.0

TABLE 3.2
Family Size

Family Members	Number of Respondents	Percent of Sample
less than 2	25	1.8
2	145	10.4
4	274	19.7
6	340	24.4
8	312	22.4
10	159	11.4
12	52	3.7
14	20	1.4
16 and over	6	0.4
no reply	60	4.3
Total	1393	100.0

TABLE 3.3
Father's Occupation

Professional	25.6%
Merchant	13.4%
Clerical	16.6%
Laborer	1.4%
Retired/unemployed	27.9%
Unclassified	15.1%
	100.0%

TABLE 3.4
Who Are You? (ID1)

	Total	Percent of Those Who Responded
a. Family Name	217	17.6
b. Specific Nationality	212	17.2
c. Religious Affiliation	83	6.7
d. Arab	89	7.2
e. Arab Muslim	43	3.5
f. Other	588	47.7
Total	1232	99.9

TABLE 3.5
How Do You Identify Yourself? (ID2)

	Number of Respondents	Percent of Those Who Responded
a. I am the child of X person	251	19.0
b. I belong to X tribe	190	14.4
c. I believe in X religion	625	47.2
d. I am a citizen of X	258	19.5
Total	1324	100.1

After religion (47.2 percent), the major points of reference for the sample were the state (19.5 percent) and the family (19 percent). Significantly, tribal affiliation rated a weak fourth among the choices. Citizenship and family affiliation rated almost equal as choices of identification. Since they are complementary in providing the student with security, this might be expected. Nevertheless, the two combined (38.5 percent) are still secondary to religious affiliation. Although no specific question was asked in this regard, one may assume that the Iranian revolution played a role in the religious awakening of the youth.

It was hypothesized that students would answer the question, "Where are you from?" (ID3), by indicating the Gulf states or the Arab world in a general manner. This was not the case, however, as all the students named their respective countries.

Concerning their friendships, 74 percent of those who answered ID4 indicated that they had friends of their own nationality, while 26 percent indicated that they did not (95 students failed to answer this question). Table 3.6 shows the insignificance of chi-square analysis: students are still deeply culture bound.

Asked to give the number of their friends of their own nationality (ID5), 67.6 percent of those who answered this question said they had

TABLE 3.6
Age Related to Identity AGE(X1)

(y) Variables	X²	DF	MO	X²S	CC	CCF	CS	MR	SR	B	Beta	P*
ID1 Who are you?	154.468	40	161	.000	.333	-.005	.422	.020	-.019	-.002	-.003	.013
ID2 How do you identify yourself?	39.145	24	69	.026	.169	-.018	.251	.065	-.061	.007	.002	.011
ID3 Where are you from?	430.461	56	42	.000	.491	-.019	.236	.253	.250	.112	.164	30.795
ID4 Do you have friends of the same nationality?	24.886	8	95	.001	.137	-.061	.011	.259	.166	.000	.048	2.737
ID5 Number of the above friends	224.666	40	128	.000	.388	.250	.001	.261	-.036	.001	.001	.004
ID6 Number of friends who are not of the same nationality	128.095	40	286	.000	.322	.162	.001	.262	-.038	-.056	-.026	.991
ID7 How do you define your country?	142.402	48	60	.000	.310	.063	.009	.262	.000	-.078	-.037	1.791
ID8 Identify the Gulf states	16.249	8	561	.038	.138	.008	.378	.291	.142	.251	.150	21.409
ID9 Define the Gulf states	82.123	40	53	.000	.240	-.036	.084	.294	-.050	-.000	-.036	1.836
ID10 Locate the Arab world	11.654	8	121	.167	.095	-.038	.078	.297	.068	.126	.034	1.408
ID11 Describe the borders between the Arab states	12.633	8	108	.125	.098	.000	.497	.297	-.011	.015	.006	.052
ID12 Describe an Arab's movement in the Arab world	98.257	8	113	.000	.267	.142	.001	.297	.059	.084	.030	.857
ID13 Does the Arab world constitute one nation?	72.335	48	1351	.013	.795	-.050	.029	.305	.008	-.083	-.042	1.359

Identity Questions (Ys)

*X² = Chi Square
DF = Degrees of Freedom
MO = Missing Values
X²S = Chi Square Significance
CC = Contingency Coefficient
CCF = Correlation Coefficient

CS = Correlation Significance
MR = Multiple Regression
SR = Simple Regression
B = The unadjusted slope in the regression equation
Beta = The adjusted slope in the regression equation
F = F test

TABLE 3.7
Why Are the Gulf States Arab?   (ID9)

		Percent of Those Who Responded
a. They are related to the Arab land	323	24.1
b. Arab tribes lived there historically	334	24.9
c. The inhabitants speak Arabic	445	33.2
d. They follow Islam	202	15.1
e. Kinship with other Arab states	15	1.1
f. Other reasons	21	1.6
Total number of respondents	1340	100.0

fewer than ten. Asked to give the number of their friends of nationalities other than their own (ID6), 42.5 percent of those who responded said they had fewer than ten, while 25.8 percent said they had no friends of another nationality. The F test confirms the hypothesis that students associate more with their compatriots than with outsiders, although the percentages might lead one to think otherwise. In general, the results of ID4, ID5, and ID6 show that the research sample is very limited in terms of friendship and communication.

On the question of identifying the Gulf states (ID8), 95.7 percent of those who answered this question knew them all, while 4.3 percent did not. However, 40.3 percent of the total sample of 1,393 (561 students) failed to answer this question. Given the cultural inability to admit ignorance, these numbers could well be added to those who were unable to identify the Gulf states, which would significantly alter the ratios. Here the F test disconfirms the research assumption that students associate themselves with their respective countries rather than with the Gulf states as a whole. However, in other sections of the questionnaire, students consistently identified with their own country over other choices, so that this finding may be incomplete.

Answers to ID9 ("Why are the Gulf states Arab?") are given in Table 3.7 (53 students failed to answer this question).

In formulating ID10 ("Locate the Arab world"), it was assumed that the majority of the sample would agree with the statement that the Arab world extends from the Atlantic Ocean to the Gulf. The results clearly show that this is not the case. Of those who answered this question, 36.2 percent agreed with the statement, while 63.8 percent disagreed (121 students failed to answer the question). The results would seem to indicate an emphasis on local nationalism as opposed to pan-Arabism.[5]

The questions on the borders between the Arab states and the freedom of movement between them (ID11 and ID12) elicited some interesting responses. It was hypothesized that the sample would agree that there are borders and obstacles to freedom of movement between the Arab states. The F test reveals the opposite, perhaps indicating a degree of wishful thinking among the students.

Of those who answered ID11, 48.9 percent agreed that there are borders and that travel from one Arab country to another is a complicated matter. On the other hand, 51.1 percent denied that there are borders or obstacles to travel between the Arab states (108 students failed to answer this question).

In the next question (ID12), respondents were asked to describe the procedures involved in traveling between the Arab states. Of those who answered this question, 55.8 percent described the process as "easy," while 44.2 percent described it as "complicated" (113 students failed to answer the question). Several points should be noted here. While Gulf Arabs find travel between the Gulf states a relatively simple matter, this is not the case for non-Gulf Arabs, who experience great difficulty in traveling to Gulf states. Entry procedures can involves searches, delays, many signatures, tips, and general harassment. Thus, the respondents may have been thinking of the ease of movement between the Gulf states, or perhaps projecting their dreams of Arab unity.

Response categories to ID13 ("Does the Arab world constitute one nation?") were as follows: a) Yes, because there are accepted borders; b) Yes, because of a common language; c) Yes, because of a common religion; d) Yes, because of common traditions; e) Yes, because of economic unity; f) Yes, because of political unity; g) Yes, because of common goals; h) Other. Only 42 respondents out of the total sample of 1,393 answered this question. The F test disconfirmed the hypothesis that the students would choose language and religion as the basis for their ideal of one Arab nation.

Discussion

Nationalism is the feeling of belonging to one's nation and identifying with its language, religion, race, etc. It is this feeling of unity that causes people to perceive themselves as members of a nation or to demonstrate "at least . . . their desire to create nations where none existed before."[6]

For the inhabitants of the Arab Gulf states, the feeling of Arab nationalism is now a matter of the past. As Fouad Ajami has stated,

Political ideas make their own realities. Often in defiance of logic, they hold men and are in turn held by them, creating a world in their own image, only to play themselves out in the end, shackled by routine problems not foreseen by those who spun the myth, or living past their prime and ceasing to move people sufficiently. Or, political ideas turn to ashes and leave behind them a trail of errors, suffering and devastation.[7]

The idea of one Arab nation extending from the Atlantic Ocean to the Gulf proved to be a myth for our respondents (see Table 3.8).

Nationality Related to Identity Variables

It was hypothesized that in response to the question, "Who are you?" (ID1), students would identify themselves first and foremost as Arabs, which would indicate a sense of Arab nationalism. However, only 7.2 percent of those who answered this question identified themselves as Arabs. Another 3.5 percent identified themselves as Arab Muslims (see Table 3.4). The number of students who identified themselves by their specific nationality was more than twice the number of those who identified themselves as Arabs. Chi-square significance and F test reveal that when students are nationalists, they are not Arab nationalists but patriots.

Nevertheless, the greatest number of students chose the response category "other," using it to express their own feelings and ideas. For example, many Bahraini students (63 percent) expressed the wish to see a revolution. The Bahraini regime was particularly unpopular with the students, who saw it as unresponsive and oppressive. Qataris, Kuwaitis, and Emirate students were especially interested in personal issues.

It was hypothesized that students would respond along nationalist lines when asked, "How do you identify yourself?" (ID2). Instead, the largest percentage (47.2 percent) indicated that religion provided them with their self-concept. Chi-square analysis and F test both disconfirmed the original hypothesis. The correlation coefficient also showed an inverse relationship between nationality and ID2 (see Table 3.8). The most deeply involved in religion were students from the U.A.E., followed by Saudi Arabia, Qatar, Bahrain, and finally Kuwait.

In response to ID3 ("Where are you from?"), all of the students named their respective countries, as mentioned earlier, but 4.5 percent added the adjective "Arab."

It was hypothesized that the majority of the sample would have friends of their own nationality as an indication of sharing common interests. Chi-square analysis of the results showed the reverse. Kuwaiti students were the least involved with their compatriots, followed by Bahrainis and then students from the U.A.E., while Qataris and Saudis had the most friends of their own nationality. Again, the Kuwaitis associated the least with non-Kuwaitis. The Qataris were second, followed by the Bahrainis, the Emirate students, and finally the Saudis.

It is well known that Saudis are a tribal people and still associate mainly within a tribal structure, especially in central Arabia. However, the Saudis in this sample were mostly from the eastern part of the country, which may explain why they were the most willing to associate with others. Eastern Saudis may have political and social reasons for associating with foreigners.

When asked, "How do you define your country?" (ID7), only 22 percent of the sample chose the response option of "an Arab land"; 20 percent chose "the star of the Gulf"; 35 percent chose "the beloved land"; and the rest opted for "rich," "beautiful," and "other." The original hypothesis was that the sample would define their countries as Arab. Chi-square and other statistical analysis disconfirm this hypothesis, as shown in Table 3.8.

What makes the Gulf states "Arab"? The Arabic language was the reason chosen by 33.2 percent of those who answered ID9; 24.9 percent said that the reason lies in the historical existence of Arab tribes in the area; 24.1 percent chose geographic location; and 15.1 percent said that Islam is the reason. The inverse relationship of the simple correlation, shown in Table 3.8, indicates that the multiplicity of nationalities in the sample led to the multiplicity of opinions on this issue.

Surprisingly enough, only 36 percent of the sample agreed with the statement that the Arab world extends from the Atlantic Ocean to the Gulf, while 64 percent disagreed (ID10). Although this is what students are taught in school and hear repeated in the media, their responses indicate that they reject it. This is consistent with the students' general tendency to reject the idea of Arab nationalism. The Arab world is seen not as one nation but as a collection of nations. Emirate students were at the top of the scale in holding this view, followed by Qataris, Bahrainis, Saudis, and finally Kuwaitis. It seems that the Kuwaitis are the most idealistic in their conception of the Arab world.

In response to the question on the borders between the Arab states (ID11), some 49 percent of the sample said that there are none while some 51 percent said that there are, as mentioned previously. The highest percentage in the former category were Saudis, followed by Emirate students, Bahrainis, Kuwaitis, and finally Qataris. It seems that the Gulf students' opinions are a reflection of their own situation. Their countries are the richest in the Arab world and they are welcomed in most Arab states. Furthermore, the Gulf states are relatively open to travel between themselves, while an Arab from a non-Gulf state requires an entry visa. This suggests that the sample did not relate to Arab problems as a whole.

ID13, which asked for the reason why the Arab world constituted one nation, drew a very poor response, perhaps indicating an awareness of the problem of pan-Arab nationalism. Only 42 students answered the question while 1,351 students declined to answer. Of those who answered the question (3 percent of the total sample), 15 percent chose language and 12.5 percent chose Islam as the main factor. However, the refusal of the majority of the sample (97 percent) to answer this question would seem to be an indication of the students' rejection of the idea of "one Arab nation."

Gender Related to Identity Variables

Do male and female students from the Gulf states differ on the question of identity? It was hypothesized that males and females would respond similarly on this issue. Chi-square analysis shows that there are clear differences (see Table 3.9).

A breakdown of the responses to ID1 ("Who are you?") according to gender is given in Table 3.10. Males identified themselves by their family name more often than did females, while females answered more frequently in terms of nationality, religion, and Arab nationalism. Generally speaking, a weak correlation coefficient is shown in Table 3.9 when ID1 is considered as a dependent variable and gender is the independent.

In answer to ID2 ("How do you identify yourself?"), females and males identified themselves in terms of religion in approximately the same proportions, but differed in terms of the other options (family, tribe, and state), with females showing more association than males by a slight margin. On the whole, Table 3.9 tends to confirm the hypothesis that males and females tend to respond to this question in similar fashion when nationality is taken as an independent variable. Similarly, in response to ID3 ("Where are you from?"), both males and females mentioned the name of their own country, although females tended to elaborate more.

In answer to ID7 ("How do you define your country?"), 37.6 percent of the females, as opposed to 28.5 percent of the males, defined their country as "the beloved land," while the percentage of males and females who chose the option "the star of the Gulf" was almost equal (females, 20.4 percent; males 19.6 percent). Some 31.8 percent of the males, as opposed to 18.5 percent of the females, chose the option "Arab." Table 3.9 shows the acceptance of the research hypothesis that males and females share similar views on this question, as F test indicates.

Male and female responses to ID9 ("Why are the Gulf states Arab?") were similar. While one-third of the sample (33.2 percent) indicated that the Arabic language is the main factor identifying the Gulf states as

TABLE 3.8
Nationality Related to ID Questions

Ys	X^2	DF	MO	X^2S	CC	CCF	CS	MR	SR	B	Beta	F
ID1	293.225	35	162	.000	.438	-.078	.002	.893	.893	85.299	.828	3806.993
ID2	204.001	21	73	.000	.365	-.114	.001	.893	-.049	-5.973	-.016	1.793
ID3	7023.191	49	45	.000	.915	.892	.001	.894	.067	2.846	.029	4.753
ID4	118.923	7	97	.000	.289	-.050	.029	.894	.056	.011	.014	1.190
ID5	205.110	35	138	.000	.374	.068	.005	.895	-.072	-.220	-.001	.013
ID6	157.711	35	296	.000	.354	.048	.036	.895	-.073	-4.238	-.014	1.359
ID7	258.768	42	70	.000	.404	.097	.001	.895	.053	2.646	.009	.486
ID8	12.061	7	567	.098	.119	.095	.001	.896	.175	10.218	.043	8.560
ID9	84.269	35	62	.000	.244	-.071	.004	.899	-.080	-.014	-.012	1.103
ID10	62.533	7	130	.000	.217	-.066	.006	.899	-.018	3.782	-.007	.303
ID11	46.082	7	118	.000	.186	.055	.020	.899	-.050	-9.676	-.028	5.013
ID12	105.866	7	122	.000	.277	.175	.001	.897	.061	8.834	.022	2.251
ID13	15.573	18	1353	.622	.529	-.080	.001	.897	.097	6.375	.023	1.902

Identity Variables

TABLE 3.9
Gender Related to ID Variables

Ys	X^2	DF	MO	X^2S	CC	CCF	CS	MR	SR	B	Beta	F
ID1	34.236	5	163	.000	.164	.159	.002	.163	.159	.024	.095	10.520
ID2	3.526	3	74	.317	.051	-.054	.321	.170	-.054	-.029	-.032	1.459
ID3	90.546	7	47	.000	.251	-.022	.251	.174	-.022	-.000	-.002	.006
ID4	12.481	1	99	.000	.099	-.026	.272	.176	-.026	-.000	-.035	1.452
ID5	15.951	5	134	.007	.111	.024	.256	.179	.024	.016	.040	2.399
ID6	27.831	5	292	.000	.157	-.001	.388	.179	.001	.018	.024	.803
ID7	48.857	6	67	.000	.188	-.021	.211	.181	-.021	-.025	-.035	1.503
ID8	7.160	1	566	.007	.098	.025	.264	.183	.025	-.009	-.016	.241
ID9	12.801	5	59	.025	.097	-.003	.410	.183	-.003	.000	.021	.621
ID10	3.116	1	127	.077	.051	-.013	.190	.184	-.013	-.074	-.057	3.868
ID11	13.880	1	115	.000	.105	-.033	.002	.187	-.033	-.054	-.063	5.222
ID12	8.585	1	118	.003	.083	-.009	.478	.187	-.004	-.026	-.027	.682
ID13	4.277	6	1352	.639	.307	.063	.001	.202	.063	.065	.095	6.562

Identity Variables

Arab, 28.3 percent of the males and 35.3 percent of the females chose this answer.

On the definition of the Arab world as extending from the Atlantic Ocean to the Gulf (ID10), there was a significant difference in the responses of the males and the females. Here females seemed to take a more realistic view, for while 60.1 percent of the males accepted this definition, 65.6 percent of the females rejected it. The inverse relationship of the correlation coefficient disconfirms the research assumption. This finding also applies to ID11 and ID12, concerning the borders between the Arab states. The majority of the respondents did not answer ID13.

Socioeconomic Status Related to Identity Variables

In their study on *Alienation and Expatriate Labor in Kuwait*, Farah, Al-Salem, and Al-Salem noted that "the indigenous labor force is concentrated in the finance sector and the government bureaucracy."[8] According to recent Kuwaiti government statistics, 76.2 percent of the Kuwaiti workforce is employed by the government and 80 percent are white-collar workers.[9]

The same generally holds true for other Arab Gulf states, as reflected in the research sample. The majority of the respondents' fathers were either merchants, white-collar workers, or professionals. Students who indicated that their fathers were employed as manual laborers did not exceed 2 percent of the total sample.

In answer to the question, "Who are you?" (ID1), nearly one-half (47.7 percent) of the respondents chose the option "other" over the response categories of family, nationality, race and/or religion. The children of manual laborers were the highest in disassociating themselves from the above-mentioned subvariables (61.1 percent), followed by the children of the merchant and tradesmen class (58.5 percent), the white-collar or clerical class (49 percent), and finally the professional class (42.2 percent).

The research hypothesis suggested that the respondents would identify themselves first by family name, then by state, religion and/or race. Taking socioeconomic status into consideration as an independent variable, chi-square analysis reveals a significance of .000 and a correlation coefficient of .038; and finally, the F test result of 10.740, as shown in Table 3.11, disconfirms the research hypothesis. This suggests that identity in the Arab Gulf countries is in a state of crisis.

Socioeconomic status correlates negatively (−.003) with ID2 ("How do you identify yourself?"). While some 47.2 percent of the sample as a whole identified themselves wth their religion, the white collar class was at the top (53.2 percent), followed by the professional class (51.9

TABLE 3.10
Who Are You? (ID1)

	Males	Females
a. Family name	22.3%	15.8%
b. Specific nationality	13.1%	18.8%
c. Religious affiliation	1.2%	8.8%
d. Arab	7.1%	7.3%
e. Arab Muslim	3.9%	3.2%
f. Other	52.5%	46.0%
Total	100.1%	99.9%

TABLE 3.11
Socioeconomic Status Related to ID Questions

Ys	X^2	DF	MO	X^2S	CC	CCF	CS	MR	SR	B	Beta	F
ID1	52.897	20	613	.000	.252	.038	.076	.109	-.099	-.059	-.101	10.740
ID2	30.822	12	556	.002	.188	-.188	.382	.143	.094	.192	.091	10.572
ID3	146.963	28	535	.000	.382	.166	.001	.148	-.060	-.035	-.064	4.298
ID4	28.528	4	576	.000	.183	-.005	.420	.158	.011	.000	.059	3.727
ID5	23.601	20	590	.260	.168	.000	.487	.166	.057	.042	.044	2.677
ID6	32.898	20	674	.034	.209	.024	.186	.168	.039	.003	.002	.005
ID7	31.588	24	551	.137	.190	.020	.221	.172	.045	.043	.025	.739
ID8	3.416	4	856	.490	.079	-.034	.096	.173	.014	-.025	-.018	.297
ID9	27.701	20	544	.116	.177	-.004	.047	.182	.058	.000	.045	2.537
ID10	12.510	4	589	.013	.123	-.022	.197	.187	-.027	-.220	-.073	5.864
ID11	7.871	4	573	.096	.097	-.020	.221	.187	.003	-.017	-.008	.089
ID12	.862	4	578	.429	.032	-.039	.071	.202	.075	.168	.074	4.655
ID13	23.127	18	1371	.185	.715	-.031	.120	.213	.076	.061	.039	1.019

Dependent Variables

percent), the working class (47.1 percent), and finally the merchant class (37.1 percent).

The father's occupation variable correlates positively with ID3, "Where are you from?" (.166). Its significance, however, is very weak (.001).

Responses to ID4, ID5, and ID6 showed that working and merchant class respondents had fewer friends than either the white-collar or the professional class respondents. The correlation coefficient test shows an inverse relationship between father's occupation and ID4, "friends of the same nationality" (−.005). White-collar and professional class respondents seem to associate more with others than the working and merchant class respondents do.

In response to ID7 ("How do you define your country?"), students chose the option of "the beloved land" more often than any other, with white-collar and professional class respondents choosing this response somewhat more often than respondents from the other classes. However, statistical analysis shows no difference on this question when socio-economic status is taken into consideration.

In response to ID9 ("Why are the Gulf states Arab?"), one-third of the total sample chose the Arabic language as the reason. However, statistical analysis shows an inverse relationship between socioeconomic status and this choice of response (−.004). The higher the respondent's social status (as indicated by father's occupation), the less he chose language as the defining characteristic.

In response to the statement that the Arab world extends from the Atlantic Ocean to the Gulf (ID10), 94.4 percent of the working class respondents disagreed, as compared with an average of 65 percent of the merchant, white-collar, and professional class respondents who disagreed. Hence there is also an inverse relationship between social class and ID10 (−.022). In general, the children of working-class fathers seemed to be more aware of the problems in the Arab world than others in the sample.

Summary

In conclusion, one can say that students in the Arab Gulf states appear to be experiencing an identity crisis. The only formulated identity they have developed within the past ten years has been the sense of citizenship, which may be attributed to the generous benefits available to them as citizens through the educational, medical, and social welfare systems of the Gulf states. However, this raises the question of what changes could take place if such benefits were to come to an end one day.

Pan-Arab nationalism, a sanctified concept for some thirty years, had lost its meaning by the 1970s, and today receives lip service in the interest of the state only. Pan-Arabism is a myth as far as the students in our sample are concerned. What is true of Arab nationalism is also true of the pan-Islamic movement: there is a vast difference between theory and practice. The wealthy Muslims of the Gulf states who talk about the distribution of wealth according to Islamic theory do not necessarily practice what they preach.

In summary, identity in the Arab Gulf states is unfocused, with no commanding loyalties exhibited. It would seem that the powers that be might do well to mobilize this potent force into positive channels for the good of the individual and the state.

Notes

This paper is part of a series on political socialization in the Arab Gulf states of Kuwait, Bahrain, Qatar, the United Arab Emirates, and Saudi Arabia, sponsored by the University of Kuwait. The author would like to express his deep appreciation to Dr. Ahmad Dhaher, Amal Al-Mulla of the Kuwait Institute for Social Research, Najat Al-Kohaji, and Dr. Maria Al-Salem.

1. For a general survey of the literature on identity, see Robert Alford, *Party and Society* (Chicago: Rand McNally, 1963); Gabriel A. Almond and Sidney Verba, *The Civic Culture* (New Haven: Princeton University Press, 1963); Reinhard Bendix and Seymour Martin Lipset, *Class, Status and Power: Social Stratification in Comparative Perspective* (New York: Free Press, 1966); Herbert Hyman, *Political Socialization* (Glencoe: Free Press, 1959); and Erik Erikson, "Identity and the Life Cycle," in *Psychological Issues* (1959).

2. Sigmund Freud, "Group Psychology and the Analysis of the Ego," in *The Complete Works of Freud*, vol. 18 (London: Hogarth Press, 1955), p. 105. This study, dealing with mass psychology and individual reactions, was first published in 1921.

3. In this respect, see Easton and Hess, "The Child's Political World," *Midwest Journal of Political Science* 6 (1962):229–246.

4. The ruling families in the Gulf stem from the Al-Anaiza tribe, which emigrated in the middle of the eighteenth century. In Kuwait, the Al-Sabah family rules; in Bahrain, the Al-Khalifa; in Qatar, the Al-Thani; in the U.A.E., the Al-Nehyan, the Al-Qawasim, and others; and in Saudi Arabia, the Al-Saud.

5. See Fouad Ajami, "The End of Pan-Arabism," *Foreign Affairs* 57 (Winter 1978/79):355–373.

6. Rupert Emerson, *From Empire to Nation* (Cambridge: Harvard University Press, 1960), p. 89.

7. Ajami, "The End of Pan-Arabism," p. 355.

8. Tawfic E. Farah, Faisal Al-Salem, and Maria Al-Salem, *Alienation and Expatriate Labor in Kuwait* (Cambridge, Mass.: Migration and Development Study Group, 1980), p. 7.

9. Kuwait, Ministry of Planning, *Annual Statistical Abstract* (1979), pp. 110 and 124.

4

Islam, Pan Arabism and Palestine: An Attitudinal Survey

Stewart Reiser

The central theme of this paper is that there is perhaps a more useful and less monolithic manner of inquiry into Arab attitudes towards the Arab-Israeli conflict. This means looking at the multi-layered identities that co-exist within one individual in the Arab world. Thus an Egyptian Muslim's attitude towards the Arab-Israeli conflict may be somewhat influenced by his political self-identification as either an Egyptian (state) nationalist, an Arab nationalist or as a Muslim "living in Egypt." The individual's perception of Israel or their attitude towards the resolution of the Arab-Israeli conflict may be influenced by their identity as a member of a particular ideological or communal group.

Communal identity within the Arab world has been the subject of recent re-examination by Arab and Western observers alike. Arab society has been confronted with the task of political self-definition since the creation of the modern Arab states at the close of World War One. Prior to this, under the Ottoman Empire, religious affiliation and family, clan and ethnic loyalties of the people, did not conflict with the overriding political system. It was only during the final decades of the Ottoman Empire that Islam, as the primary focus of loyalty, was challenged by Arab, Kurdish and Turkish nationalisms. With the West's creation of the Arab states, the transnational phenomenon of Arab nationalism grew. This phenomenon was partly a response to the cultural affinity that the Arabic-speaking people shared and partly a reaction to Western imperialism.

Reprinted with permission from *Journal of Arab Affairs* 3, 2 (Fall 1984):189–204. Copyright 1984 by the Middle East Research Group, Inc.

Pan-Arabism has been the attempt to give some practical and political expression to this shared cultural affinity. Concurrent to the process of developing Arab nationalism, state nationalism was also being forged as political, bureaucratic and economic interests consolidated power within the separate Arab states. To a certain extent this has led to marked inter-Arab conflict, conflict between the advocates of separate sovereign states and those advocating the unification of the "Arab Nation" into one Arab state. This conflict high-lighted the Nasser period of Middle Eastern politics. Nasser's broad transnational appeal reflected not only the anti-imperialist and anti-Zionist component of Arab nationalism but was also associated with his program of socio-economic reforms for large segments of the population. Since the death of Gamal Nasser most observers of the region measure the vitality of the Pan-Arab movement by the actions and interests of the national leaders and conclude that the *raison d'etat* and calculable interests of the established states have finally and irreversibly supplanted the Arab ideal. Others look at the same historical evidence and conclude that Pan-Arabism's ebb may be a temporary phenomenon, part of a dialectical process which contains within it seeds of recovery and return. Still others, such as Tawfic Farah who conducted a student survey, similar to the one later presented in this paper, at Kuwait University, conclude that the vacuum created by the "demise" of Arab nationalism is now being filled by religious belief on one level and identification with the nation-state on the other.

There still has not been a resolution to the identity crisis within the Arab world. Speaking of his homeland, Lebanon, sociologist Halim Barakat states that . . .

> There is no agreement between the sections of society on principles and no true interaction between these sections. The citizen feels loyalty to his group and his region more than to his homeland. . . .[1]

This description also fits Arab society in general, since there is no consensus on principles, no true dialogue, no loyalty to homeland. To this should be added the existence of conflicting cultures, the non-separation of religion and state, conflicting motivations and the lack of national character.

These contrasting and conflicting political and ideological orientations in the area and within each state almost guarantee that there can be no solid consensus on "Islamic" or "Arab" values or how these values should be reflected in the arena of public policy. Inconsistency often passes for irrationality and is largely a consequence of the yet unresolved clash of ideals and value systems and the overall ideological fragmentation. This clash continues not only between conflicting groups but also within the minds of many individual Arabs.

II

There have been several Arab student surveys over the past few decades.[2] The students surveyed in the Northeastern University study came from 12 Arab states, as well as Palestinians from Israel and other countries. They were chosen through three random sample surveys which were conducted in 1979, 1980, and 1981. The names and addresses of 1,612 Arab undergraduate and graduate students at Northeastern (and Boston) University were obtained through the International Student Office at Northeastern and after two follow-ups, 595 students responded. A 36-item questionnaire in three parts was prepared and administered to the respondents. The first part focused on their past and present attitudes toward their primary political and cultural associations. This first series of questions attempted to provide the student respondent with a sufficiently broad vehicle with which to address the issues of political/cultural association. Questions were structured so that the students could check the category that most reflected their attitude, and also provided them with opportunities to expand and discuss their choice. Some sample questions included: "How do you most strongly identify yourself?" "Why?" "Considering the potential gains and losses of merging your state with others, would you choose to retain your separate state, integral unity, federation or a looser confederation within a larger Arab state?" "Why?" "Would you choose some type of merger with other Arab states for the purpose of a stronger religious community or would you prefer the current territorial *status-quo* with the strengthening of religious values through law in your existing state?" "Why?" etc. Their definitive choices of association were state nationalism, religious community association, Arab nationalism, family and clan association, and regional-integration (i.e. "Greater Syria", an integrated Maghreb, etc.).

The second part of the survey concerned past and present attitudes toward the Arab-Israeli conflict, both in terms of means and desired objectives. Lastly, in the third part of the survey, the respondents' personal background was sought. This included their country-of-origin, religion, the degree of religious conviction held, whether this had increased or decreased since leaving home, the level of their fathers' and mothers' education, their respective occupations, the students' age, gender, major at the university and occupational goals, and the length of their stay in the United States as well as the university. In many cases follow-up interviews were held.

The study had several working hypotheses and this paper will limit itself to three of them. The first is that there may be a correlation between the ideological and communal association of individual Arab students on the one hand and their attitudes toward the Arab-Israeli conflict on the other. The second, with the alleged increased importance of state nationalism and identification with the states' existing boundaries, it is essential to examine attitudes towards the Arab-Israeli conflict controlled by the independent variable of the respondent's country-of-origin. And third is that in order to "test for" Islamic approaches towards the conflict, several independent variables must be kept under control. Muslim Arabs must be compared to their Christian counterparts in their attitudes and, of perhaps equal importance, there must be a further control of the individual's degree of religious conviction.

III

Over half of the respondents in the Northeastern study (53.1 %) gave Arab nationalism as their primary association. The two affiliations which had predominated in the Kuwait study, religious association and state nationalism were chosen by 38.7% of the Northeastern respondents (14.4% and 24.3% respectively). While the rationales for associating with a wider community called the Arabs, and in many cases advocating the merger of their states into a larger Arab nation, varied, several dominant themes emerged. "The desire for a stronger, more rational economy," "greater political and economic independence from the Superpowers," and "increased military power against regional enemies" were those themes elaborated upon in the printed survey and in follow-up discussions.

There are several speculative reasons for the political opinions in the Northeastern study varying so substantially from the Kuwait survey. [3] One is that there existed a large measure of suspicion among the student respondents, even here in the United States, as evidenced by a full 84.9% anonymity. Living away from one's domestic political system may allow students increased freedom to choose differently. This preference for anonymity may reflect the desire of speaking one's mind while minimizing the risk of any government tracing political positions to individuals. Perhaps the least speculative and most relevant explanation for the strength of Arabism as a political identification lies in the particular professional and career orientations of the Northeastern University respondents. Nearly 74% of the aggregate were engineer and related "technical" science majors. For those aspiring to enter this growing class, a wider Arab or regional arena within which to apply their skills may have its attractions. Regional projects and transnational ventures may seem more rational for personal and national growth to these youth than those with other career aspirations. In fact, 70.4% of those majoring in engineering, the physical sciences and technology-oriented disciplines chose Arab nationalism or regional integration as their community orientation. This compares to 58.1% of the aggegate of Arab students choosing these two communities. With this summary of group affiliations and political associations as a background it is now time to inquire into the correlation between political association and attitudes toward the Arab-Israeli conflict.

In order to provide the respondents with ample opportunity to express their attitudes towards the Arab-Israeli conflict, the students were presented with a set of alternative choices for each of two separate categories. The categories were desired objectives in the Arab-Israeli dispute and second, preferred means by which to attain these goals. The choices of goals were:

1. A secular bi-national state located on land which is now the West Bank, Gaza and Israel.

2. A Palestinian state on the West Bank and Gaza, independent of and at peace with both Israel and Hashemite-led Jordan (i.e., the East Bank.) This West Bank Palestine would be led by either the P.L.O. or local Palestinian nationalists.

3. A Palestinian state on the West Bank and Gaza, led by the P.L.O. or local nationalists, federated (or more loosely confederated with Hashemite Jordan) and with peaceful relations with Israel.

4. A unitary West Bank/Gaza/East Bank state, led by the P.L.O. (no Hashemites) and with peaceful relations with Israel.

5. An Arab Palestine on territory now Israel, the West Bank and Gaza *with* the expulsion of the Israeli Jews.

6. An Arab Palestine located on the territory which is now Israel, the West Bank and Gaza. *No* expulsion of the Jews, but not a "bi-national state" (i.e., No special political rights for Jews, no accommodations for future immigration, etc.).

While there exist degrees of difference between the six options, the clear cut-off point was between those student respondents willing to accept both a Palestine (independent of or connected or absorbing Jordan) and peaceful relations with Israel and those who desire to see Israel (in its present *de jure* pre-1967 boundaries) eliminated. The sets of solutions, therefore, reflecting the "accommodationists" are numbers 2, 3, and 4. The overall numbers of students choosing these three options was 192 or 32.3% of the aggregate. Choices 1, 5, and 6 called for the elimination of the sovereign state of Israel and a total of 403 students or 67.7% of the aggregate chose these objectives. Among the 53.1% of those who identified themselves as Arab nationalists, a total of 84.8% chose options 1, 5 and 6 and only 15.3% chose options which allowed for the continued existence of an independent Israel. The other communal association which reflected "militant" objectives was the very small (30 students out of nearly 600) group identifying themselves as advocates of a "Greater Syria." All chose either option #1 or #5.

Approximately 14.5% of the aggregate body of respondents chose religious association as their primary political/communal association. Their responses were considerably more moderate and accommodating towards the continued existence of Israel, with 47% choosing the three options that included peace with Israel and 52.9% choosing the three which called for its dissolution.

The last communal association of any statistical significance is that of state nationalism. (Those 18 respondents, 3.1% of the aggregate, who gave as their primary political association their family and clan *all* chose one of two "accommodatic" objectives; while the unanimity is interesting, the 3.1% is too limited for any conclusion.) Those who chose the nation-state as their focus of identity registered 24.3% of the aggregate, the second largest group of respondents. By far they also registered the most moderate set of goal choices. While 44.1% of the state nationalists chose the three opinions calling for the dissolution of Israel, 55.9% accepted its existence concurrent with a political/territorial solution to the Palestinian problem. If these trends reflect similar attitudes in the region, and Tawfic Farah's study at Kuwait University (which found state nationalism and religious association replacing the "discredited" Arab nationalism) is valid, then public sentiment towards some accommodation with Israel may, indeed, go deeper than the trial balloons and "leaks" to the Western press by segments of the Arab leadership. In any case, there appears to remain a strong correlation between those Arabs attached to an ideology of unification of segments of the Arabic-speaking world on the one hand and the desire for the elimination of the state of Israel on the other.

The four types of means that the respondents had to choose from were:

Military and economic means against Israel and economic pressure against the United States.

Military and economic means against Israel.

Economic means against both, coupled with diplomacy.

Diplomacy without the use of military or economic means.

The choices of preferred means of the respondents appear to correspond closely with those results concerning favored solutions to the conflict. The strongest advocates of the use of military force and economic pressure against Israel (or against Israel and the United States) were the Arab nationalists and "Greater Syrian" advocates; 85% of those who identified themselves as Arab nationalists chose options 1 and 2. All 30 respondents who identified themselves as "Greater Syrians" chose military means. Those choosing the religious community as their primary political association were also strongly militant, but almost 24% of them chose using economic pressure and diplomacy without the accompaniment of military force. The state nationalists, of the four groups with statistical significance, were again the least militant with only 36.4% of their total (of 145 respondents) desiring to use force as a means towards their desired political goals.

The next issue which the statistical survey examined was country-of-origin as an influencing factor of Arab attitudes towards Israel.

As earlier stated, the Northeastern University Survey findings indicate that 32.3% of the aggregate of respondents chose options 2, 3, and 4 (which accept Israel as a permanent state in the region) while 67.7% chose options 1, 5, and 6, which do not.

Among the "accommodationists" the Iraqi student body at Northeastern is the most willing to accept Israel as a permanent state in the region, with 67% choosing these three options. It should be noted that most of the Iraqi respondents were surveyed after the start of the Iraqi-Iranian war and one may speculate that this has influenced their desire for accommodation with Israel, despite the official "Rejectionist" policy of their leadership. Egyptian students also chose the three options which included peace with Israel at a high rate, theirs being 62% of their aggregate, as perhaps could be anticipated by the Camp David accords as well as the events leading up to the treaty. And, approximately 45% of those from Syria chose peace (as against 32.3% of the Arab aggregate). The remaining five sub-sets of students were all strongly militant and registered between 73.0% and 81.8% against peace with Israel. The Lebanese militancy, as indicated by only 26.6% of the Lebanese respondents choosing accommodation (as compared to the greater willingness to compromise with Israel in Suleiman's 1973 survey) is most explainable by the ravages of the Lebanese civil war. The survey found that those who identified themselves as Maronite Christians rather than as just Christians described themselves as much more religious and more willing to have peaceful relations with Israel than their non-Maronite Christian counterparts.

The Palestinians, both within Israel and within Arab states including Jordan, proved to be, along with the respondents from Bahrein and the United Arab Emirates, the most militant of all the surveyed students. Twenty percent of the respondents from Bahrein and the U.A.E. chose accommodation, with 25% of those from Libya doing the same. Palestinians from Israel chose the 3 options accepting Israel at 20% of their total, while those from Arab countries including Jordan, did so at 18.2%.

On the one hand, there was a strong correlation between the national origins of the respondents and their goal orientations and their choice of means on the other. With two exceptions (students from Syria and those from Iraq) the student bodies which were most militant in goal orientation were also the more militant in preferred means (choosing options 1 & 2). Those students who picked the least militant goals were those who favored economic pressure and diplomacy to resolve the Arab-Israeli conflict rather than the use of military force. In the follow-up interviews as well as in the written survey, many students who chose goal options 2, 3, and 4 (which would accept a compromise with Israel if it included a Palestinian national solution) insisted that it was only through the use of force that the Arab states and Palestinians could get Israel to accept that type of solution. In some cases, the respondents stated that "Israel only understands force"; in most cases, however, it was treated as an "acceptable" means towards a desired end.

The last issue which this paper will address is the religious influence upon the conflict. The historic "militancy" of Islam has characterized many analyses of the Arab-Israeli conflict as well as other inter-cultural/religious conflicts in which Muslims have participated. Due to the large percentage of Lebanese involved in the Northeastern survey a large portion of the Arab aggregate (approximately 40%) were Christian. This enabled us to compare Muslim and Christian Arab attitudes toward Israel. To this was added the second independent variable of the degree of religious conviction held by each respondent.

The next section of the survey tested for solutions to the Arab-Israeli conflict with the respondent's religion and degree of religious conviction as independent variables. Once again options 2, 3, and 4 were compressed into a single category which indicated willingness to accommodate Israel in the region and options 1, 5, and 6 into a category which did not. Recalling that 32.3% of the Arab aggregate chose accommodation we found that 35.8% of the Muslim Arab aggregate were willing to recognize Israel, 35.8% of the religious Muslims were willing to recognize Israel, 35.7% of the non-religious Muslims were willing to recognize Israel, 24.6% of the Christian Arab aggregate were willing to recognize Israel, 36.7% of the religious Christians were willing to recognize Israel, 13% of the non-religious Christians were willing to recognize Israel.

These results are in sharp contrast to the conventional assumptions of a "militant Islam." Muslim Arabs were more willing to compromise with the State of Israel than their Christian counterparts by 11.2% (35.8% as compared to 24.6%). Furthermore, within the Muslim aggregate, there was no statistical difference whatsoever between religious and non-religious Muslim students in their willingness to compromise with Israel. This should lead observers of the region to at least question notions concerning Islam's emotional impact upon attitudes held towards Israel in the more deeply religious circles. Within the Christian Arab aggregate, however, there was considerable difference in attitudes between those who described themselves as religious (Christians) and those who did not. While 36.7% of the religious Christians showed a willingness to compromise with Israel (making them, very narrowly, the most "accommodating" group), only 13.9% (of the 123 *non-religious* Christian respondents) were willing to make peace with Israel. This group was, by far, the most militant of the four groups within the survey. In both the written survey and in many follow-up interviews it was disclosed that most of these non-religious Christians were self-defined Arab or Syrian nationalists from Lebanon who opposed both the Maronite-dominated phalangist organization and its affiliation with Israel.

Seventy-five percent of the aggregate Arab respondents chose to use military force (option 1 and 2) to attain their goals. The following statistical results emerged when religion and degree of religious conviction were introduced as independent variables. Seventy-seven percent of the Muslim aggregate were willing to use force, 75.8% of the religious Muslims were willing to use force, 82.8% of the nonreligious Muslims were willing to use force, 71.0% of the Christian aggregate were willing to use force, 48.5% of the religious Christians were willing to use force, 91.7% of the non-religious Christians were willing to use force against Israel.

The answers of the Northeastern respondents seem to indicate that on the whole Muslim Arabs were somewhat more willing to use military means against Israel than their Christian Arab counterparts (77.9% as compared to 71.0%). Within the Muslim aggregate, the non-religious were more inclined to do so than their religious counterparts (82.8% as compared to 75.8%). The most interesting finding was the comparison within the Christian aggregate. *Non-religious* Christians were significantly more inclined to use military means than their religious counterparts by over 40% (91.7% as compared to 48.5%), and once again, were by far the most militant of all four groups.

While this study represents the attitudes and views of nearly 600 Arab students living and studying in America and is not a sample of Arab students in general, and certainly not of the overall Arab population, the conclusions made are hopefully suggestive for future research.

IV

The attitudes of the student respondents in the Northeastern survey may be instructive since the sample does represent a significant cross-section of one articulate and upwardly mobile sector of Arab society, and a group which may feel freer in their political expression due to their anonymity and distance from home.

One can conclude from the attitudes surveyed that there has been a small (8%) but measurable increase in the acceptance of Israel among Arab students studying in America during the past decade.[4] Secondly, both militant or compromising attitudes held by student respondents towards Israel appear to be strongly correlated with political ideologies and connections to communal association and political self-identity of the respondent. Those respondents who associated themselves with a larger nationalist body such as "Arabism" or the "Greater Syria Movement" tended to be far more militant than those respondents who chose the religious community as their primary communal association. Each of these two groups, in turn, were far more militant than the "state nationalists" who are satisfied with their national territorial status quo and existing boundaries within the Arab world. Thirdly, when the national origin of the respondents is used as an independent variable in measuring attitudes towards the Arab-Israeli conflict, wide variables were again registered by the students. As in the 1973 study, students from Egypt were the most willing to reach a compromise with Israel; similarly Syrian students remain accommodating; those of Palestinian origin remain the most opposed to compromise. The major shifts in attitudes over the past decade were the Lebanese towards militancy and the Iraqis towards accommodation. It appears that each national set of respondents has either remained the same or changed in response to actual events (i.e., the civil war for the Lebanese, the war with Iran for the Iraqis, and the continued occupation of the West Bank and Gaza by Israel for the Palestinians), rather than any inherent approach to conflict that is culturally derived.

Lastly, within the culture or "system" of Islam there appears to be more elasticity in legal interpretation (vis-à-vis laws of war and peace) than many observers of the area discussing Jihad have generally implied. This historical/judicial elasticity seems reinforced by the statistical findings in this study measuring the impact of religion and the degree of religious conviction upon attitudes towards the Arab-Israeli conflict. Reviewing the Northeastern Survey's statistics that measure attitudes towards both the resolution of the Arab-Israeli conflict as well as the means by which to achieve this goal, there seems no evidence that there are monolithic cultural determinants of these attitudes. In each of the survey's categories of questions measuring attitudes towards goals or acceptable means, non-religious Christians were significantly more militant than their religious Christian counterparts or religious or non-religious Muslims. There seems no evidence of either an "Arab" or "Muslim" approach to the Arab-Israeli conflict. Rather the individual's approach to the conflict is closely related to, shaped by, and reshaped by his manner of identifying his community and this community's definition of justice. This observation might give us pause before evoking the spector of "militant Islam" as a major obstacle to accommodation in the Middle East.

Notes

1. Halim Barakat, "Alienation and Revolution in Arab Life," *The Jerusalem Quarterly*, No. 4, Summer 1977 (The Middle East Institute, Jerusalem), pg. 118.

2. Levon H. Melikian and Lufty N. Diab, "Group Affiliations of University Students in the Arab Middle East," in *The Journal of Social Psychology*, Vol. 49, 2nd half (Provincetown, Mass: The Journal Press, May 1959), pp. 149–159; Saad E.M. Ibrahim, "Arab Images of the United States and the Soviet Union Before and After the June War of 1967," in *The Journal of Conflict Resolution*, Vol. XVI, No. 2 (Ann Arbor, Michigan, June, 1972); Paul D. Starr, "The October War and Arab Students' Self-Conceptions," in *The Middle East Journal*, Vol. 32, No. 4 (Washington, D.C.: The Middle East Institute, 1978), pp. 444–456; Michael W. Suleiman, "Attitudes of the Arab Elite Toward Palestine and Israel," in *The American Political Science Review*, Vol. 67, No. 2 (Washington, D.C.: The American Political Science Association, 1973), pp. 482–489; John Edwin Mroz, *Beyond Security: Private Perceptions Among Arabs and Israelis* (New York: Pergamon Press, 1980).

3. Tawfic Farah, "Group Affiliations of University Students in the Arab Middle East (Kuwait)," *The Journal of Social Psychology*, Vol. 106, 1978, pp. 161–165 and *Political Behavior In The Arab States* (Boulder, Colorado: Westview Press, 1983).

4. Suleiman, *op. cit.*, p. 485.

5

The End of Pan-Arabism

Fouad Ajami

Political ideas make their own realities. Often in defiance of logic, they hold men and are in turn held by them, creating a world in their own image, only to play themselves out in the end, shackled by routine problems not foreseen by those who spun the myth, or living past their prime and ceasing to move people sufficiently. Or, political ideas turn to ashes and leave behind them a trail of errors, suffering and devastation.

An idea that has dominated the political consciousness of modern Arabs is nearing its end, if it is not already a thing of the past. It is the myth of pan-Arabism, of the *Umma Arabiyya Wahida Dhat Risala Khalida*, "the one Arab nation with an immortal mission." At the height of its power, pan-Arabism could make regimes look small and petty: disembodied structures headed by selfsh rulers who resisted the sweeping mission of Arabism and were sustained by outside powers that supposedly feared the one idea that could resurrect the classical golden age of the Arabs. As historian Bernard Lewis summed it up little more than a decade ago, allegiance to the state was "tacit, even surreptitious," while Arab unity was "the sole publicly acceptable objective of statesmen and ideologues alike."[1] What this meant was that states were without sufficient legitimacy. Those among them that resisted the claims of pan-Arabism were at a disadvantage—their populations a fair target for pan-Arabist appeals, their leaders to be overthrown and replaced by others more committed to the transcendent goal. Now, however, *raison d'état*, once an alien and illegitimate doctrine, is gaining ground. Slowly and grimly, with a great deal of anguish and of outright violence, a "normal" state system is becoming a fact of life.

No great idea passes from the scene without screams of anguish, protests of true believers, and assertions by serious analysts that the idea still stands—battered, transformed but standing nonetheless—and debate about the vitality of pan-Arabism continues, for it is still far from accepted that the idea has been eclipsed. Writing in the July 1978 *Foreign Affairs*, Walid Khalidi reaffirmed the vitality of the pan-Arabist idea. He observed that the Arab system is "first and foremost a 'Pan' system. It postulates the existence of a single Arab Nation behind the facade of a multiplicity of sovereign states. . . . From this perspective, the individual Arab states are *deviant* and *transient* entities; their frontiers illusory; their rulers interim caretakers or obstacles to be removed." Before the "super-legitimacy" of pan-Arabism, the legitimacy of the Arab states "shrinks into irrelevance." In such a system, "explicit or transparent *raison d'état* is heresy."[2] What is normal for others is abnormal in the Arab world. Since Arab states are really deviant entities, which in time will pass from the scene, they are to be constrained in what they do for statehood. Nothing less than a pan-Arab superstate will do.

A second view is that of Mohamed Hassanein Heikal, once the propagator of Nasserist ideology and today one of the bearers of the myths—in President Sadat's pejorative description, one of the high priests of the Nasserist temple. Heikal, who once made the distinction between Egypt as a state and Egypt as a revolution, and who defended the right of the "Arab revolution" to interfere in the internal affairs of Arab countries, now grudgingly concedes that the state has triumphed over the aspirations of pan-Arabism. He has recounted a conversation he had with Secretary of State Kissinger during the latter's shuttle diplomacy in the Middle East in which he told Mr. Kissinger that Egypt was not merely a state on the banks of the Nile, but the embodiment of "an idea, a tide, a historical movement." To this Mr. Kissinger is reported to have said that he himself could not deal with latent intangible forces, or negotiate with an idea.

The Sadat diplomacy—of which Mr. Heikal is a critic—seemed to sustain the Kissingerian view. The idea that Heikal once brandished in the face of Nasser's rivals has lost its lure and power. Everyone, laments Heikal, recognizes that "the idea, the tide, the historical movement" is absent and that the party sitting across the negotiating table is the Egyptian state with its limited frontiers, resources and calculable interests.[3]

Heikal has reiterated this view that the Arab system is on the defensive, that "it has been forced to retreat in disarray," in this journal. Egypt, "for so long the mainstay of the Arab system," has opted out of it; the opportunity afforded by the October War of 1973 to put the system on solid foundations was lost, with the fault presumably in the decision-maker's judgment. Faith intrudes, however, for Heikal ends on an upbeat note. The Arab system may suffer a temporary setback, but it could bounce back (presumably when the Egyptian decision-maker sees the error of his ways), because the Arab world possesses a vitality that makes "the real constituency of any Arab leader the Arab world as a whole."[4] Once again, the leader's constituency does not end with the boundaries of his state: even when the idea is violated, it still possesses sanctity and recuperative power.

The story of pan-Arabism's retreat goes deeper than Sadat's policy. And, to be sure, it has nothing to do with Mr. Kissinger's diplomacy, for, whatever the carrots and sticks in his bag, Mr. Kissinger could not remake Arab history or defeat a compelling idea. The willingness of the Egyptian state to be more like other states—to negotiate for itself—had nothing to do with Mr. Kissinger's diplomatic tactics, but was rather the result of changes and transformations within Arab politics itself. Reason of state had already begun to prevail in inter-Arab affairs, and pan-Arabism had lost its hold over the popular imagination several years before Kissinger appeared on the scene with a distinct preference for an "Egyptian solution" and an aversion to dealing with "historical movements."

II

Pan-Arabism's retreat began in 1967 after the Six Day War, which marked the Waterloo of pan-Arabism. In the immediate aftermath of the war there was no competing system of legitimacy—in fact, very little if any legitimacy remained in Arab politics as a whole. The regimes had survived, but the defeat had dishonored practically all of them and had devastated, in particular, the pan-Arabists in Cairo and Damascus. No regime could have gone its separate way then. The "radical" regime in Cairo would capitulate to the will of the oil states led by Saudi Arabia, but the oil states would not press their victory too far or too hard. The military defeat was sustained directly by the armies of Egypt, Syria and Jordan—for all practical purposes and in terms of inter-Arab politics, by Egypt—but the defeat had underlined the vulnerability of the Arab system of states, the bankruptcy of the Arab order and its guardians, whether radical or conservative. The champions of pan-Arabism were defeated in the Arab system; the idea had lost its magic. Yet particular states were still captives of a status quo erected by the defeat, which they could neither undo nor indefinitely live with.

Opportunity to break out of that situation and to assert reason of state would arise with the October War. The irony is that the war which Mr. Heikal and others looked at as an opportunity to revive the Arab system, was precisely the event that would enable reason of state to challenge the then feeble but still venerated pretensions of pan-Arabism. The logic that triumphed in October 1973 was not the pan-Arabist one held up by Nasser and the Baath, it was the more limited notion of solidarity preferred by those states that had long opposed pan-Arabism. What President Sadat was to do subsequently was read the results of October 1973—more accurately perhaps, to use the results—and to stake out a large territory of independent prerogative for Egypt and himself. What might have been an Egyptian temptation between 1967 and 1973, particularly under President Sadat in the second half of that period, could be done in the aftermath of the October War because it was only after that war that the man at the helm of the Egyptian state was in command. The "honor" of the state had been redeemed. Egypt's sacrifices and what Mr. Sadat called "the size of the victory" on the Egyptian-Israeli front—presumably larger than it was on the Syrian-Israeli front, as it had been nonexistent on the Jordanian and Palestinian front— would be used to legitimate a break with the Arab system.

Times had changed; so had the leader in charge. Whatever his frustrations with the Arab system—and they were plentiful—Nasser was too much a captive of that system to break with it in the same manner and to the same degree as Sadat. Given his personal makeup, his history, the constituency he had acquired, and the images he had manipulated, the best Nasser could do was moderate his policies and set the stage for someone less tied to the policies of the past. Even in defeat Nasser was still a pan-Arab hero: his victories lay in the Arab system, for after 1967 there was very little left in Egypt to point to with much pride.

Whatever his dreams were prior to 1967, Nasser was a changed man after the Six Day War. He was willing and able—or almost able—to strike a bargain with none other than King Faisal of Saudi Arabia, and for the last three years of his life he managed to forge an alliance with the Jordanian monarch, who had long been one of his political rivals. Finally, he would accept the Rogers Peace Plan and implicitly renounce much of what he had stood for in the past. His pan-Arab constituency (that part of it which did not defect, that is) was of course willing to extend to him the benefit of the doubt. His reconciliation with Saudi Arabia was stormy and problematic enough to exonerate him in the eyes of his followers. His alliance with King Hussein provided rather more material for disillusionment, for his ally was the enemy of the Palestinians. But here again, as Malcolm Kerr so aptly put it, Nasser's "incredible luck stayed with him into the grave," for, to most of his followers, he "died as a martyr to the cause of Arab brotherhood" as a result of the strain of the Jordanian civil war negotiations and his

concern for the plight of the Palestinians.[5] As for his acceptance of the
Rogers Peace Plan, that could easily be brushed aside. To this very day
his followers maintain that it was a tactical decision, buying time to
prepare for another military round. The burden of the past was far too
heavy to have allowed Nasser the same margin for maneuver even if
he had wanted to abandon the pan-Arab cause.

Anwar Sadat had never excited a pan-Arab audience and had never
been a hero. But if he lacked the hero's stature, he also lacked the hero's
reputation, and was free of the chains that tie heroes to their great
deeds. If anything, Sadat would find it a bit gratifying—and this is only
human—to slay the myth of his predecessor, a man he had once known
as an equal and who had managed to rise above Sadat and other
colleagues to heroic proportions in no small part through the love and
devotion of people in distant Arab capitals. Sadat could hope to compete
with his predecessor in Egypt proper, but in the Arab world his
predecessor was larger than life. Perhaps in Sadat's "Egyptianness" there
is a desire of sorts to move from Nasser's shadow into a smaller arena
where his predecessor is more subject to errors and to a normal, more
tangible audit.

With the pan-Arab hero out of the way, the conservative Arab states
would find it easier to deal with his successor, a less ambitious man,
more accepting of boundaries and ideological differences. That is why
Sadat could enlist those states in a joint endeavor like the October War,
a feat which Nasser might never have been able to accomplish. That
Sadat would eventually go further down the road of autonomy than
the limits preferred by the oil states is one of the supreme ironies of
recent Arab politics. Where the oil states once feared Egypt's meddlesome
politics, they lived to experience the fear of her disengagement from
pan-Arab responsibilities. The threat that once emanated from her
radicalism and pan-Arabism receded; a new threat came from her separate
and independent nationalism. Of all the Arab states, Egypt is the largest,
the most politically stable, the most legitimate within her boundaries.
This enabled Egypt to give pan-Arabism concrete power, and then, when
she tired of it, to turn inward. The oil states had wanted from Egypt
an abandonment of the pan-Arabist ideology and acceptance of the logic
of the state system, and they got that. What Sadat's diplomacy was to
show was that states—or, more precisely and aptly, the leaders of states—
could read their interests differently and independently.

III

Sadat's diplomacy was the most dramatic illustration of the weakness
of pan-Arabism and objectively the most important, if only because

Egypt had been, as Mr. Heikal rightly states, "the mainstay of the Arab system." But throughout the preceding decade there had been other "revolts," other "separatist" attacks against the monolithic pan-Arab doctrine. It is only within the context of those other attacks that the Sadat diplomacy can be correctly situated in Arab politics.

The Palestinians launched the first post-1967 attack against pan-Arabism. Given their predicament, their economic and political dependence upon the Arab states and their lack of a territorial base, theirs had to be a different kind of attack. But there was no doubt that those who rallied around Yassir Arafat and George Habash in the aftermath of the Six Day War had given up on pan-Arabism—the first group in the name of Palestinian nationalism, the second in the name of social revolution. The duel that raged between the Palestinians and the Nasserites from early 1965 until Nasser's death in 1970 was in essence a fight about the independent rights of Palestinian nationalism. If the Arab states could not protect themselves against Israel, let alone do something for the Palestinians, then the latter were to construct their own independent politics. In the final analysis, it was Arafat's brand of nationalism, with its pledge of nonintervention in the internal affairs of Arab countries, that found its way into the organized Arab state system, rather than George Habash's revolution. Arafat's narrow focus on Palestinian nationalism and his avoidance of social and ideological issues were in keeping with the new tenor of Arab politics, and that is why Arafat's course found a reasonable measure of support in Riyadh: in his strict Palestinian nationalism there was an acceptance of reason of state. That acceptance was not applicable to the two "sanctuaries," Jordan and Lebanon, hence the two civil wars in which the Palestinians came to be involved.

Another crack in the pan-Arab edifice was the virtual end of the Baath Party, the pan-Arab party that took seriously its mission of bringing about the one Arab nation. A shell called the Baath remains, and it claims power in both Iraq and Syria, home to the Baath in the post-World War II years, but President Hafez al-Assad is cut of different cloth. A cautious member of a minority sect, he harbors no illusions about Arab unity and is probably the first leader in modern Syrian history to make peace with Syria's national situation and to accept the limitations of geography and resources. Since his rise to power in 1970, he has managed to rid Syria of a great deal of its romanticism and extremism, and to move it to the center of Arab politics. To do so, he put an entire tradition behind him by accepting a reconciliation with King Hussein, and abandoning the infantile Baathist notion of bringing Egypt into the pan-Arab fold and making her do their bidding for them. He has also tried, as his cumulative record in Lebanon would demonstrate, to tip the scales against those with a penchant for extreme solutions. Thus, in June 1976, he intervened against his former allies—the leftist Palestinian/Muslim alliance—and then in February 1978 against the Maronite Christian militias when it became clear to him that their aim was nothing short of partition.

The threat of a partitioned Lebanon is yet another serious challenge to pan-Arabism in a decade of setbacks. This challenge comes from an area that never accepted the idea of Arabism but made a peculiar kind of peace with it, namely, Christian Lebanon. As long as the Arabists accepted Lebanon's unique identity and situation, Lebanon could find its role and place in the "Arab family" as a link between the Arabs and the West: as a place for those who played and lost in the game of politics and needed a place to write their memoirs or plot their return to power; as a playground for Saudis and Kuwaitis who wished to escape the climate and puritanism of their own countries; as a banking haven for Syrians who wanted to flee from the politics and intrigues of the military and the economic irresponsibility of would-be socialists. Lebanon, so it was believed, could have it both ways: live off the Arab world yet think of itself as a piece of the Occident. Arabism was far away; one could pay homage to it and go about the business of trading, publishing, smuggling, banking.

This worked as long as the Arab-Israeli conflict was removed from Lebanon's soil—a situation that changed after 1970, when the Palestinians, expelled from Jordan, made their political home in Lebanon. Then the glib, superficial Arabism of Lebanon met a test it was destined to fail. The leaders in the Christian community who had known the Arab system and made their peace with it lost to those for whom Arabism and Islam were synonymous, and who believed in their own cultural supremacy and the backwardness of the Arabs. Convinced that they were being abandoned by the West (they too had heard of the "decline of the West"), resentful of the post-October 1973 wealth and prominence of the Muslim Arab states, losing control over a country that had gotten too "Palestinianized" and radicalized for their taste, aware that the demographic facts were shattering the myth of Christian majority, the Maronites would do what would have been unthinkable yesterday: after a brief reliance on a Syrian connection, they opted for a break with the Arab system—an alliance with Israel and a full commitment to partition.

Through it all, the advocates of partition would be helped by the obvious culpability of the Arab states, which had exported the "sacred Arab cause"—the Palestinian issue—onto Lebanese soil. In other words, the least Arab of countries, as well as the weakest militarily, was to bear the brunt of full Israeli retaliation and to accept a parallel and competing system of authority. Sincere or not, the Palestinian slogan of nonintervention in the internal affairs of Arab countries was harder to practice than to preach. With Israel more than willing and able to retaliate for raids into her territory, the Lebanese formula would unravel. The gift of an enlarged Lebanon bequeathed by the French turned into a nightmare, and the Maronite militias took up arms, first to defeat the leftist Palestinian/Muslim alliance and then, a little later, to try to carve out their own state, bidding farewell to the pleasantries of "Arab brotherhood." They were now willing to state what had been their conviction for quite some time: that they think of themselves as a different breed; that they are apart from the Arab world, not geographically but culturally of a different world. The Syrian army may win a confrontation or two, but what must be honestly and candidly dealt with is a bid for partition and creation of a sovereign Maronite state. If anything, Syrian assaults steel the will of the militias and silence those in the Christian community who still believe that things could be managed with a slightly reformed version of the old status quo.

IV

In an otherwise across-the-board break with the universalism of pan-Arabism, it was only the young group of officers who came to power in Libya in September 1969 who would raise the old banner in the decade that followed the 1967 defeat. Qaddafi and his fellow officers were more royalist than the king, more true to Abdul Nasser than Nasser himself, nostalgic for the young Nasser and bent upon reenacting his drama with all its noisy color and vitality. Libya, insulated from the Arab world, was thus to go through the same stage that Nasserites and Baathists had gone through in the preceding decade. The principal difference between Qaddafi's group and yesterday's unionists was that the former combined, perhaps for the first time, two forces that had generally been at odds in recent Arab history: oil and pan-Arabism. From Egypt and Syria the unionist movement had been a claim by poor states for the "collective" wealth of the Arab world. The Libyan case was to provide just the opposite: an affluent society wanting to unite with its poorer neighbors.

Determined to realize the old dream, Qaddafi would seek unity with as odd a candidate as Bourguiba's Tunisia, but Egypt was the real focus of his aspirations. For four years he would urge unity upon both Nasser and Sadat, although one suspects that the offers were made in a different spirit to each: he would "offer" Libya to Nasser, while he wanted to "steal" Egypt from Sadat.

In both the Tunisian and latter-day Egyptian cases, Qaddafi was urging unity on two older men for whom he had little if any regard, whom he thought he could eventually push aside. To a Muslim Arab soldier like Qaddafi, Bourguiba can only seem like a compromised Francophile, symbol of a by-gone age in which Arabs accepted the supremacy of the West and aped its ways. As for the pre-October 1973 Sadat, Qaddafi could hardly be blamed for the low opinion he held of him—after all, that was a more or less universal judgment. During that transitional and difficult period when Sadat lacked his own source of legitimacy, many of Nasser's followers in and outside of Egypt came to think of Qaddafi—"*al walad al majnun,*" Sadat called him, "the crazy boy"—as the spiritual son and true heir of Nasser. As it turned out, the source of Qaddafi's appeal lay more in Sadat's seeming ineptitude than in anything that Qaddafi himself had done. Thus, when Sadat finally made good on his promise to break the military stalemate, the Qaddafi appeal came to an end. The October War might not have been the glorious achievement that Sadat made it out to be, but it was an achievement nonetheless. Egypt was once again a country with a leader, and Qaddafi's bid for unity could be pushed aside. Reenacting the past had had its day.

Neither the fire and passion of the Libyan revolution nor its money could turn history around and revive an exhausted idea. Since their seizure of power in 1969, Qaddafi and his fellow offcers have gradually come to see the differences among Arabs that had previously eluded them. The contrived boundaries had a reality after all. (They ought to know that, for their own rather strict immigration policies contradict all their talk of pan-Arabism.) Here and there a few writers and publicists—not to mention some troublemakers—prospered on Libyan money repeating Qaddafi's slogans about his Third Theory, or carrying out his wishes in Beirut and Cairo. But this was not to be Qaddafi's era, for he was already an anachronism. With its wealth and small population and its relative isolation from the traumas and wounds of Arab history, Libya may go on a little longer with more sound and fury about pan-Arabism, but its experiment and ideas are irrelevant to the needs and situations of other Arab states.

A social scientist at Kuwait University has supplied us with important evidence substantiating the demise of pan-Arabism and suggesting the shape of things to come. Taking a sample of students from practically all Arab countries, he administered a questionnaire to nearly 500 undergraduates at Kuwait University with the aim of ascertaining their views on pan-Arabism, family, state and religion. What he found was a remarkable assertion of Islamic sentiment and of patriotism associated with particular Arab states—in other words, the vacuum left behind as a result of the demise of pan-Arabism is being filled by religious belief on one level and by loyalty to the state on another. His data led him to conclude that the discussions of "one Arab nation" and "Arab brotherhood" are myths and exhausted slogans.[6]

This shift in belief corresponds to concrete changes in the distribution of power in the Arab system. Power has shifted to the state (Saudi Arabia) that has long been a foe of pan-Arabism and has traditionally seen itself as a guardian of the *turath*, the heritage, or Islam, to be more precise. Muslim universalism is a safer doctrine than the geographically more limited but politically more troublesome idea of pan-Arabism; the "48 Muslim countries and 700 million Muslims" is a safe and distant symbol, giving a semblance of "super-legitimacy" without posing a threat to reason of state. Summit conferences like the one held in Lahore in 1974 and institutions like the Islamic Economic Conference appeal to those who wish to speak of the resurrection of Islam without shackling the power of the state. No one wants to unite Saudi Arabia and Bangladesh, Indonesia and the United Arab Emirates. The only challenge that Islamic sentiment might pose would come from far below the world of state elites, where a militant, popular kind of Islam may reject—as it does in Iran, and to a lesser extent in Egypt—the world view and preferences of state elites. But that, at least in the Arab context, is a different problem from the disruptive doctrine of pan-Arabism, for it is a challenge contained within the boundaries of the state.

V

The boundaries of Arab states have been around now for nearly six decades. It is not their existence which is novel, but their power and legitimacy—the power (as much as that power exists in the modern state system) to keep pan-Arab claims at bay and effectively to claim the loyalty of those within. They are no longer as "illusory and permeable" as they used to be. The states that lie within them are less "shy" about asserting their rights, more normal in the claims that they make.

The Arabs who had once seemed whole—both to themselves and to others—suddenly look as diverse as they had been all along. The differences, smothered over by ideology and by a universalistic designation, can in no way be ignored or suppressed. Indeed, the more they are blanketed over by a thin veneer of superficial universalism, the more dangerous they become, if only because they create resentment on the part of those who do not feel the designation and who judge that Arabism places them at a disadvantage—that is, it used to ask some of them to fight and die while others did not, or to use their territory as sanctuary for guerrilla raids while others were safely insulated by ceasefire lines and U.N. troops, or to pay for the economic inefficiency and large populations of sister states.

The Arab system of states will have to search for a new equilibrium, for a more limited and perhaps more workable system, because concrete and irreversible changes have already taken place to make interstate boundaries harder and more legitimate. Six factors that enabled pan-Arabism to slight boundaries and to play havoc with sovereignty are either things of the past, or are undergoing fundamental metamorphosis:

1. The universalism of pan-Arabism derived to a considerable extent from the universalism of the Ottoman Empire of which the Arab states had been a part for four centuries. In other words, scholars, officials and officers slipped from one universalist system into another. It was an understandable response to the nationalism of the Young Turks: if the Turks were a nation, so too were the Arabs. But whatever unity was lent to the Arab society by the universalism of the Ottoman system now belongs to the past. The Ottoman experience has been committed to history, and six decades after its collapse it is becoming a fading memory.

2. Arab nationalism rested on the power and popularity of the pamphlet and the book; it was conceived and spread by intellectuals, mostly those in exile. From Europe, where publicists like Neguib Azoury, Shakib Arslan, and later Michel Aflaq of the Baath Party conceived their ideas, the distinctions among Arabs seemed negligible, almost nonexistent. It was theory written from afar by theorists concerned with and consumed by large-scale distinctions between rival and whole civilizations.

Now the power of intellectuals is waning, with a definite backlash in the Arab world against the written word and intellectuals. The beneficiaries are either men of affairs schooled in the hard knocks of politics—a Hafez Assad rather than Michel Aflaq—or development-oriented elites. In contrast to the literary intellectuals who dominated the early stage of Arab nationalism, the new elite is a more sober, less grandiose group—less likely to emphasize the abstractions of Arab unity, more sensitive to the realities on the ground or more committed to specifc tasks. A nationalism that fails to create a political order cannot withstand the dissolution of its creed, and the intellectuals were temperamentally unfit to create such a concrete order. It is one thing to polemicize about the "one nation" and its metaphysical base, but quite another to erect it on the ground.

3. The anticolonialism of the mandate years lent a great deal of unity to the Arab system, as an entire generation was traumatized by what they saw as the Arabs' betrayal by the West. The Balfour Declaration and the Sykes/Picot agreement made their imprint on a large number of Arab nationalists, wherever they were, and forged a strong bond of

unity among officials, publicists and officers who thought in terms of the Arab and the West.

However, what we observed of the Ottoman Empire pretty much applies as well to the anti-Westernism of the mandate years. Britain and France, the two powers whose deeds and diplomacy haunted and traumatized a generation of nationalists, have been cut down to size; they made their last stand in the Suez affair and since then their diplomacy has, on the whole, been sympathetic to the Arab states. London is no longer a hostile capital where diplomatic schemes are hatched against the Arabs; in fact, it has become familiar and accessible, with whole sections that have been "Arabized." The British, once resented and admired masters, now covet Arab investments and worry about the penetration of their society by Arab capital. France has become synonymous with Charles de Gaulle: an admired symbol of nationalism and, from 1962 onward, a "friend" of the Arab states. Beyond this, there has been a subtle and steady "growing up," a realization by Arabs that they have no monopoly on trauma, so to speak, that they are not the only ones whose ambitions have been thwarted and to whom history has dealt a raw deal or two. Worldly success in the aftermath of October 1973 is to a great extent responsible for this shift.

4. There was a mobile, trans-state elite that moved from one Arab state to another; they knew and understood one another and their horizons transcended the boundaries of a single state. They "believed implicitly in the existence of an Arab nation: in schools, in barracks, in the Ottoman parliament, in exile in Cairo, and in the Sharifian forces they had come to know each other and acquired the ease of discourse which possession of a common language and a common education gives."[7] Some of these men formed the nucleus of the group that rallied around the Hashemite Prince Faisal as he came out of the Arabian Peninsula to be crowned in Syria and later (having been driven out of Damascus by the French) to rule over Iraq.

That mobile structure of dynasts, officers, officials and scholars has by now been replaced by more "parochial" elites as the usual complex of bureaucratic interests has developed in each of the Arab states. The change may be best captured by comparing the leading Arab dynasty in the early and middle parts of this century to the leading dynasty today. The Hashemites thought of the Arab world as their domain. They ruled in the Peninsula and, with the help of the British, established monarchies in Damascus (Prince Faisal's short-lived Arab kingdom), Transjordan and Iraq. Of all that, a modest throne remains in Jordan where a skilled but hemmed-in monarch tries his best to survive and to reconcile conflicting claims and pressures. Today's leading royal house, the Saudi family, is committed to its own sovereignty in the blessed (materially and spiritually) piece of land it has. The victory of the more "local" Ibn Saud over the "pan-Arab" Shariff Hussein half a century ago may have been the first victory (albeit of a dynastic/tribal kind) for reasons of state over the more grandiose ambitions of pan-Arabism. Below the dynastic level, the same shift in favor of parochial elites is equally evident in the usual occupations that states generate. To be sure, technocrats, teachers and skilled workers migrate in large numbers from the populated Arab states to the richer oil states, but these are people who migrate for a living and are content to leave power to the host governments.

5. The Palestine defeat in 1948 was seen as an injury to the pride and integrity of the entire Arab world—not strictly as a Palestinian defeat, but as a pan-Arab one. The creation of Israel was a deeply wounding and traumatizing experience, a symbol of Arab weakness and backwardness, a reminder that whatever the Arabs were in the past, whatever their old glories and achievements, they were now in decline, at the mercy of others, no longer sovereign in their own region. Having vowed to undo the "shame" of the defeat, it became difficult for any state to take itself out of the conflict.

The unity forced onto the Arab world by the Arab-Israeli conflict has eroded—perhaps less dramatically than in other areas, but eroded nonetheless. Whatever the future shape of the conflict between the Arab states and Israel, the Sadat diplomacy has dragged the Arabs—with great numbers of them shouting, objecting, feeling violated and betrayed—into the modern game of states. The conflict is no longer about Israel's existence, but about its boundaries; and in inter-Arab affairs, the leading military state has for all appearances rejected the inter-Arab division of labor that assigned it the principal obligation for a pan-Arab cause.

6. Finally, from 1956 (after Suez) until Nasser's death in 1970, or until the 1967 defeat, the power of pan-Arabism derived from the power of charismatic leadership. Prior to the emergence of Nasser as a pan-Arab savior, the idea had been an elite endeavor of publicists, intellectuals and a few officers. Nasser would take the theories and the emotions to the masses, give pan-Arabism its moment in the sun, and then its tragic end in 1967.

The politics of charisma, however, have passed from the scene. T. E. Lawrence once expressed a stereotype about the Arabs that has managed to stick: "Arabs," he said, "could be swung on an idea as on a cord. . . . Without a creed they could be taken to the four corners of the world (but not to heaven) by being shown the riches of the earth and the pleasures of it, but if on the road, led in this fashion, they met the prophet of an idea, who had nowhere to lay his head and who depended for his food on charity and birds, then they would all leave their wealth for his inspiration."[8] Today the idea and the prophet are gone: the man who could in a speech excite youth in West Beirut, Amman and Baghdad against their governments is no longer there, and this has contributed to the normalization of the Arab state system.

The circumstances that produced the ebb of Nasserist charisma may be *sui generis*, but the end of Nasserism is a piece of a bigger puzzle. It is the end of that stage of Third World history represented by men like Nasser, Nehru, Sukarno, Nkrumah—dreamers who sought what one of them, Nkrumah, described as the "kingdom of politics." In that kingdom they sought answers to questions of identity and self-worth, dabbled in dreams and intangibles, but their politics were bound to come to an end, for the sort of nationalist fervor they embodied triumphs for a moment but cannot last forever.

The exhaustion of the nationalist fervor generally signals a coming to the fore of economic issues and demands, of problems that do not lend themselves to solo performances, to the magic touch of charisma. Less colorful leaders, whose links to the nationalist struggle are often tenuous, are the ones who have to satisfy the new needs. With defeat in 1967, charisma turned to ashes and the conservative oil states made their financial help contingent upon a new style and kind of politics. The romantic phase of nationalism is over, then, as it falls upon the second generation to accomplish the technical and often grim tasks of governance. Anwar el-Sadat's recent autobiography, *In Search of Identity*, is really the last of its kind.[9] The next time an Egyptian head of state writes an autobiography, I suspect that identity will not be the principal thread; he may have to name it "In Search of Productivity" or something similarly routine. Whoever he turns out to be, he may well be envious that one of his predecessors "philosophized" about revolution, while the other talked of identity.

VI

Whether the Arabs like it or not, what they are left with and what they increasingly must acknowledge is a profound fragmentation of the Arab existential and political crisis. We know the themes and memories that lent unity to their consciousness and history: one language, the classical golden age of Islam, the decline of the Muslim order, the universalism of the Ottoman Empire, the yearning for independence, the traumas of being initiated into an international system in which they were not full participants, the Palestine defeat, the Six Day War, and finally October 1973. Particular regimes and leaders aside, Arab states are stuck with one another, and the shared themes and concerns could conceivably provide a basis for a working regional order—or, if pushed too far, for disaster and continuous discord.

The shared themes and concerns must not obscure the fragmentation. There is no longer a collective Arab crisis and there is no use pretending that it exists. To illustrate, let me briefly sketch the separate and quite different dilemmas of several populations in the Arab world.

In Egypt, the serious life-and-death issue is economic, and the main struggle is for human worth and dignity in a crowded, economically pressed society. For a young educated Saudi, Kuwaiti or Libyan, the sky is the limit: huge projects to run, European vacations, investments, offers from foreign businessmen and people with all kinds of schemes, dreams and gadgets.[10] For a young and equally skilled and educated Egyptian, the overwhelming reality he has to deal with is unemployment or a dead-end job in a sluggish bureaucracy and the impossible dream of making ends meet, the nightmare of finding and affording an apartment in Cairo, where rentals have gone sky-high thanks in part to the abundance of petrodollars. Is there a mystery to the frustration of the young Egyptian, his suspicion that he must go to Sinai and face Israeli arms while others talk of pan-Arabism in London and Paris? Is this not the reality that President Sadat so masterfully evoked when he spoke of "nightclub revolutionaries"? The wealthy Arab states have been somewhat helpful to Egypt, but Egypt's economic needs are staggering, and it is these needs and grievances that enabled the Egyptian President to do what he did on the foreign policy front.

Whether Sadat's diplomacy stands or falls, it will do so on its own merit, judged in terms of what it will or will not do for Egypt; charges of treason, or tribunals against Sadat by Iraq or Libya will be to no avail. But foreign policy can be a ruler's escape, and victories and virtuoso performances are easier to pull off in distant places than at home. The noted Egyptian analyst Lewis Awad has recently argued that much of what Nasser did in foreign policy was sheer escapism.[11] The same temptation may again present itself, this time by irrelevant talk about threats in the Horn of Africa, challenging the Soviet Union, and the like. For Egypt, the real threat is at home: a huge population that must be fed and educated; a decaying capital; an overcrowded society that must seek an economic role in the surrounding region, and must therefore avoid too sharp a break with its neighbors.

The Fertile Crescent offers a striking contrast to the Egyptian case. There, the crisis is political; it is a crisis of political legitimacy, of taming political passions, of fnding a framework that satisfies the aspirations for self-determination. Lebanon and the Palestinian question are the two outstanding political problems and, barring some unforeseen solutions to both, that area is destined to suffer more of the bloodshed and violence that have become its lot.

Without a territorial base of their own, the Palestinians would still have it within their power to disrupt the Arab system of states. This power derives not only from their presence in Lebanon and Jordan, and their influence in Kuwait, but also from their appeal to an overwhelming body of opinion throughout the Arab world that wants what it thinks an appropriate resolution to the Palestinian question: self-determination for the Palestinians. Both historical-emotional factors and the cold logic of reason of state overlap here, for it is believed that the best way of taming Palestinian radicalism is to contain the Palestinians within their own state, either autonomous or linked to Jordan, and that only then will the Arab system of states be effectively normalized.

The Palestinians, too, have come to see it this way. Whereas it was once heresy to speak of an independent Palestinian state—after all, Palestine was supposed to be part of a larger Arab entity—the Palestinians have come to realize that they too require the normalcy of statehood. Their view has come to converge with the recognition of most Arab states that their own reason of state vis-à-vis Palestinian claims is best served by the Palestinians acquiring their own territory with all the responsibilities such a process usually entails. This explains President Sadat's insistence during the Camp David negotiations on a linkage between an Egyptian settlement and a framework for the West Bank and Gaza Strip, and explains as well Saudi Arabia's cautious response to the summit.

All of the crucial or affected Arab states see in the resolution of the Palestinian question an enhancement of their own sovereignty: the Lebanese could then begin to put together a shattered country whose economic role is perhaps irretrievably lost; the Saudis and the Kuwaitis would feel more secure about their own wealth, less susceptible to disruption; the Egyptians—and even the Syrians—would be freed from a military confrontation that they could neither win nor disengage from without damage to their interests and legitimacy. The Jordanian position is admittedly the most thorny and troublesome, for it is clear that there are, in inter-Arab politics, two claims to the West Bank: Jordanian and Palestinian. King Hussein's claim rests on Jordan's sovereignty prior to 1967; the Palestinian claim is the more standard nationalist claim of a people to their territory, and it is that claim which the Arab states honored during the Rabat summit of 1974.

Since then, there has been an undeniable erosion in the power of the Rabat resolution that declared the Palestine Liberation Organization "the sole, legitimate representative of the Palestinian people." President Sadat's call upon the Jordanian monarch to "shoulder his responsibility" indicated where the Egyptian President stood. King Hussein's reluctance to get off the fence displays the caution of a man deeply pessimistic about the intentions of the state that currently holds the West Bank. And, in the absence of some firm signs that Israel is eventually willing to relinquish the West Bank, King Hussein is likely to continue to do what he has been doing for the last decade, namely, staying within the limits of an overall Arab consensus, and urging restraint and caution on the part of other Arab actors. But should signs of an Israeli change of heart materialize, the inter-Arab struggle for the West Bank, now somewhat subdued and repressed, would come to the fore. Hard choices would then have to be made by the Jordanian monarch, by the Palestinians themselves, by the Syrians, who claim both sides of the fight as their friends, and by the Saudis, who help to subsidize and sustain both the PLO and Jordan.

In the oil states, there are the problems of managing great wealth and then of setting that wealth and what it builds next to the violence and instability of the Fertile Crescent and the poverty of Egypt. Saudi Arabia, the leading oil state, understands what John C. Campbell calls the "political fragility" that lies beneath its prosperity.[12] Having helped exorcise the area of Nasserism, the Saudis were willing to deploy the oil weapon in the October War, to subsidize the two Arab combatants and, when the war was over, to try to keep them together. Their distinct preference is for a "moderate" Arab system of states based on a reasonable measure of consensus. The preferred Saudi design is what I have described elsewhere with no claim to originality as a "trilateral" design, a triangular system of power bringing together Saudi Arabia, Egypt and Syria.[13] The Saudi predilection for this arrangement explains most of Saudi Arabia's inter-Arab politics as of late: try to bring Sadat back into the Arab fold without squeezing him too hard; bail out Hafez Assad, subsidize his incursion into Lebanon, and make sure that he does not tilt toward the rejectionists.

Above and beyond particular foreign policy decisions, the oil states will continue to experience the difficulties of living in a militarized, impoverished part of the world, as well as the dreams and possibilities spawned by great wealth. They can help their neighbors and try to buy a reasonable measure of stability, but they cannot remake or keep the entire region afloat, tame all its passions, deal with all its grievances. They can influence other Arab states but cannot dictate their policies because they have difficulty "converting" the medium of power they have—money—into other assets. This was most poignantly demonstrated by President Sadat's margin for maneuverability in his dealings with Saudi Arabia. "Petro-power" has more sway in Arab life than it did a decade or two ago, but it is a vulnerable kind of power; with the logic of numbers and demography so heavily stacked against it, it needs allies, protection and a great deal of subtlety and caution.

For quite some time—if only because of pan-Arabism's noise and refusal to play by the rules of the game of states—a view prevailed in the West and among some of the Arabs that, if pan-Arabism were to subside, all would be well. States would be left to undertake what states undertake within their boundaries; the conflict with Israel would be resolved, or at least transformed and made more like other conficts, less lethal, less resistant to resolution. There is a great deal of merit to that view, but the politics of states can also kill, can dislocate, destabilize and erupt into turmoil and violence. With economic development approximating a new *raison d'état*, states can lose their legitimacy because they fail to deliver the goods—not intangibles such as identity, but tangibles such as jobs, education and food.

In a world of states we cannot be sanguine about saying that a state system has been normalized. The state next door may move in, not in the name of something lofty and metaphysical like pan-Arabism, but, again, for something more tangible—to preempt the dangers of an unstable state next door (Syria and Lebanon), or to avert the troubles of an erratic leader and to annex a wealthy neighbor at the same time (Egypt and Libya). Counter-elites and young officers may rebel, not in the name of pan-Arabism, but because they have a better cure for the ailment of the state. And in a situation of that kind, "betrayal" of obligations to other states could be a convenient justification for a political game that remains dangerous and deadly.

There are plenty of things to work out and fight over in the Arab system of states: the "responsibility" of the rich states; the "rights" of the poor states; the usual struggle for primacy and advantage among the resourceful and skilled states; the quest for self-determination on the part of the Palestinians; the restoration of civil order and legitimacy in Lebanon; the struggle of the most economically pressed, yet preeminent Arab state for economic solvency and viability. The passing of pan-Arabism means just that: the end of one set of troubles. Normalization of the Arab system, on the whole positive and overdue, brings in its train its own troubles, inflicts its own wounds, commits its own errors.

Notes

1. Bernard Lewis, *The Middle East and the West* (New York: Harper and Row, 1964), p. 94.

2. Walid Khalidi, "Thinking the Unthinkable: A Sovereign Palestinian State," *Foreign Affairs*, July 1978, pp. 695–96 (emphasis added).

3. Mohamed Hassanein Heikal, in *Al Anwar* (Beirut), April 15, 1978.

4. Mohamed Hassanein Heikal, "Egyptian Foreign Policy," *Foreign Affairs*, July 1978, p. 727.

5. Malcolm Kerr, *The Arab Cold War* (New York: Oxford University Press, 1971), p. 155.

6. Tawfic Farah, "Group Affiliations of University Students in the Arab Middle East (Kuwait)," Reports and Research Studies, Department of Political Science, Kuwait University, 1977. I am deeply grateful to Professor Farah for sharing with me his findings and for a helpful discussion of the issues discussed here.

7. Albert Hourani, *Arabic Thought in the Liberal Age* (New York: Oxford University Press, 1962), p. 292.

8. T. E. Lawrence, *Seven Pillars of Wisdom* (Harmondsworth [England] and Baltimore: Penguin, 1962), p. 41.

9. Anwar el-Sadat, *In Search of Identity* (New York: Harper and Row, 1977).

10. Malcolm Kerr, "The Dilemmas of the Rich," Near Eastern Studies Center, University of California at Los Angeles, 1977.

11. Lewis Awad, *The Seven Masks of Nasserism* (Beirut: Dar al Qadaya, 1977) (in Arabic).

12. John C. Campbell, "Oil Power in the Middle East," *Foreign Affairs*, October 1977, pp. 89–110.

13. Fouad Ajami, "Stress in the Arab Triangle," *Foreign Policy*, Winter 1977–78, pp. 90–108.

6

The Arab Road

Fouad Ajami

With the Israeli evacuation of the last portion of Sinai on April 25, 1982, once again a major turning point in the Arab-Israeli conflict has arrived. In historical terms, the withdrawal will signal the beginning of the fourth phase of that conflict.

The first one was the initial struggle for Palestine. It opened with the Balfour Declaration of 1917 and closed with the establishment of Israel in 1948. The second phase was that of the 1948–1967 status quo. It closed with the Six Day War of 1967. The third phase has now just ended. It saw the eruption of two wars—the war of attrition along the Suez Canal and the October war of 1973. It closes with the Israeli evacuation from Sinai and the normalization of relations between Egypt and Israel.

The fourth phase will, in large measure, witness a return to the first one: Once again it will focus on the quest for statehood in part of the land of Palestine. In this phase the principal issue will be the future of West Bank and Gaza Strip. Much as the Arab states talked about Palestine and the rights of the Palestinians in the preceding two phases, the question of Palestine was not the dominant one. It lay dormant between 1948 and 1967, when wider pan-Arab issues took precedence. Between 1967 and 1982 the main effort revolved around the determination of the Arab political order to retrieve what was lost to Israel in the Six Day War. Its driving force was Egypt's sustained effort to challenge the intolerable outcome of 1967.

The fourth phase of the conflict opens in a world radically different from the one in which the first struggle was fought. But some of the

Reprinted with permission from *Foreign Policy* 47 (Summer 1982). Copyright 1982 by the Carnegie Endowment for International Peace.

features of the first phase still survive. Outside actors are still involved. Their patronage and aid are solicited to help alter the balance of power on the ground. International resolutions still put forth moral claims. Hard as the Israelis insist on the prerogatives of conventional military power, for they are no doubt supreme there, the strategies employed in the first phase of the conflict still remain. This time the Palestinians try to use them to break the hold of their powerful enemy on contested territory. These are features of what the Syrian scholar Sadik al-Azm called Palestinian Zionism—a mixture of guerrilla warfare and diplomacy, an attempt to enlist the resources and help of others in a nationalist quest; the claim that the consummation of that kind of ideal would bring a measure of order and stability into the region, that the interests of mighty powers from afar—Britain yesterday, America today—would be better served if that kind of nationalist quest is honored and upheld.

No fate decrees that the Arabs and Israelis will back into the past and play out old themes. They might do so. In the Middle East as elsewhere the past is a powerful contender for what men do with their lives and their future. The temptation to go back into the past is considerable. On the Arab side, as painful as this conflict has been, it has been manipulated by officers and kings, by old-style politicians and new revolutionaries, by confrontation states and ones more removed from the direct burden of the fight. In Israel there is the fear of a society that feels threatened by an international economy of oil and investments that makes the country less significant today than it was yesterday; there is a lack of fit between its military pre-eminence, which remains overwhelming and decisive, and its political and economic position in the world. The temptation in Israel to lash out at this kind of development—at the perceived fickleness of friends who have allowed the logic of economics to take precedence over loftier considerations—should in no way be underestimated.

But for the Arab state system, putting old wine in new bottles will not be sufficient to deal with the problem. For what Israeli Prime Minister Menachem Begin has in mind for the West Bank and Gaza Strip is political and economic absorption into Israel. On the West Bank in particular the evidence cannot lie: the extension of Israeli settlements into urban areas, the requisitioning of land, the pre-emption of water resources, the flight into "anthropology" so common in situations of occupation where the occupier escapes from the urgency and legitimacy of the nationalist claim by talking about village councils and notables, about the unrepresentative nature of those who press the nationalist issue. Thus the old cliché that time is on the Arab side is no longer persuasive. Soon the facts erected on the West Bank will make any transfer of authority an impossible nightmare. The settlements that began as so-called archaeological expeditions are now armed fortresses, a law unto themselves.

In the fourth phase the Arab state system will be confronted with a decision it has so far refused to face up to: It will have to concede openly the 1948-1967 status quo to challenge the post-1967 status quo. For the Arabs now face an Israeli determination to stay in place after the last withdrawal from Sinai. Thus the Arabs will need to put together a viable interstate order: that upholds the Palestinian claim to the West Bank and Gaza and removes the shackles imposed on the Palestinians by inter-Arab politics; that sustains a sufficiently legitimate consensus to withstand the predictable assault from those in the Arab world still unable to accept a historic compromise between the Israelis and the Palestinians; and that accommodates itself to the return of Egypt into the Arab mainstream without excessive expectations about what Egypt would and would not do, could and could not do, within the context of a repaired Arab consensus.

"I Shot the Pharaoh"

Three decades ago the Arab scholar Albert Hourani wrote something about the Arab encounter with Israel before the 1948 climax that aptly summed up the legacy of those years and that of the years to come. In the years before 1948, he observed, "The Arab governments made no preparation, either for peace with its concessions or war with its sacrifices."[1]

Each path had its attendant dangers. To offer concessions was to risk the charges of treason and defection, to be seen as acquiescing in the dismemberment of one's world and civilization. The threat of opportunists passing themselves off as purists always lurked; the best was always the enemy of the good. Yet war was its own hell. Its burden could not be distributed fairly among a multitude of Arab players. Even in a world where Arabism made its claims, the question of Palestine did not figure with equal intensity in the universe of all Arabs. Many resented that men were somehow being dragged into a fight on behalf of others. And it has been hard for the men who govern to speak candidly about Israel's military advantage. To concede it was to concede in front of one's own people the backwardness of one's own civilization, its vulnerability to the might and organization of others.

It was with this legacy that Egyptian President Anwar el-Sadat fought—with courage at times and incoherence at others. And it is with this legacy that the dominant order in the Arab world will have to break: with more coherence than Sadat, if only because those who do it next will not be the solo performer that Sadat was, and because theirs will be an easier task, for Sadat did not labor in vain.

Sadat's Arab rivals err when they interpret his death as some kind of Egyptian verdict on the diplomacy he undertook. Sadat was not killed because he had gone to Jerusalem or because he sought peace with Israel. He was killed because he hemmed in his own country with the massive wave of arrests a month before his death; because he had manipulated forces—Moslem fundamentalism—whose fury he under-estimated; because the man who had once appealed to his country's desire for safety and to its instinctive dread of great crusades had lived to become too controversial and erratic; because in his appeal to people and lands beyond Egypt, the self-styled *fellah* who prided himself on his roots in the land came to lose touch with his own world.

To be sure the separate peace with Israel contributed to Sadat's fate and end. His enemies in the Arab world could not topple him. But their vehement denunciations of him led him to seek greater acceptance at home through greater obedience. The Camp David process contributed to the growing doubts in some circles in Egypt about the country's Islamic vocation. The old dream of turning Egypt into a piece of Europe that had once tantalized some Egyptians came to be revived in Sadat's Egypt. Re-emerging as the dream did embodied in Sadat and some of his entourage, it fed its nemesis: Moslem fundamentalism, the militant yearning for authenticity, a frightened kind of nativism that sees its mission to call the country back to its roots and identity.

Sadat subjected his country to mighty and ultimately dangerous crosscurrents. The opening to the West dragged what had been under President Gamal Abdel Nasser a relatively austere culture pitted in a taxing military struggle into a dizzying new world of glamour and possibilities. But the political system remained largely authoritarian, its symbols deliberately evocative of the past, of paternal authority, of shame, of the simplicity of the village. This combination is tough and became ruinous. It is doubtful whether many societies have the dexterity to perform an act of this kind. It is clear that Sadat's Egypt did not.

"I shot the Pharaoh," said one of Sadat's young assassins during the trial. Yet even as the words were being uttered another pharaoh was in place. He would, judging by his record so far, do things with greater caution. But he would stay on Sadat's course, for no other way out existed for Egypt. Thus Egypt would proceed to retrieve what Sadat had worked for and then go beyond him.

No one in Egypt or elsewhere in the Arab world could ask Sadat's successor to decline what Sadat had sought and more or less secured for his country before his death. He was able to swallow his pride and deal with Israel and with Begin. Because the alternatives seemed riskier and bleaker still, he took his country on what seemed to other Arabs a reckless and defiling path. In a very deep way Sadat may have expressed the desire of his country to get out of that blind alley into which the Arab-Israeli fight leads those who engage in it—forever doomed to repeat old arguments, to be haunted by the same ghosts, to fall prey to the same shadows.

Sadat's obsession became an almost neurotic desire to drag his Arab rivals into the spotlight, to make them face what they knew about the issues of war and peace with Israel but would not admit in public. Their evasions fed his own impatience. A year or so after his journey to Jerusalem, he had reached the point of no return with the more moderate Arab players. In many ways, some of his own—and Egypt's—deeds caught up with him. Because Sadat abandoned Jordan in favor of the Palestine Liberation Organization (PLO) at the 1974 Rabat summit meeting—which designated the PLO as the "sole, legitimate representative" of the Palestinians—as a way of covering his flank and preparing for the next round of negotiations with Secretary of State Henry Kissinger and Israel, his call in 1978 upon Jordan's monarch to shoulder his burden and participate in Camp David was doomed. The Jordanians had marched to Egypt's drums before, and they had paid for it—massively in the Six Day War and on a lesser scale during the Rabat summit.

Then too Begin's deeds in the aftermath of the Egyptian-Israeli peace left Sadat vulnerable in the eyes of those in Egypt and elsewhere in the Arab world who were ready to judge Sadat's diplomacy by its performance. The Begin policies on the West Bank, the raid on the Iraqi nuclear reactor a mere few days after a meeting between Begin and Sadat, and the massive raid on the heart of Beirut left Sadat in an untenable position. Sadat had argued that his peace with Israel would tie Israel's hands. But precisely the opposite had happened, or so it seemed. Sadat had claimed for his peace much more than it was capable of delivering. The fact that no one else in the Arab world had that kind of power either in no way worked in his favor. It only increased Arab opposition to Sadat in direct proportion to the mounting frustration. Gradually, Sadat's pursuit culminated in what may not have been what he intended when he went to Jerusalem: a separate peace between Egypt and Israel.

Right from the start President Hosni Mubarak seemed to heed some of the lessons of his predecessor's fate: No man can lead other Arabs by belittling them; he cannot indulge in fantasies about Egypt's identity with the West at a time when the crowded Egyptian society has sought to solve its Malthusian crisis by exporting its people to the rest of the Arab world; he needs a measure of non-alignment in international affairs and some distance from his superpower patron.

But by the same token the Egyptian state has no apologies to offer those in the Arab world who wish Egypt to repent and change its ways. Vulnerable as Sadat's course was to all kinds of charges, it was all along helped by the absence of a rival Arab project. Sadat's Arab opponents could rail against him and belittle his achievements, but many of them had long lived on slogans, had long failed to read the world as it is. His repeated violations baffled his Arab rivals. At each point they lamely insisted that Egypt would draw a line for him, that he was destined to falter in the face of massive economic troubles at home, of Israel's behavior in the region, and of continued Arab opposition. In one Arab view of things, the Egyptian path could be dismissed as the idiosyncrasy of the man at the helm of the Egyptian state. But the course was more than Sadat's; it was sustained by Egypt's will.

The Arab Audit

Egypt and the Arab states must now begin to draw up a new contract. The dominant parties in the Arab world will have to come up with a realistic assessment of what has come to pass in Arab politics of recent years and what it is the Arabs seek in the years to come. In a curious kind of audit, there has been a draw of sorts between Egypt and the other Arab states. On one level Egypt sustained its own course: The recovery of national territory is no small matter. But the country had to use up the life of a president to do so, and the kind of peace that was reached contributed to a sense of cultural crisis. The country could survive on its own economically when it had to do so. But here too a price had to be paid. An American safety net had to be provided for Egypt's precarious act. And dependence on the United States came with all the doubts and anxieties that such reliance rekindles in a land where domination by foreigners had left such deep wounds and anxieties.

The audit on the non-Egyptian side is equally complex. Egypt's rivals could console themselves that they had held out, that they had tried their best to keep together a working Arab system without Egypt, that the old propensity to depend on Egypt had to be broken, and that they had gone a long way in that direction. But the years from Sadat's initiative until his death were less than brilliant ones for them. The gap left by Egypt was nearly impossible to fill, and this void contributed to some of the drift in recent years.

The Iranian revolution opened up a new front for the Arab world and presented the Arab states of the Persian Gulf with particularly acute problems. The gulf had not become a region apart from the Arab world, as so many of the Reagan ideologues were fond of saying when they came to power. Things as old and elusive as historical memory and as tangible and new as labor migration from the poorer Arab states to the gulf states continued to knit the two regions together. But the Arabs of the Persian Gulf had their own agenda. They were closer to the fire of the Iranian revolution. The politics of wrath and virtue represented by the Ayatollah Ruhollah Khomeini was more frightening to them. When Saddam Hussein of Iraq took it upon himself to vanquish the Iranian revolution, he presented the Arab system with yet another issue on which its differences had to play themselves out.

As Khomeini draped his appeal in Islam's colors, Saddam Hussein tried to re-Persianize Iran and to draw old lines between Persians and Arabs. The battle, he insisted, was for the Arab identity of the gulf. The choice of the battle's name, Qaddisiya, evoked the old battle of A.D. 637 when Arab armies defeated the Persian Sassanid Empire. But many in the Arab world had become too sophisticated for that kind of logic. The old battle of the superpowers, too, presented non-Egyptian Arabs with many choices. The Soviet invasion of Afghanistan and the reassertion of containment and its extension to the Middle East recalled the difficult days of the Cold War. Once again there were pressures on the local actors to declare themselves. It was easy for Sadat to make his choice in regard to the duel of the superpowers. But it was harder for others.

There was, then, no easy way of papering over serious differences among non-Egyptian Arabs. The Arab state system was no longer the single-issue system that the Arab-Israeli conflict had presumed it to be. This fact would give Egytpt reprieve under Sadat. It will continue to operate in Egypt's favor in the near future.

The Palestinians' Natural Partner

Mubarak's Egypt now faces an important historical imperative at which both Nasser and Sadat failed in their very different ways—that of finding a realistic and tolerable place for Egypt in the Arab order without the extremes of hegemony (Nasser's trap) and sullen revolt and contempt for others (Sadat's final station). It is an imperative for Egypt; it is so for other Arabs as well. No other issue, not even the Palestinian question perhaps, has loomed as large in recent Arab politics as that of Egypt's place. Under Nasser, Egypt's classic advantages—its demographic weight, its steady statehood, its cultural pre-eminence—were turned into the main force in Arab political life and consciousness.

Egypt's classic advantages remain. The other Arabs know it: They know it even when they deny it. But they also know something of which Hourani spoke sometime ago and that has become more poignant today: "They are not unconscious of the inner weaknesses of the country: the extremes of poverty and wealth, the constant growth of population, and the inner isolation and uncertainty of the Westernized Egyptian intellectuals." Since 1967 the scales have tipped against Egypt. The country is battered, its infrastructure a nightmare, its people uncertain about what kind of socioeconomic and political order can answer the staggering problems of so unwieldy a country.

The arrogance with which Egypt thought of itself relative to other Arabs both during the liberal period prior to Nasser and then under the Free Officers regime of Nasser and Sadat no longer corresponds to the Arab world as it is. Rather like America's relationship to its West European allies, the realities and impressions of the past are at odds with the current distribution of power. It hurts to see one's advantages slipping away. But it hurts more to act as though they were not.

Part of Egypt's arsenal has included the idea that Egypt remained the one state that could redeem Arab rights in Palestine. Just exactly what was meant by that was never clear. But the promises made and the maximalist assertions would in time undo those who made them. Egypt did not have that kind of power. The manner in which Sadat turned away from the Arab world was in large measure a product of his country's incapacity to step back gracefully from yesterday's inflated expectations and assertions.

Now that considerable burden has been removed from Egypt's shoulders. The Palestinians for one had long rebelled against the trusteeship of other Arabs. In taking a measure of responsibility for their own fate, they make the Egyptian search for a new role more commensurate with the country's power and limitations all that much easier to bring about. Other weapons and claimants have entered into the Palestinian arena: Palestinian nationalism, the wealth of the oil states, the claims of more militant believers in Damascus and Baghdad that the Arab nationalist mantle and, hence, the fight for Palestine belong to them. The Egyptian claim has become more modest. As it was expressed by Egypt's Minister of State for Foreign Affairs Boutros Boutros-Ghali, the Egyptian mission is to get the Arabs and Israelis to accept the existence of each other.

The retreat from yesterday's burden took time: The legacy was too deep to be liquidated with a single stroke. Sadat was in many ways a transitional figure. He could begin to step away from the legacy, but precisely because it haunted him and because he was so much a part of the past, he could not do it without shrillness and incoherence. It now falls to others to inherit a less traumatic and burdensome legacy. Primacy is assigned to the Palestinians themselves, as Sadat himself had agreed at Rabat in 1974. He was a shrewd man. In pressing for an end to the Arab tutelage over the Palestinians, he was freeing Egypt.

The talk about liberating Palestine would no longer be available for Egypt to manipulate, but Egypt would still be left with a considerable role to play. The Egyptians are the natural partners of the Palestinians, and it is the Palestinians who in the phase to come may actually do their best to bring about an Egyptian re-entry into Arab politics that is as non-traumatic as possible.

Of the principal Arab states, Egypt and Saudi Arabia have no claims on Palestine. Both are status quo powers. Both are geographically distant enough from Palestine, secure enough in their own ways, to wish the Palestinians well and to see in Palestinian statehood and self-determination an honorable and decent way out for all parties concerned. Jordan, Syria, and Iraq are different.

Jordan governed the West Bank from 1948 until the Six Day War. Jordanians and Palestinians have shared a political community of bloodshed and intrigue as well as geographic proximity. Two Jordanian monarchs have governed Palestinians: They did it with a mixture of paternalism, repression, and genuine benevolence and care. Ruler and ruled came to know each other, sometimes very well, sometimes too well. They lived through the struggle for Palestine that issued in the creation of Israel. For them, more than for other Arabs, the event was directly experienced. Then they lived through the Six Day War, which marked their lives with a common sense of defeat and tragedy. In 1970—during Black September—they faced each other in a bloody chapter yet to be forgotten by either.

But they have shared even more; for life, even political life, is rarely that simple. In a history of uncertainty and turbulence, the Jordanian monarchy has provided the Palestinians with a desperately needed sense of continuity and order. In a world where fate is always cruel and capricious, King Hussein has been there after so many mighty storms have come and blown over. Many traditional and privileged Palestinians felt, and still feel, more comfortable with his kind of order than with the radicalism of Palestinian intellectuals and activists in Beirut. At the Rabat summit, the Palestinians made a bid for their own separate political quest, and Hussein accepted it.

Since then he has scrupulously observed it. But suspicions linger: Would he not want the return of the West Bank to his realm? Would he not at the right moment strike a deal with Israel and make possible a Jordanian solution—placing the West Bank and Gaza under Jordanian rule? For obvious reasons these questions worry the PLO. For in inter-Arab politics there exist two claims to the West Bank: the Palestinians' and Jordan's.

In pursuit of these claims, the support of Egypt and Saudi Arabia is pivotal. The Egyptians have been, if only because of their distance and because of their broader horizons, most willing to sponsor independent Palestinian politics against other Fertile Crescent claimants. In the pre-

1948 years they supported Haj Amin el-Husseini against Ibn Hussein Abdullah of Jordan. Nasser's Egypt followed the same path: Egyptian will and Egyptian support created the PLO at an Arab summit in 1964 and continued to support its chairman, the demogogue Ahmad Shukairy, against King Hussein. Even Sadat, only days before his death, would still speak of trying to shelter the PLO against the might of its would-be rivals in the Fertile Crescent.

If Egyptian support is pivotal to the Palestinians in the long run to check the claims of Jordan, the PLO needs Egyptian participation in a somewhat altered Arab balance of power in the short run to ease the hold of Syria on the Palestinians. Since 1976, when the Syrians came into Lebanon in full force, the PLO has lost a good deal of its room for maneuver. The more isolated Syria grew from Egypt on the one side and from the Saudi-Jordanian-Iraqi working alliance of the last two or three years on the other, the more Syria sought to control Lebanon and the Palestinians.

Then there remains the essential imperative for the PLO to talk with Israelis, to explore the possibilities of a compromise between Israel and Palestine. In a task of this kind, the Syrians (and the Iraqis) have been more royalist than the king. But the Palestinians cannot afford this kind of purist politics. And to break from the Syrian grip, they need the backing of other Arabs who understand that the Palestinians must retain some margin for maneuver if their cause is to survive.

So far the Palestinian movement toward an explicit acceptance of the re-partition of the land of Palestine and toward a two-state solution has been done in a "guarded, almost cryptic way."[2] But the pressure will continue to mount within the Palestinian community on the West Bank and among the Palestinians scattered throughout the world for a more explicit position in favor of a two-state solution. And the pressure will be all the more intense because the PLO's political base in Lebanon has become more slippery and more dangerous than ever. The Palestinian-Shi'ite alliance forged in the early 1970s on the fringes of Beirut has collapsed there and in southern Lebanon; moreover, the Lebanese Phalanages, now pre-eminent among Lebanese Christians, await the opportunity to drive out the foreigners—that is, the Palestinians—and re-create their fantasy of the pure country they imagine Lebanon to have once been. The break with ambiguity on the part of the PLO and the Palestine National Council will require self-restraint in the Arab world and political backing for a new Palestinian policy based on territorial compromise with Israel. The Egyptians have talked with Israelis in full daylight, creating a community of interest between Egyptians and Palestinians.

There is yet a more obvious factor in Arab politics that will weigh in on Egypt's side: Saudi power. The rupture with Egypt was not to Saudi Arabia's liking. The bridges burned were, for the most part, burned by Sadat: He was too flamboyant and erratic for Saudi taste; he wanted others to take risks they could not take.

To a certain extent the role of balancer of the Arab system, traditionally played by Egypt, came to be played by Saudi Arabia. But Saudi Arabia's course has been more cautious and defensive. The Saudis do not wish to dominate the other actors but to defend a viable and conservative order in the Arab world. In this kind of undertaking the Saudis now have a good deal in common with the Egyptians. If there are any prospects for a measure of stability and order in inter-Arab politics in the years to come, the Egyptians and the Saudis will have to build and sustain it. It will have going for it Egypt's weight and Saudi wealth. Its task will be the old one played by status quo powers in the aftermath of upheaval and drift: to provide an antidote to wild schemes and to demonstrate that a dominant political order has answers to pressing ailments, that its caution, its tangible assets, and its understanding of the world are safer bets than the call of uotpian schemes.

To go this far in conjecture about the material with which a post-April 1982 Arab consensus could be put together is to confront the seemingly insoluble question of inter-Arab politics—namely, the place of Syria in such a scheme. Syria has frustrated those who have sought to understand it. At times many have asked why Syria should even matter, since it does not have the standard ingredients of which countries that matter are made. But the country does matter. Syria's main asset, in contrast to Egyptian pre-eminence and Saudi wealth, is its capacity for mischief. Its location in relation to Israel, its Soviet connection, its army, and its presence in Lebanon and therefore its hold on the PLO give Syria a measure of power.

But there is deep trouble at home. Control of Damascus may give a Syrian regime a sense of place in Arab politics and history. But since the mid-1970s the base of the Syrian regime has become increasingly narrow and the regime thus more repressive. Some of its key cities are in a state of near civil war. Much of the regime's talent has gone into staying in power. In the long run that kind of regime may be doomed. Pacifying cities with heavy artillery cannot be indefinitely relied upon. Sooner or later the trigger is pulled one too many times.

In its regional behavior the regime now in power has hitherto shown more caution than its utterances would suggest. In the words of one American scholar on Syria, Yahya Sadowski, it has been "balancing relations with the USSR by an 'opening' to the West, supporting the Palestinians while not provoking an Israeli assault, and proceeding with the 'socialist transformation' at home while steadily strengthening ties to the monarchies of the Arab Gulf." This kind of course led Shlomo Avineri to write: "Syria is at the moment a status quo power, despite its belligerent and radical public image."[3] The balancing act so skillfully performed by the Syrians is by its very nature precarious. Lebanon is a quagmire with no end in sight. The confrontation with Israel can at any time turn deadly and serious, and the Syrians can then stumble into a situation of no return where no third alternative exists to a grim fight on one side or an intolerable level of psychological and political humiliation on the other.

But if the general Syrian course does not change and if indeed Syria is and remains basically a status quo power, its attempt to play the moderate Arab center against the rejectionists can be tipped in favor of the former. For such a development to occur, substantial Saudi aid is essential. Aid and a measure of legitimacy can make the course of this or a future Syrian regime easier to navigate. Aid will allow the regime to pacify some of its opponents. A greater measure of legitimacy might serve to make the Syrian regime less brittle at home, less exacting in its dealings with the PLO.

The custodians of the Arab system know, even if they do not admit it in public, that the Syrian regime holds the Palestinian cause hostage. Syrian President Hafez al-Assad secured that power when he moved into Lebanon. Should compromise between Israelis and Palestinians loom anywhere on the horizon, the Syrians, worried about their own bid for the restoration of sovereignty on the Golan Heights, would have some powerful cards to play. There is a basic asymmetry between the Palestinian claim for the West Bank and Gaza and the Syrian claim to the Golan. The power of the first is felt with greater cultural and emotional intensity in the Arab system. The power of the second is more tangible: It is backed by a formidable military force strong enough to disrupt any peace process. That is why Arab aid to Syria is of paramount importance; and that is why movement on the West Bank and Gaza in inter-Arab politics must proceed with parallel fidelity to the Syrian claim on Golan.

The principles yet to be worked out between Israel and Syria are the ones that came to pass between Egypt and Israel: exchange of territory for peace and recognition, restoration of sovereignty with limits on deployment of troops and weapons, and emplacement of international peace-keeping forces. This prospect is enough to give the most hopeful person reason for despair. For its requires almost utopian restraint on the part of both parties. The room for maneuver here would be provided by the international consensus on the illegality of Israel's claim to the Golan; by a sufficient volume of Arab aid to Syria; by movement in the Arab system to resist Syrian unilateralism in Lebanon; and by the fact that the Syrian presence in Lebanon, although formidable, is not without some cracks.

In the period before any serious developments on the Golan Heights become possible, Syria might insist on pre-eminence on the ground in Lebanon. But the PLO must acquire some freedom in the phase to come if it is not to be suffocated by the Syrians. It must be given the latitude in the Arab world to brace itself for what it must inevitably come to do in the next phase: concede what happened in 1948 to press its claim for the West Bank and Gaza. To take this step it needs wider Arab sanction and, as stated at the beginning, a break in the Arab world with the legacy of how the encounter with Israel has been handled and used.

A New Ideological Climate

When the Arab states last met at the Fez summit in November 1981 to endorse the Saudi peace plan, the old legacy prevailed. The leaked Fez proceedings·make for interesting, if depressingly familiar, reading. The delegate from the Democratic Republic of Yemen warned that the plan's adoption would cause a split between the Palestinian people and the PLO. Iraq, now stalemated in its war with Iran, came to attack Syria and to talk about the security of the Persian Gulf. Syria had some words to say about the treason of the Egyptian regime and the old argument that the time was not yet ripe for a resolution of the kind proposed by Saudi Arabia. The Saudi argument that this is the most that the Arabs could hope for, that they had to speak the language of the age and seek a solution within the framework of international legitimacy, did not carry. The best was again the enemy of the good.

The argument made by some observers that the Fez summit faltered because Washington failed to extend prior endorsement of the Saudi plan is an argument masquerading as sympathy for the Arab states but really resting on a thinly veiled notion that the Arabs are not yet serious and autonomous people in their own right. Indeed, to make that kind of argument is to misunderstand the manner in which those who sponsored the resolution and those among the Arabs who supported it wanted to proceed. It underestimates the very deep feeling in large stretches of the Arab world that much in Arab political life has been abdicated to the will of distant powers. The plan had to prevail first in Arab councils. For in the kind of climate that prevails today in the Arab-Moslem world, the clumsy embrace of powers from afar can kill and can delegitimate.

But the outcome of Fez notwithstanding, the Arab state system must try again to put forth an answer of its own to the dilemma of the Palestinians. The Saudi proposal is an affirmation of a two-state solution—an Israeli one and a Palestinian one. The Arab state system should say so in the next phase, and with sufficient clarity. If and when the Egyptians return to claim their place an inter-Arab politics, those among the Arabs who want to see the adjustment of the Arab world to the realities of power and order in the world will be joined by an effective ally. That kind of adjustment might then stand a chance.

It will be said that such an adjustment will not suffice to deal with Israel's military might. Strictly speaking, this claim is true. But it is equally true that the prevailing Arab policy had no answer of its own to the frightening level of Arab weakness displayed in 1981 when Israel raided the Iraqi nuclear reactor and Beirut, and annexed the Golan Heights. This kind of weakness has to be repaired in the classic manner in which states bridge such military gaps and build an effective deterrent. But into the next phase, at least, the Arabs should move with an affirmation and an explicit readiness to work out the terms of the compromise between the Israelis and the Palestinians. The Arabs would no longer deny the statehood of another people. The burden of denial would be shifted, more starkly than ever before, to the other side. This shift may not amount to much on the scales of raw military power. But combined with the rights of 1 million Palestinians to whom the West Bank and Gaza are home (as compared with the messianic claims of 20,000 settlers) it is, at least, a beginning.

On yet another level it could be said that the Arabs should be spared the follies of such an initiative because this kind of step is no longer good enough for Israel, because it has been overtaken by events, because the Israel led by Begin and Defense Minister Ariel Sharon no longer seeks or needs Arab recognition. This suggestion merits three comments. First, if Arab recognition of Israel is no longer the prize and goal it used to be, all should understand that this signifies a fundamental change for the worse in terms of this conflict. Second, even if this step were for now overtaken by events, the case for an Arab recognition of Israel within the pre-1967 borders would remain compelling. Above all it would rest on the need on the part of the Arab states to conduct this conflict within the assumptions, the restraints, and the language of the state system: They no longer have the luxury of quibbling about the statehood of the region's dominant military power. This step has to be taken if Egyptian-Arab relations are to have a chance; for the gap between an Arab world still mired in the vocabulary and negations of the past and an Egypt with full diplomatic relations with Israel is susceptible to all kinds of trouble. Third, there is the question of the other Israel, the one that remains opposed to Begin's view of things and that may still see in Arab recognition a promise of a new beginning.

If the dominant political order in the Arab world gropes its way to this kind of conclusion, it will be helped by something in the air, something ephemeral yet tangible: The balance between the sensibility of the dominant order and fundamentalist rebellion under Islam now favors the former. The fundamentalist surge that found an expression in Iran's upheaval and in which Arabs participated in a vicarious way has stalled. Altogether, there is perhaps a new ideological climate in which the world of caution and order can be given a chance.

From the beginning of the Iranian revolution it was not Iran's materiel force that worried its Arab neighbors. They could balance and deal with such a threat. To borrow the terms of Edmund Burke's classic discourse on the French Revolution, there was Iran as "faction" and "sect," and there was Iran as a "state," and the sect was more terrifying. Its center was in Iran and its circumference was all over the Moslem world. "The faction is not local or territorial but it is a general evil . . . where it least appears in action, it is still full of life. In its sleep it recruits its strength and prepares it exertion. The social order which refrains it feeds it. It exists in every country . . . and among all orders of men in every country." Throughout 1979 and 1980 Iran was a land in which nothing seemed to matter: not commerce, not industry, not conventions and laws, "a land where nothing rules but the mind of desperate men."[4]

Two years or so after it had come to power, the Iranian revolution has stalled, not because Saddam Hussein has taken it on in battle, but because it has failed at home, because it has overreached itself and because many in the Moslem world who had hoped against hope that the mullahs would let others live and participate in power have come to know better. The sect has been defeated; it remains to deal with the revived Iranian state.

By the time Iranian President Abolhassan Bani-Sadr had fled to Paris and the revolution had begun to devour its secular children, the romance of the Iranian revolution that had played havoc with the Middle Eastern system had effectively diminished. Not even the likelihood of victory on the battlefield against Iraq can bring back to life the threat of Iran as a model. The initial power of the revolution lay in the power of its example. The lure of virtue and messianism looked appealing not because of some demented quality within the civilization but because the secular alternatives presented by the powers had failed. When the revolution played itself out in the way it did at home, it left many with a sense of defeat and disappointment. But conceivably it left the door open for the dominant political order to pick up the pieces and start again.

There exists no assurance about how civilizations will behave, how long a period of grace a political order has before it is pressed by frustration from below. But there is a basis for arguing that the bets on the Iranian revolution and, hence, on the call of fundamentalism, are in and that the skeptics have prevailed. For all the imagery from afar of an Arab and Moslem world forever in the throes of crisis and radical change, this remains an innately conservative culture, with the caution and pragmatism of the vulnerable merchant culture it happens to be. Saints, revolutionaries, zealots, and Mahdis have made their frequent appearances on its landscape. But home, property, and order have prevailed, all the more so in the aftermath of turbulent storms.

Ambiguous Arbiter

Were the dominant order in the Arab world to hold and to find the will to define the terms of its encounter with Israel along the lines of a two-state solution, it could put the American arbiter face to face with its own confusions and would make it confront dilemmas it has so far avoided.

Since 1967, and more so since the American decade in the Middle East ushered in by the October war, it cannot be said that the United States gave the best of itself in its understanding of, let alone its conduct toward, the Middle East. Did it wish to support comprehensive settlement, or did it prefer piecemeal solutions? Did it believe that the settlements on the West Bank were an "obstacle to peace" as President Carter maintained or that they were "not illegal" as President Reagan and his people asserted when they came to power? Did it believe that the acquisition of territory by force was inadmissible or that such action involved "juridical matters," in the words of Secretary of State Alexander Haig, Jr., which were "subjective matters" that "could be argued to eternity"? Did it really believe that by talking about the Soviet threat it could frighten others into forgetting their own priorities and rivalries and enlisting in a crusade against Soviet power? Did it have any deeper wisdom about the ultimate shape of some kind of Middle East settlement—above and beyond having Haig assure Israel and Secretary of Defense Caspar Weinberger assure the Arabs of America's support and affection?

It has been nearly a decade since *Pax Americana* projected itself into the Middle East—so full of hubris, yet so ill prepared. The structure that emerged bore the flaws and weaknesses of its inception: It was put together at a time of general U.S. decline elsewhere in the world, asserted by an embattled American president fighting for his political life. The Middle East was to be, so it was hoped, what Southeast Asia turned out after so much blood and treasure not to be: a place where U.S. power makes a difference, where the ends of policy and its means are kept in proportion, where vital interests are easily visible, hence relatively easily defensible before public opinion.

The invitation of the local actors made things all that much easier. American support and America's presence were sought by Israelis and by a formidable wing of the Arabs—by the rich to keep things from falling apart, by the economically pressed to sustain them while they go about doing other things. The distant power would provide the technology of war and sponsor the diplomacy of peace. Each side to the Arab-Israeli conflict would see in U.S. support what it wished. The Arabs wanted the superpower patron of their enemy to make their enemy give way and relinquish territory; some wanted the United States to shelter them from the inevitable—the obligation to come to terms with Israel to recover the occupied territories. Israel wanted the means to uphold the status quo.

The superpower caught in the middle would make its claim, as the Kissinger memoirs *Years of Upheaval* continually reiterates, on its power to deliver territory in return for peace and recognition. For all its hectic activity in the region, the U.S. arbiter would remain ambiguous—"constructive ambiguity," as Kissinger would say—about its own view of the final terms of an Arab-Israeli settlement. It would seek refuge behind refusing to impose a settlement—as though to state its own policy was tantamount to having its way. But ambiguity could only work as long as the positions of the protagonists on the ground remained more or less ambiguous themselves, as long as the territory held by the militarily stronger party remained negotiable, as long as time bought was bought for good and clear purpose and used to get Arabs, Israelis, and Palestinians away from the brink.

The great investment of a decade culminated in an Egyptian-Israeli settlement—no small endeavor itself. But this, it might be said, was all along in the cards. That much is visible to anyone with cursory familiarity with Israeli political memoirs of the 1940s and 1950s. It was with Egypt that Premier David Ben Gurion and his contemporaries wanted to come to terms and for obvious geopolitical reasons. *Pax Americana's* achievement rested on that and on the fact that Sinai was and remained negotiable territory.

Now in the new phase the logic of U.S. unilateralism in the area is face to face with its own contradictions, shortcomings, and history. Ambiguity has brought the Arab-Israeli conflict to this point, and the American magician may have no more tricks up his sleeve. Candor and a courageous American decision on the future of the West Bank and Gaza will have to replace the magician's act, for few observers are taken in anymore. Even *Pax Americana's* principal achievement in the area, the Camp David agreements, bought with so much treasure and such a massive presidential commitment, has been allowed to erode. Ambiguity has allowed one party to the treaty to turn the world on the West Bank upside down and yet still maintain that it is in compliance with what it agreed to at Camp David.

Every time a great power takes itself into alien lands, it takes not only its military might and its material resources. With the baggage goes something of itself, of its own self-image, of its sense of the just, the outrageous, of things that can and cannot be. For better or for worse, America is a party to the confrontation between Israeli and Palestinian and to the next phase of the Arab-Israeli conflict. In the multitude of decisions made and deferred, of sympathies extended or denied, it will be making judgments about others and judgments about itself.

Notes

1. Albert Hourani, "The Decline of the West in the Middle East II," *International Affairs*, April 1953, p. 166.

2. Edward Said, "Ending Ambiguity: Reflections on the Palestinians," *The Nation*, December 5, 1981, p. 605.

3. Shlomo Avineri, "Beyond Camp David," *Foreign Policy* 46 (Spring 1982), p. 28.

4. Edmund Burke, *Works of the Right Honorable Edmund Burke* (London: 1803), vol. 8, p. 255.

7

Arab Nationalism:
A Response to Ajami's Thesis
on the "End of Pan-Arabism"

Hassan Nafaa

The Arab world constitutes a particular regional system. Interactions between its components, whether cooperative or conflictual, have therefore a special and peculiar set of dynamics. Many factors push the region toward highly cooperative interactions, even toward complete unity: the same language and culture, a shared historical experience, and present problems held in common. Other factors pull it in the opposite direction: unequal distribution of human and natural resources, substantial differences in political systems, ideologies and constitutions, as well as serious psychological and sociological heterogeneity.

Arab nationalists emphasize the common features among the components of the Arab system, trying to cultivate those features toward the construction of a viable common future; their opponents, for their part, advance their own characteristics and argue that divisive features predominate. Each side interprets history to underline its respective arguments. Clearly the debate between proponents and opponents of "one Arab nation from the Gulf to the Ocean" might be argued endlessly and to little avail, on the rhetorical plane; but the fact of Arab nationalism cannot be argued away. It is a major political and social phenomenon,

This paper was originally presented at the 22nd Annual Convention of the International Studies Association, Philadelphia, March 18–21, 1981.

Reprinted with permission from *Journal of Arab Affairs* 2, 2 (Spring 1983):173–199. Copyright 1983 by the Middle East Research Group, Inc.

as well as a mobilizing ideology that has shaken the whole region since the last years of the nineteenth century.

Nasser's Egypt succeeded, if not in achieving Arab unity, at least in synchronizing the interactions between its components and in helping the emergence of a specific Arab system with Egypt at its core. But the defection of Egypt from the Arab system after the conclusion of a separate peace treaty with Israel resurrects the debate on pan-Arabism. Many articles and studies have been devoted to the issue. The analyses have been very different, some even antagonistic. Walid Khalidi still believes in the vitality of pan-Arabism, seeing in it a sort of "super-legitimacy," in contrast to which the legitimacy of Arab states "shrinks into irrelevance."[1] M.H. Heikal points out that the actual crisis of the Arab system is a temporary one and that the Arab system has important assets that can well turn the tide in its favor once again.[2] Carl Leiden concludes, after an analysis of Arab nationalism today, that "Arab nationalism is not likely to disappear but its peak in the twentieth century seems to have passed; other nationalisms have taken its place while the turbulent politics of the Middle East continues."[3] F. Ajami occupies the opposite end of the continuum, with an extremely clear stance: "An idea that has dominated the political consciousness of modern Arabs is nearing its end, if it is not already a thing of the past. It is the myth of pan-Arabism."[4]

The current debate is characterized by passions and confusion, which do not help in understanding the role of pan-Arabism and its dynamics. In this debate concepts such as Arab nationalism, pan-Arabism, Nasserism, and "Arab system" tend to be used synonymously, though they are not. Even at its peak, Nasserism was not generally considered identical with Arab nationalism. In 1965 Hans Tuetch argued that "pan-Arabism constitutes the intellectual mainstream of Arab nationalism. But to confer the term 'Arab nationalism' exclusively on pan-Arabism, or in its most violent side, current Nasserism, would be grossly misleading. Arab nationalism means different things to different groups: it is by no means a simple movement. Pan-Arabism has many facets, and Arab nationalism has assumed three principal forms, which partly or entirely exclude each other."[5]

This essay attempts to clarify the role of pan-Arabism and to explain its significance within the foreign policies of Arab states. In the context of the current debate, the best approach may be to conceptualize the basic assumptions of the extremist thesis that predicts the "end of pan-Arabism" expressed by Ajami. An analysis of these assumptions could clarify the nature of pan-Arabism itself, the dynamics of its development, its present crisis and its possible future.

II

Ajami devoted three articles to this issue. The titles of his articles are expressive and revealing: ranging from "stress in the Arab triangle"[6] to the "struggle for Egypt's soul,"[7] both of which, by Ajami's logic, lead to "the end of pan-Arabism."[8] Before proceeding, we must first conceptualize the assumptions and hypotheses that led Ajami to his conclusion. Three concepts emerge. The first relates to the internal dynamics of pan-Arabism, or the mutations in socioeconomic structures of the components of the Arab system; the second relates to the external dynamics, or the mutations in the environment, a target of classic pan-Arabism; and the third relates to "conjuncture," or the mutations in the leadership of the pan-Arabic movement.

Ajami considers that the "universalism of pan-Arabism derived to a considerable extent from the universalism of the Ottoman Empire, of which the Arab states had been a part for four centuries."[9] So Arab nationalism has been a natural response to Turkish nationalism/imperialism. But the Ottoman Empire is now no more than a memory. Western colonialism established new boundaries within which specific Arab states emerged; and each one, for the past sixty years, has progressively consolidated its own legitimacy and its specific nationalism. Furthermore the "mobile structure of dynasts, officers, officials, and scholars has by now been replaced by more 'parochial' elites as the usual complex of bureaucratic interests has developed in each of the Arab states."[10] So a particular nationalism has emerged in each of the Arab states, and its constituency is the *raison d'Etat*, a concept which is by nature, in Ajami's sense, antagonistic to the concept of pan-Arabism since the constituency of pan-Arabism is the whole Arab world. In other words, the *raison d'Etat* of any state and the exigencies of pan-Arabism cannot have any sort of interaction other than conflictual.

Ajami sees the antagonism between the "reasons of state," and pan-Arabism as a continuous trend characterizing the dynamics of the Arab movement since its beginning. For him the past of Saudi Arabia presents an interesting case: "the victory of the mere 'local' ibn Saud over the 'pan-Arab' Sharif Hussein half a century ago may have been the first victory (albeit of a dynastic/tribal kind) for reasons of state over the more grandiose ambitions of pan-Arabism."[11] Egypt represents an interesting and more evident case in the present. Egypt's defection from the Arab system is viewed as a process which started, according to Ajami, after its defeat in 1967. Egypt was "tired of fighting others' fights,"[12] but Nasser was too closely allied with pan-Arabism to be able to effect a dramatic divorce with the Arab system. Nasser meant to be considered a hero till the end; Sadat was not a hero and little attached to pan-Arabism. His commitment was to "Egypt first," to keep "Egypt Egyptian." The October War gave Sadat the long-awaited occasion to free himself from the claims of other Arabs. He wanted a modern Egypt allied with the West, and to do so did not hesitate to conclude a separate peace with Israel. Ajami seems to believe that the conflict with Israel was perceived by Egypt as an Arabic (not Egyptian) one; that Nasser's pan-Arabist politics were solely his own; and that Sadat's politics, including his rapprochement with Israel and the West, represented the real Egyptian position. "What was the dividing line between Sadat's own transgressions and Egypt's will?" Ajami asks, and then answers himself, "The other Arabs could go through the motions of distinguishing between their denunciation of Sadat and their professed respect for the Egyptian people. But the distinction was difficult to make in practice, and many suspected that Sadat was not a solitary individual, that he really did represent Egypt's inner self, her willingness to set aside the sacred struggle and accept a separate peace."[13]

Ajami considers that pan-Arabism is challenged not only by the different reasons of state and the redistribution of powers among the Arab states that makes of the oil states (the natural foes of pan-Arabism) important actors in the Arab and international system, but also by the economic, sociological, and psychological antagonism which this redistribution (or disequilibrium) generates among the populations of the Arab states. Ajami emphasizes that "for a young, educated Saudi, Kuwaiti, or Libyan, the sky is the limit: huge projects to run, European vacations, investments, offers from foreign businessmen and people with all kinds of schemes, dreams and gadgets.[14] For a young, equally skilled, educated Egyptian the overwhelming reality has been to deal with unemployment or a dead-end job in a sluggish bureaucracy, and the impossible dream of making ends meet, the nightmare of finding and affording an apartment in Cairo, where rentals have gone sky-high, thanks in part to the abundance of petrodollars."[15] Ajami emphasizes the Egyptian feelings against the Arabs, which allegedly gave Sadat the needed support to justify his visit to Jerusalem and to pursue anti-Arab politics, in a cynical manner: "Beyond the confines of diplomacy and politics, two popular concerns gave Egypt's diplomatic defection and its battle with the oil states personal meaning and drama. In a country where land is scarce and valuable, concern was developing over real-estate acquisitions by rich Arabs; there was a feeling that outside Arab capital was making Egyptians strangers in their own land. There was also widespread discontent over the fact that Cairo had become the Bangkok of the Arab world, that outside Arab capital was violating Egypt's honor and integrity and its women. The land acquisitions and the issue of sexual liberties were serious and sensitive matters. The leadership did not have to dwell on these themes; they were there in the country's popular films and magazines and in Egypt's endless chatter. Arab wealth challenged Egypt's sense of self: possessed by arriviste Bedouins, it underlined the cruelty of a world gone awry."[16]

So if we want to aggregate these fragmented elements and polish away the rhetorical veneer, we can say that pan-Arabism has been defeated, according to Ajami, on both governmental and popular levels. On the governmental level, Arab regimes behave according to their separate *raisons d'Etat*, which push them in divergent directions: Egypt's pushing her to seek solutions to her own problems with the West, Saudi Arabia's pushing her to conserve her wealth through a loose pan-Islamic framework. Arab reasons of state could never converge in the framework of pan-Arabism. And on the popular level of public opinion, the development of particular and antagonistic nationalisms within the boundaries of Arab states, accompanied by the concentration of wealth in the less populated and less developed parts of the Arab world, generates grievances and bitterness among the Arab populations. Because of this, the aspirations of Arab peoples are not likely to find comfort or satisfaction in a pan-Arabist ideology.

To substantiate his allegations concerning the demise of pan-Arabism in public opinion, Ajami refers to a field study undertaken by a social scientist at Kuwait University.[17] It was designed to elicit the opinions of 500 undergraduates about pan-Arabism, among other issues. This study, according to Ajami, "has supplied us with important evidence substantiating the demise of pan-Arabism and suggesting the shape of things to come . . . [for among its findings] was a remarkable assertion of Islamic sentiment and of patriotism associated with particular Arab states."[18]

As the changes in the internal structure of the Arab states (here, the redistribution of power among them) have contributed to the demise of pan-Arabism, so too have mutations in the Arab environment acted.

Ajami's reasoning seems to point up three targets that aided in the emergence of Arab nationalism and, later, the maintenance of unity in the Arab system: the Ottoman Empire, the colonialism of the Mandate years, and Israel. All three targets of analysis have brought profound mutations, either by their progressive shaping of the Arab scene or by the change these targets wrought in Arab perceptions; whichever the case, these three targets have represented a challenge to the integrity of the Arab world.

The Ottoman Empire, under which the Arab world saw itself as a whole, is now a thing of the past. Further, the anticolonialism that once unified an entire generation which saw the Balfour Declaration and the Sikes-Picot agreement as a betrayal of the Arabs by the West, is no more a target of Arab nationalism. "Britain and France, the two powers whose deeds and diplomacy haunted and traumatized a generation of nationalists, have been cut down to size: they made their last stand in the Suez affair, and since then their diplomacy has been, on the whole, sympathetic to the Arab states. London is no longer a hostile capital . . . [and] France has become synonymous with deGaulle: an admired symbol of nationalism and from 1962 onward, a 'friend' of the Arab states."[19]

As for Israel, it doesn't represent the same target it used to be in the past. The defeat of Palestine has been perceived as a defeat of all Arabs. But now "the unity forced onto the Arab world by the Arab-Israeli conflict has eroded . . . Sadat diplomacy has dragged the Arabs into the modern game of states. The conflict is no longer about Israel's existence but about its boundaries; and in inter-Arab affairs the leading military state [Egypt] has for all appearances rejected the inter-Arab division of labor that assigned it the principal obligation for the pan-Arab cause."[20]

It is interesting to observe the symmetric and asymmetric situation engendered by the development of plurinationalism in the Arab world in light of the Arab-Israeli conflict, according to the logic of Ajami's analysis. For Ajami "the Palestinians launched the first post-1967 attack against pan-Arabism . . . [and] there was no doubt that those who rallied around Yassir Arafat and George Habash in the aftermath of the Six-Day War had given up on pan-Arabism. . . . The duel that raged between the Palestinians and the Nasserites from early 1968 until Nasser's death in 1970 was in essence a fight about the independent rights of Palestinian nationalism."[21] Ajami also considers Egypt's defection from the Arab system a nationalist move. This logic suggests that Israel became the sole target of Palestinian nationalism (not pan-Arabism), while pan-Arabism as an ideology became itself the target of all kinds of nationalism—the Israeli nationalism, of course, but also the Egyptian, the Saudi, and Palestinian nationalisms.

Ajami considers that the "idea [of pan-Arabism] had been an elite endeavor of publicists, intellectuals and a few officers. Nasser would take the theories and the emotions to the masses, give pan-Arabism its moment in the sun, and then its tragic end in 1967." Here pan-Arabism and Nasserism are intimately tied: "The power of pan-Arabism derived from the power of [Nasser's] charismatic leadership." But Ajami does not explain in his analysis why and through which mechanism an Egyptian phenomenon (i. e., Nasserism) became an Arab one and why the Arab masses identified themselves and their inspirations with those of Nasser, nor why an ideology and a political movement which existed before Nasser would end with his death (physic or moral).

However, Ajami recognizes that "the circumstances that produced the ebb of Nasserist charisma may be *sui generis*," but he excludes immediately any eventual resurrection of Nasserism: "The end of Nasserism is a piece of a bigger puzzle. It is the end of that stage of Third World history represented by men like Nasser, Nehru, Sukarno, Nkrumah . . . [who] sought answers to questions of identity and self-worth, dabbled in dreams and intangibles, but their politics were bound to come to an end, for the sort of nationalist fervor they embodied triumphs for a moment but cannot last forever."[22]

So the end of pan-Arabism according to Ajami is not an isolated phenomenon. Its death is a part of the death of the whole Third World that once tried to find an identity.[23]

III

Ajami carefully avoided defining the pan-Arabism which he believes had ended. He made of pan-Arabism a great monster and assigned himself the task of defeating it, then he discovered that the monster had an immortal function and could not be defeated; so he acknowledged the function of the monster, but at the same time tried to give the impression that the function he assigned to the monster is a new one and not those it used to exercise. "Arab states," Ajami said, "are stuck with one another, and the shared themes and concerns could conceivably provide a basis for a working regional order—or, if pushed too far, for disaster and continuous discord." And this is precisely what pan-Arabism tried to implement: to find the basis of a working Arab order (unless Ajami means by regional order a Middle-Eastern one). The form of this order is not of much importance: what is more important is that it works. A working Arab system requires a precise definition of its goal, its objectives and a description of the way it can implement them. If Ajami simply rejects the revolutionary pan-Arabism model (Nasserism) and claims to substitute for it a system of independent states, one must admit that this system of states did exist, but didn't work and never had the support of the masses.

Ajami seems to confuse the idea and its implementation, the ideology and the political movement. The idea of "one Arab nation with an immortal mission" has never been translated into a viable political project. It is still a slogan, like that of the Communist Manifesto: "Workers of the world, unite!" To say that pan-Arabism has died because it failed to achieve the one Arab nation is like saying Marxism does not exist anymore because it failed to unify the workers of the world!

Pan-Arabism is an idea (or ideology) and a political movement. The political movement tried to transform the idea into a political design or project for the society it considers its constituency. Neither the idea nor its political movement exists in a vacuum. Both are the product of the social, economic and cultural structure in which they take place, and their transformations and mutations are conditioned by changes in the societal structure and its interaction with its environment.

The history of pan-Arabism, the idea and the political movement, shows that pan-Arabism has constants and variables. The constant has always been the objective, which was and still is independence and unity; the independence of each Arab state is the condition for unity. These objectives have never been subject to doubt or even controversy. The variables, which have been subject to controversy and endless debate, concerned the content of independence, the form and the ways of achieving it, but not the substance.

The leadership of the pan-Arabist movement passed from Arab feudalists and dignitaries, to kings and royal families, to the *petite-bourgeosie* constituted around an alliance of military, bureaucrats and intellectuals. In each stage the content of pan-Arabism, in terms of the target, the ways and the forms of unity, the kind of society it works for, its implementation, et cetera, changes. It is worthwhile to note that pan-Arabism, like any nationalist movement, is a recipient of different intellectual streams: religious fundamentalism or reformism, secular thought with its two branches, liberalism and Marxism, et cetera.

IV

To prove the demise of pan-Arabism, Ajami argues that the evolution of Arab states since the colonial mandates has been characterized by the emergence of local nationalisms around bureaucratic interests. This is a fact. But Ajami forces the analysis and sees in local nationalisms and pan-Arabism antagonistic and irreconcilable concepts. This is not accurate.

First: local nationalism is the outcome of both colonialism and modernism (which, for some Arab states, coincide and, for others, are different phenomena). Western colonialism in Arab states did not start at the same time and has no single label. The difference in timing and colonial labels prevented the creation of a unifed pan-Arabism movement. It is interesting to note here that pan-Arabism started in the Eastern Arab world, and that its objective in the beginning was the establishment of an Arab state in the Mashreq (including the Peninsula, Syria, Palestine, and Iraq). Egypt and the Maghreb were outside the pan-Arab interaction. The pan-Arabist movement engendered some unity of action and coor-dination, even after the colonial mandates in Mashreq in the aftermath of World War I. It was natural that the struggle against colonialism found its constituency in the more solid, and legally easier to organize, local nationalism. However, the amount of interaction between different local nationalist movements, on the one hand, and between them and the proponents of pan-Arabism, on the other hand, intensified during the struggle against colonialism and with the increasing danger of the Zionist movement in Palestine. It is very interesting to notice the parallelism between the intensification of the struggle for independence and the *increasing* Arab interaction. The very nationalist Egypt became interested in the Palestine question and a passionate dialogue between Arab nationalist intellectuals (i.e., Sati Al-Husri) and the proponents of Pharaonic Egypt (Ahmad Lotfi El-Sayed) or Mediterranean Egypt (Taha Hussein) or Islamic Egypt (The Ulema of Al-Azhar) started in a very creative way. Egypt was still researching its real identity. An Egypt, nationalist and royalist, became the host of the Arab League Headquarters and entered into war against Israel in 1948.

Local nationalisms and pan-Arabism were pursuing the same objective: independence. It would be absurd to find any antagonism between these two nationalist movements as a whole. The crisis between Arab states in the aftermath of independence, which occurred separately and through the struggle of fragmented local nationalisms, is of the same nature as the crisis within any nationalist movement in the aftermath of independence: the social questions surface along with the ideological differences hidden by the exigencies of unity against the common enemy. The absence of democracy in the Arab states prevented a unification of unionist forces in the different Arab states (this step was easy and legally possible within the boundaries of each state), and the positions of the heads of Arab states made them the legal voices of local nationalism. But in a state where democracy is absent and institutions are dead, it would be inexact and simplistic to identify the heads of states with separate nationalisms. A gap between the political positions of the heads of states and nationalism inspiration could exist.

To underline his assertion, Ajami argues that the strife between Nasser and the Palestinians rallied around Arafat and Habbesh was a strife between pan-Arabism and Palestinian nationalism, and that Sadat's defection from the Arab system was "a march forward to the past" to "Egyptian Egypt"—in other words, another kind of strife between pan-Arabism and the local Egyptian nationalism.

The Palestinian example needs little comment. After all, the Palestinian defeat was first a defeat of Palestinian nationalism. The challenge she was facing was unique in the Arab world: Jewish settlement, progressively armed and organized in terrorist groups, coupled with the British occupation and Mandate. Palestinian history in the aftermath of 1948 was slowly, but surely, moving toward the reconstitution of its own national liberation movement, not as an anti-pan-Arab movement, that would be absurd, but as its *avant-garde*. The Israeli occupation of a portion of Palestine, then of the whole Palestine, denied even the existence of a Palestinian people. The existence of a specific Palestinian identity was vital for both the specific Palestinian cause and for pan-Arabism. The Palestinian struggle was to take a place in the pan-Arab system, not out of it. The strife with Nasser was about the democracy in the system, perhaps about the leadership, but it was a strife within the system that gave it more vitality.

Egypt's "struggle" to get out of the system is another story. It is "a piece of a bigger puzzle," to use the terminology of Ajami. The disarabization of Egypt was a part of her denasserization. It was a long process whose parts are organically linked. After all, Nasser was an Egyptian phenomenon, an output of the Egyptian socioeconomic and cultural dynamic in its interaction with the Egyptian environment. One may ask what was original in the Nasserian system. He may have done nothing original, but he certainly had something of the genius about him. Nasser's internal and international politics were syntheses of all Egyptian political and cultural trends, and had something of each. His virulent anti-Western attitude came from the Egyptian soul, from H. Abdoh, the pioneer Islamic reformist who felt the danger coming from the West, to all Egyptian nationalist traditions whose consciousness assimilated the lessons and the memory of Western challenges: the defeat of Egypt's Mohammed Ali, the economic penetration, the military occupation, the Palestinian defeat and Israeli threat. He would face the challenge; but Nasser's anti-Western attitude was as ambivalent as was the attitude of Egypt herself vis-à-vis the West. She feared domination but needed science and technology; Egypt also feared indoctrination of the atheistic East. Nasser never sent students of social science to the East. Social science students of Nasser's Egypt went always to the West, military and applied scientists to the East. Nasser was undoubtedly culturally West-oriented. As for Nasser's non-aligned international policy, it had its roots in Wafd foreign policy: the Egyptian position and vote in the U. N. during the Korean affair show that Egypt was already at the core of inter-Arab interaction. What he wanted was a real independence and development for Egypt. But he did not conceive the Egyptian national security separate from Arab national security. Nasser met the Arab masses on the road of struggle against military alliances: they identified their struggle with his own. Once again, the Egyptian nationalist and revolutionary cause coincided with pan-Arabism. Pan-Arabism itself also had an incredible popular dimension: the Arab nationalist feeling was there, it simply found the leader it was waiting for in Nasser who gave all this his personal and peculiar style.

In Egypt the agricultural reform, the Islamic reform (through the reform of University Al-Azhar), the construction of the Aswan dam, the Egyptianization of the economy, then its socialization, all gave Nasser true popular support. The Moslem Brotherhood despaired (by failing to assassinate him), the Egyptian Communist party decided to dissolve itself voluntarily, and the Wafd party is dead (morally and physically). Egypt became Nasser and Nasser became Egypt.

That was the beginning of Nasser's personal drama which led to the defeat of 1967. The millions of Egyptians who rushed in the streets all over Egypt, asking Nasser to stay as the head of the state were simply afraid of the future. In Egypt there was Nasser, still physically alive, and there was nothing else: a complete political vacuum in between. Nasser had to bear the burden and try to pull Egypt out of her tragedy. Nasser gave all his attention to the Army. Before he died he knew that Egypt needed radical changes. He saw the Egyptian students and workers shouting for them; but Israel was on the other side of the Suez Canal and the rebuilding of the Army was his vital priority. He died before effecting this reform. The real personal tragedy for Nasser may have been his failure to build a strong and militant political movement capable of leading the Egyptian people on the road traced by him. After his death Nasserist thought suddenly appeared, not as syntheses representing Egyptian soul, but as an assemblage of heterogenous and fragmented ideas easy to defeat. Each of the former political groups and parties had something to blame on Nasser. Egypt was still living the tragedy and the bitterness of the defeat, and all that had nothing to do with pan-Arabism.

In his struggle for power Sadat succeeded in gaining the support of the Army against the Nasserist left wing in the government and the Union Socialist Party. Sadat gained power, but he remained at the stake until the October War, which was a partial military victory, but it had a tremendous psychological impact. Sadat appeared to have achieved what Nasser failed to implement. Now Sadat could proceed to transform Nasser's Egypt into a true Sadat-Egypt. With an army happy over its performance in the war, a bureaucratic economic structure, and a complete political vacuum, without any organized forces, Egypt was easy to govern. She needed reform: democracy, economic effciency, and amelioration in the standard of living, without hurting the independence of the country. Sadat exploited to the fullest all Nasser's errors and reversed completely the socioeconomic structure and, consequently, the international allies of Egypt. Without entering into the details of the mechanisms of change, the process started with the economic open-door policy and finished with Sadat's visit to Jerusalem, the peace treaty and consequently the defection of Egypt from the Arab system.

Was Sadat pushed to this policy by an Egyptian nationalist movement tired of fighting others' fights and claiming the withdrawal of Egypt from the Arab system, as Ajami asserts, or was it a logical outcome of his socioeconomic policy and his rapprochement with the USA? Ajami seems to be more preoccupied with justifying Sadat's treaty with Israel than in analyzing the impact of the treaty from the Egyptian nationalist point of view, so that he can underline his assertion about the antagonism between Egyptian nationalism and pan-Arabism.

It is true that Sadat was cheered by thousands of Egyptians who went to receive him on his return to Cairo after his visit to Jerusalem. But it will be misleading to see in this event national support for what happened after signing the treaty. The visit to Jerusalem was one thing, the treaty another. After all, Sadat's speech in the Knesset expressed exactly the Arab consensus obtained in Rabat in 1974. But the treaty was a deviation from and a violation of this consensus.

From a nationalistic point of view, the establishment of an Israeli Embassy in Cairo while the Israeli military occupation continued in a portion of Sinai, and the special situation of Sinai, even after the end of its military occupation in 1972, diminishes the Egyptian sovereignty over it. Furthermore, it does not give Egyptian nationalism any source of pride. On the other hand, the military facilities conceded by Egypt to the USA seem to be a direct outcome of the treaty, or at least intimately related to it. In the context of an Egyptian-Israeli settlement the foreign military presence on Egypt's soil has no justification, from an Egyptian nationalist point of view.

It is significant that the slow move toward a democratic system and a pluralist party system was stopped immediately after the treaty. A "referendum" on May 27, 1978, effectively outlawed the newly reconstituted Wafd party. The June 7, 1979, parliamentary election was organized to prevent the reelection of the deputies who criticized the treaty. During these elections criticism of the Egyptian-Israeli treaty was outlawed by the referendum.

In such a context it is difficult to assert that Sadat policy which engineered the Egyptian defection from the Arab system was also that of Egyptian Egypt. This is proof, in a way, that what is good for Egyptian Egypt is also good for Arab-Egypt.

We do not believe it necessary to comment on some issues Ajami found important to throw in the debate such as what seemed to Ajami an Arab violation of Egypt's honor, Arab sexual liberties, and their avidity for Egyptian real estate. As for Egyptian feelings about Arabs and pan-Arabism as a reaction to such behavior, we would say that stereotypes always exist and can be exaggerated, manipulated and exploited for political purposes. But we do not believe that they could have a serious or general negative effect on the Egyptian belief in pan-Arabism and their common destiny. After all, the Egyptians are not dupes and they know the "Egyptian Open-Door Policy" means just that doors are open for those who have money—and money has no nationality! One may wonder why Arab capital was making Egyptians strangers in their own land, while American capital would not. Egypt's defection from the Arab system will not save, in this particular issue, either her honor or her real estate.

More serious is Ajami's reference to the questionnaire of Tawfic Farah. I doubt that any objective political scientist would draw the same general conclusions and extrapolation that Ajami did about the future of pan-Arabism on the basis of a sample of 500 undergraduates in the same university.

Without casting doubt on the objectivity of the study or the integrity of the researcher, it is not out of place to mention here a recent meticulous study by Saad ed-din Ibrahim, an eminent Egyptian sociologist of the American University in Cairo, based on a field study of Arab public opinion and the problematics of Arab unity.[24] Ibrahim administered a questionnaire to 5,557 Arab citizens from all social milieus in ten Arab states: Jordan, Qatar, Egypt, Palestine (in exile), Kuwait, Lebanon, Morocco, Sudan, Tunisia and North Yemen. The poll covers all aspects of pan-Arabism: images and perceptions by Arabs of each other, the belief in Arab unity, its form, timing, et cetera. It provides valuable statistics that pan-Arabism and the belief in Arab unity and in a common destiny is deeply rooted in the Arab consciousness. We cannot go through an analysis of these important data here. Let us take one example concerning Egypt, which seems to be the crucial target of Ajami, and the feeling of Egyptians about Arab unity and the preferred forms of cooperation between Arab states. Only 3 percent do not believe in any sort of cooperation and prefer that each Arab state run its own affairs the way it wants, without caring about the others; 23.4 percent prefer a coordination of policy through the Arab League; 59.6 percent for a federal state (military and foreign policy unity with complete independence for other issues); 13 percent prefer one Arab-nation state with a central government.[25]

This important study put it clearly: pan-Arabism is a popular reality and the unionist steps are always cheered by the Arab masses in different countries, in spite of the official crisis and quarrels between Arab states and despite the failure of the previous projects. It means also that pan-Arabism is not a political statement or position. On the individual level, it is a feeling for the past and an aspiration for a better future, a component of the personality, sociologically and psychologically speaking.

V

Ajami asserts that pan-Arabism is a thing of the past and should be so because the external challenges which provoked a collective solidarity and formed a common consciousness and feeling among the Arabs do not exist any more: the Ottoman Empire has vanished into the past, as have the colonial powers (who became friends); and Israel is now accepted, *de facto*, by almost all the Arab states including the PLO. The only remaining problem concerns Israel's boundaries, not its existence. Even this problem seems to Ajami an inter-Arab problem about the West Bank. "Should signs of an Israeli change of heart materialize," Ajami said, "the inter-Arab struggle for the West Bank, now somewhat subdued and repressed, would come to the fore. Hard choices would then have to be made by the Jordanian monarch, by the Palestinians themselves, by the Syrians, who claim both sides of the fight as their friends, and by the Saudis, who help to subsidize and sustain both the PLO and Jordan"![26] This is the assumption upon which Ajami asserts that "there is no longer a collective Arab crisis and there is no use pretending that it exists."[27] This kind of analysis is based on completely false assumptions which continue to obscure the real problem.

The struggle against the Ottoman Empire, then against the colonial powers, embodied the objective of local nationalisms and pan-Arabism alike: independence.

The struggle for independence was not simply a struggle for physical elimination of the military occupation. Nasser's attempt to achieve political independence led him to refuse military alliances and to choose the policy of non-alignment, which he perceived as the only way to conserve the political independence of small states. But this course lost him the enthusiastic and active support of the US in the early years. His battle for the development started with the Aswan High Dam, and continued logically and pragmatically toward first the Egyptianization of the economy, then its nationalization. He discovered on the way that political independence could not be separated from economic independence, and to be really economically independent one must first be the master of national resources and then be able to choose the best economic and social system in total liberty. Through an impeccable logic Nasser moved from being a target of the previous colonial power to being the target of the USA.

Pretending that pan-Arabism has no goal after the withdrawal of the colonial powers is to ignore the real motivation of pan-Arabism. Imperialism, hegemonic pretensions, and economic exploitation became targets as powerful as colonialism had been. It is not by chance that Nasser became both the symbol and the hero of pan-Arabism.

VI

The tragedy of the Palestinian people has been and still is seen as a tragedy of the Arab world as a whole. Israel is associated in the Arab mind with colonialism. Its existence became a reality only because its basis had been implanted during the colonialist mandates and occupation which covered both Palestine and the other parts of the Arab World. The Jewish immigration to Palestine grew under the protection of colonialism; and since the establishment of the State of Israel, she has been the ally of all those who have always been, or have progressively become, the target of pan-Arabism: Great Britain, France (Suez Affair), and the USA.

Israel has been an element of both integration and disintegration in the Arab world; a factor of integration in the sense that Israel is a living memorial to Arab weakness and division, which has been a stimulating factor for unity and cohesion. The desperation of the Palestinians became a destabilizing factor in the region, a fact which pushed the Arab states to search for a collective solution to their problem. And Israel has been a factor of disintegration in the sense that Israel helped the radicalization of some Arab regions, which in turn increased the divisions in the Arab world and the inter-Arab ideological struggle so much that the Arab approach to a solution became in itself conflictual.

Ajami's assertion about the erosion of the Arab-Israeli conflict as a factor of Arab unity is doubtful. Sadat's diplomacy, which in Ajami's perception, "has dragged the Arabs . . . into the modern game of states," seems to have been until now unable to approach the problem correctly. The only Arab state which has been dragged in this "modern game of states" is Sadat's Egypt. It is true that the Arab-Israeli conflict is now about Israel's boundaries and not Israeli existence, but this is not a spectacular reality. It is well known that Nasser himself tried to find a solution to the Arab-Israeli conflict and established indirect contacts with Israel in the early 1950s and later in the beginning of the 1960s; his correspondence with President Kennedy shows that he was actively seeking an acceptable solution to the conflict which would inevitably lead to recognition of the existence of Israel.

The problem is not only the boundaries of Israel but also and particularly its role in the Arab system. In this regard it is worthwhile to notice that Israel has always refused to deal with the Arab states as a whole system. For the sake of peace, Arabs are different and independent states; it must deal with each separately; but at the same time its military system and conception of national security seem to take the Arab system as a reality; and when it seeks arms and military hardware, Israel's conception of the balance of power is between itself, on the one hand, and *all* the Arab states, on the other.

This dichotomy in the Israelis' perception of war and peace with the Arab world shows clearly Israel's hegemonic design in the Arab world. Sadat's visit to Jerusalem and his treaty with Israel have this merit, that they will be seen only as contributions toward unmasking Israel's real intentions.

Ajami's assumption seems to stand on the hypothesis that the Palestinian question is nearing a solution. But in the actual context of Israeli intransigence, we do not see how the creation of an independent Palestinian state, which Ajami correctly sees as the condition for the stabilization of the "Arab-system of states," could be established without a coherent Arab-system.

So, the settlement of the Palestinians in an independent state, the role of Israel in the region, and its relation with the Arab system, will shape the future evolution of pan-Arabism.

However, the actual peace process has another new input in the region where some years ago the USA was on the defensive. Now the USA has the leading role. The solution of the Arab-Israeli conflict has been shaped by American strategy and the future settlement, if there will be any, will be the most suitable in the context of East-West relations, from the American point of view. That means that the Arab system will be challenged by the Americans' preferred Middle-Eastern system where Turkey, Israel, Egypt, and, eventually, Saudi Arabia will play a key role in the American strategy toward the USSR.

VII

There is no doubt that Nasser's charismatic leadership gave pan-Arabism a forward push and that his defeat in 1967 and death in 1970 have been a setback to pan-Arabism as a political movement. But pan-Arabism as an idea, as the aspiration for independence and unity, existed before Nasser and still exists after him. The field study we mentioned above shows that clearly.

Charisma is a social phenomenon. It means that the inspirations and the hopes of a people have been deeply assimilated by the future charismatic figure who becomes the catalyst of these hopes and inspirations. In his charisma he, in his turn, shapes these hopes and inspirations and leads his people to the materialization of their desires. The end of the charismatic figure (morally or physically) does not mean the end of inspirations and hope. The political movement he represents could suffer a serious setback, or even complete disorganization, but not the ideas he worked for, because these ideas do not basically emanate from him.

The formation of inspiration and hopes in the consciousness of a nation is an historical process which the development of the economic and social structure shapes and polishes. Once the people are not dissatisfied, oppressed and denigrated, they look for a hero. But charisma also is a social phenomenon which is likely to find a fertile ground in certain societies and in certain specific circumstances, often where the institutions of the society cease to play their organic role as social communicators. It is always more safe for a society to develop workable institutions than to wait for the hero, the charismatic figure.

VIII

What conclusions can we draw from this analysis concerning the impact of pan-Arabist ideology on the crisis of the Arab system or its disintegration?

A pan-ideology is by definition based on unification or integration, not division and disintegration. But pan-Arabism, as the intellectual mainstream of Arab nationalism, has specific characteristics of both integration and disintegration that give the interaction between the components of Arab system a specific shape:

1. Pan-Arabism is not an integral ideology. Its substance comprises a belief system of three constant characteristics: a) a feeling of belonging to one Arab nation, b) constant reference by Arabs to a glorious past and civilization of their own creation, and c) an aspiration for unity, which is considered the *sine qua non* of full participation in the actual international system of nations and civilizations. But while this belief system has won general acquiescence, there are conflictual approaches in the process leading to unity, its form, and its goals.

The intellectual sources of the pan-Arabist ideology are different and often conflictual: Islam reformist or traditionalist thought, liberal thought, and socialistic thought.

2. The evolution of the Arab world toward a system of states did not help the emergence of a pan-Arab political movement capable of developing a workable intellectual framework. The absolutism of royal families, charismatic leadership, the military *coup d'Etat*, uni-party systems are current characteristics of the internal social dynamics of Arab states. In the absence of democracy within Arab states, and consequently, of an inter-Arab democratic process which could help the formation of a pan-Arabism intellectual framework prerequisite to a coherent pan-Arab movement, pan-Arabism is confined to being a latent emotional force which has a great capacity to disrupt the Arab system of states.

3. In such conditions, a "workable pan-Arab system of states" based on the concept of *raison d'Etat* is hardly conceivable. Because in the

states where institutions are dead and the mechanism process of consensus formation is blocked, the *raison d'Etat* may be only the *raison de la famille royale* or that of a dictator. Such a system will constantly be under the pressure of centrifugal forces which are unable to express themselves through adequate legitimate channels; and, after his emergence, a powerful Arab leader could be tempted to manipulate them.

4. Egypt, for well-known reasons, occupies a central place in the pan-Arab system. Moreover, she has also a particular ideological pattern of interaction with the other components of the system. While a pan-Arabist leader has no opportunity to disrupt the Egyptian system, an Egyptian leader with a pan-Arabist ideology could, under certain conditions, disrupt the local systems of the other components of the pan-Arab system.

5. The defection of Egypt from the pan-Arab system was made possible by the pressures of internal and external forces. Internal political and social forces were more than willing to change Nasser's economic and social system, which at the same time pushed toward an active search for a peaceful settlement of the Arab-Israeli conflict; and external forces which carefully managed the Arab-Israeli conflict in a way to effect an Egyptian defection from the Arab system in forcing an Egyptian-Israeli solution, and not an Arab-Israeli solution. The failure of the Arab system of states to elaborate a common workable peace settlement with Israel helped Sadat give the impression that his choice had been compelled by the inter-Arab division.

6. The Egyptian defection from the Arab system makes her a more vulnerable and easily manipulatable chess piece in the game of American strategic policies. Egypt's separate treaty with Israel caused her defection from the Arab system and has had new ramifications affecting Egyptian real independence. This fact, added to the organic relations of Egypt with the Arab world in its human and cultural aspects, will have an impact on the Egyptian social dynamic.

The present Egyptian system has some bizarre characteristics: a liberal economic and social infrastructure with a political super-structure basically unchanged since Nasser! In other words, the present liberal Egyptian economy is channeled through the old, Nasserist bureaucracy and political system. This strange dichotomy indicates the complexity of the system and its fragility, which both make it very difficult to measure the impact of new inputs on the Egyptian social dynamic or to allow any accurate prediction.

From our analysis of the essence of the relationship between Arab nationalism and Egyptian nationalism, we could say that the future of Egyptian economic and political independence will shape the future of the pan-Arab system.

Notes

1. Walid Khalidi, "Thinking the Unthinkable: A Sovereign Palestinian State," *Foreign Affairs*, vol. 56, July 1978, pp. 695–713.
2. M. H. Heikal, "Egyptian Foreign Policy," *Foreign Affairs*, vol. 56, July 1978, pp. 714–727 (p. 727).
3. C. Leiden, "Arab Nationalism Today," *Middle East Review*, Winter 1978–79, p. 51.
4. F. Ajami, "The End of Pan-Arabism," *Foreign Affairs*, Jan. 1980, p. 355.
5. Hans Tuetch, *Facets of Arab Nationalism*, Wayne State University Press, Detroit, 1965.
6. Ajami, "Stress in the Arab Triangle," *Foreign Policy*, no. 29, Winter 1977/78, pp. 90–109.
7. Ajami, "The Struggle for Egypt's Soul," *Foreign Policy*, no. 35, Summer 1979, pp. 3–30.
8. Ajami, "The End of Pan-Arabism," *op. cit.*
9. Ibid., p. 365.
10. Ibid., p. 367.
11. Ibid., p. 367.
12. "Struggle for Egypt's Soul," *op. cit.*, p. 4.
13. Ibid., p. 20.
14. Quoted in Ajami, "End of Arabism," *op. cit.*, p. 370, after Malcolm Kerr, "The Dilemmas of the Rich," Near Eastern Studies Center, University of California at Los Angeles, 1977.
15. Ibid., p. 370.
16. "Struggle for Egypt's Soul," *op. cit.*, p. 19.
17. Tawfic Farah, "Group Affiliations of University Students in the Arab Middle East (Kuwait)," *The Journal of Social Psychology*, 1978, 106, pp. 161–165.
18. "End of Pan-Arabism," *op. cit.*, p. 364.
19. Ibid., p. 366.
20. Ibid., p. 368.
21. Ibid., p. 360.
22. Ibid., p. 368.
23. See also Ajami: "The Death of Third World."
24. Saad Ibrahim: *Ittijahat Ar-raᶜi Al-ᶜAm Al-ᶜArabi hawl masᶜalat Al-wihda: Dirasa istitlaiyyah: Arab Public Opinion and the Problematics of Arab Unity: A Field Study*, Beirut, 1980.
25. Ibid., p. 120.
26. "End of Pan-Arabism," p. 372.
27. Ibid., p. 369.

8

The Dying Arab Nation

William R. Brown

Since American troops first landed in Beirut 26 years ago, the Middle East has almost continuously occupied the attentions of American leaders. Indeed, since the 1973 Yom Kippur War, the United States has been deeply involved in a continuing effort to mediate a peaceful resolution to the Arab-Israeli conflict. Yet it is not at all clear that the United States has learned much about the region since its intensive involvement began or that American policy makers knew much about the Middle East to begin with.

Over the last quarter-century, one feature of U.S. Middle East policy has stood out above all others: its fascination with personalities. David Ben Gurion, Gamal Abdel Nasser, Golda Meir, Moshe Dayan, King Faisal, and Anwar el-Sadat then and Menachem Begin, Ariel Sharon, Yasir Arafat, and others today have all seemed larger than life, as have even mediators such as former Secretary of State Henry Kissinger and former U.S. special envoy Philip Habib. But by focusing on personalities and even on the regimes those from the Middle East have led, Americans have neglected Arab political thought and traditions, to the detriment of peace and of U.S. interests. In particular, the Arab-Israeli mediation effort has unwittingly helped keep alive issues, such as the Palestinian question, that evoke the tantalizing but obsolete and destructive chimera of pan-Arab nationalism.

The aftermath of the brutal war between factions of the Palestine Liberation Organization (PLO) in northern Lebanon provides an excellent opportunity to examine how Washington can encourage trends, such as the rise of a modern, state-oriented Arab nationalism, that can have

Reprinted with permission from *Foreign Policy* 54 (Spring 1984). Copyright 1984 by the Carnegie Endowment for International Peace.

the opposite effect—diverting Arab attentions in particular from the Palestinian question and inducing Arab states to focus instead on improving their own welfare. The first step is to understand how the Arab world's very concepts of state and nation differ profoundly from the West's.

An Intensely Personal Society

Any short overview of Arab political theory is bound to oversimplify, but it can spotlight beliefs and values that American policy must begin to acknowledge. Even before Islam began to spread throughout the Arabian Peninsula in the 7th century, Arab society revolved around the clan. The social relationships defined by an individual's obligations to these extended families gave Arab societies cohesion and a tangible concept of social justice. Leaders settled disputes informally and routinely oversaw the minutiae of their subjects' personal lives. Arab morality elevated the welfare of the group over the material welfare of the individual. Although it lacked Western-style constitutions, the Arab world eventually found a systematic set of guiding moral principles in the Koran, which is both a sacred text and a code of regulations. And this emphasis on moral welfare has continued despite the spirit of entrepreneurship that first swept through the Middle East in medieval times. Through contemporary times, Islam, unlike the West, has insisted that morality is a social not an individual virtue.

Traditional Arab rulers frequently mistreated their subjects but were seldom authoritarian. Individuals often circumvented official dictates through bribery, patronage, or family influence. Moreover, the very weak could always appeal to leaders for the magnanimous gesture that is so important in Islamic thought. The critical underlying point is that Islamic society permitted individuals to deal directly with their leaders. Whereas Western societies gradually interposed a layer of institutions between ruler and ruled, Arab society and politics remained intensely personal, and therefore Arab peoples did not develop strong states. In addition, since the days of Mohammad, Arabs have nurtured a distinct national identity. Yet unlike non-Western societies that developed in splendid isolation—China, for example—the Arab identity has been shaped by constant contact with the West.

Arab attitudes toward the West, however, are shot through with contradictions. Frequently motivated by envy, much Arab social and political development has consciously followed Western lines. Arab attempts at commercial modernization, for example, largely reflect a desire to catch up with and surpass the West. Islam itself adapted many of the tenets of Judaism and Christianity.

Yet the Arabs view borrowing from the West not as an end in itself but as a means to an end—to acquire the technology and the organizational skills to compete successfully with the West. Indeed, Arabs continue to reject explicitly Western values, considering the West to be devoid of the rich human qualities and sense of community that they prize.

The concurrent wishes to emulate Western material success and to preserve the absolutism of Islam have produced vast differences between Arab and Western states today. The West's faith in the power of reason and its belief that individuals are capable of making value-free decisions based on objective information and self-interest have encouraged the view that individuals can and should initiate political action: thus the West's belief in popular sovereignty and civic responsibility, as well as the tendency of individuals to adopt social roles, such as those of voter, citizen, or consumer. In turn, most individuals accept the various constraints that the state imposes on them and on economic, social, and political institutions.

To Arabs, however, the idea that action reflects self-interest and that individuals may originate political action are both suspect. And they reject Western social roles as one-dimensional and therefore artificial, relying instead on religious faith. They consider society's ideal political actor to be the corporate group, whose reference points are provided by tradition—which Arabs view as a concrete, tangible phenomenon. Because concepts on which the Western state rests are not accepted by Arab societies, Arabs regard the state as almost incomprehensibly abstract.

Whereas Westerners tend to regard Arabs as holding confused political allegiances, Arabs are generally completely bewildered by such outpourings of patriotism as those of the millions of Americans and Europeans who voluntarily went to their deaths in two world wars. In Moslem eyes the Western state exists largely to create and exercise power and therefore lacks the moral purpose that Arabs value in their own societies. They believe that attributing any other purposes to the Western-style state constitutes an act of self-deception.

These Arab attitudes are changing, however, and Arab countries have begun to develop the attributes of states. Oil revenues have at last given Arab states the power potential to compete effectively with the West. In Iraq, Kuwait, Libya, Saudi Arabia, and the United Arab Emirates oil income has reached critical mass and set off a political chain reaction in which Arab leaders are beginning to harness the human and material resources needed to manage a modern state. The performance of Arab governments has already improved greatly. Although Arab countries appear disorganized to many foreigners, efficiency is on the rise, and offices today routinely use computers and employ Western business techniques.

In addition, most Arab governments have accepted or claimed a formal responsibility for their states' social and economic development. Admittedly, the proposals made by many Arab governments shortly after World War II to expand rights for women, rationalize taxation systems, and implement land reform and a variety of crude socialist schemes reflected little more than a wish to pre-empt and limit Western influence over their societies. These proposals were not developed into specific legislation or decrees. And few reformers urged their societies to abandon Islam's social values.

In some Arab countries, however, reform efforts went far beyond lip service. Blessed with national outputs totaling $130 billion, Saudi Arabia and Kuwait could afford to enhance social welfare for its own sake. Moreover, the oil revolution has enriched even Arab states that do not produce oil through official subsidies, investments, and guestworker remittances. The infectiousness of ideas in the Middle East and the glaringly visible abundance of its new wealth all but guarantee that governments that fail to institute social programs will be asking for trouble.

As citizens contribute to and benefit from government programs, they will develop notions of civil rights, popular sovereignty, and civic responsibility—although it is impossible to say whether Arab societies will create Western-style states or invent new political forms that marry the ideas of both nation-state and community of faith.

Similarly, the new wealth has brought Arab leaders greater power and responsibilities and therefore greater independence as chiefs of state. The most important manifestation of this new independence has been a growing willingness and ability to ignore the obligations and defy the demands of the old Middle East system, the so-called Arab nation.

Why Arab Leaders Hate the PLO

Traditionally, politics in the Middle East have rested on this amorphous and romantic but comfortable concept, which evokes visions of a single people who share a common language, culture, religion, and history and inhabit an area stretching from the Persian Gulf to the Atlantic Ocean. Historically, the Arab people have looked to unity rather than to fundamental social change to create the strength that could command international respect.

But the dream of forging an Arab nation has hindered the development of strong Arab states in two ways. First, it powerfully concentrates the Arab mind on a concept that unavoidably represents political values and practices that flourished in the absence of strong states. Second, it constantly reminds Arabs that the political map of the modern Middle East was essentially drawn up by the European colonial powers, not by the Arabs themselves. Today's Arab states, it is argued, were created to serve European, not Arab purposes. Thus working within the context of these states—and especially leading these states—is widely condemned in the Arab world as a completely illegitimate activity. Antipathy toward the state is generally not spontaneous but tends to arise when Arab leaders, seeking victories in their continuing struggles over national emotions, accuse each other of betraying the Arab cause. Prevented by the traditional appeal of Arab nationalism from ignoring these charges, Arab leaders have had great difficulty in using Saudi, Jordanian, or Egyptian nationalism for Saudi, Jordanian, or Egyptian purposes.

Popular religion has strengthened the national themes of Arab politics. The ideal of unity represented by the Abbasside Caliphate, which lasted from A.D. 750–1258 when the Mongols destroyed Baghdad, the capital of Islamic civilization, rekindles Arab pride and self-esteem, recalling a golden age when a single Arab empire stretched from India to the Pyrenees Mountains.

In their plea for nationalist resolve, however, the Arabs have added a complicating factor that has confounded the lives of their leaders— the adoption of the Palestinian cause. A people ejected from their homeland, the Palestinians are the ultimate symbol of national sacrifice. And as the September 1982 massacres at the Sabra and Shatila refugee camps demonstrate, the Palestinians' sacrifices continue to this day.

With the birth of the PLO, a small group of purposeful men came to personify the Palestinian cause. To the surprise of the Arab state leadership, PLO leaders also successfully staked out a claim as the Arabs' national conscience and virtually pre-empted any prospective opposition. The PLO won its greatest victory at the 1974 Arab summit conference in Rabat, Morocco, where the assembled heads of state all solemnly declared Arafat and his organization to be the sole representatives of the Palestinian people. The Arabs' national symbol was effectively given control over itself.

The appeal of the Palestinian cause throughout the Arab world has forced Arab leaders to profess support formally and almost ritualistically. And because ultimately leaders are controlled by what they tell their people, the singular place given the Palestinian issue has paralyzed Arab politics. Leaders of states have not been free to pursue other goals wholeheartedly, and the Arab body politic has remained in a near coma. No wonder chiefs of state hate the PLO, as has been amply demonstrated by Jordanian King Hussein's war on the guerrillas in the Black September of 1970; the decimation of PLO forces in Lebanon by the army of Syrian

President Hafez al-Assad in 1976; rhetorical and physical attacks by Iraq and Libya; Sadat's complete disregard of the PLO when he launched his peace initiative; and most revealing, the Arab states' responsibility for or studied indifference to the disasters that have befallen the Palestinians since Israel's 1982 invasion of Lebanon.

There are limits to the hostility that the Arab states can express toward the PLO, largely because state leaders cannot afford to lose touch with their peoples completely. But their rhetorical support and occasional olive branches are merely tactical moves. Moreover, the Palestinians operate under severe constraints as well. They must constantly ingratiate themselves with their principal providers of economic aid and security. And because Palestinians are a minority within each Arab state, the state holds the ultimate power in any contest or showdown with these representatives of the Arab nation. Nationalism can inspire, but its one-weapon arsenal of raw emotion is rarely a match for the people and resources that can be commanded by the state. Thus the nation can only occasionally thwart the aims of state leaders, and state leaders have not been able finally to subdue the nation.

As a result, Arab politics have come to rest on dead center. Neither the Arab states nor the Palestinians can easily make specific commitments to one another. And all are unable to keep those commitments that are made. Further muddying the situation and confusing Arab political loyalties is the PLO's specific political design. Arafat and other Palestinian leaders depend on invoking the pan-Arab cause and therefore visions of pan-Arab unity. But all the while the PLO has been working for a Palestinian state, which cannot easily be reconciled with standard interpretations of unity.

The 1982 Israeli invasion of Lebanon showed how wide the gulf between nation and state in the Arab world has grown. For the first time, Israeli troops invaded an Arab capital far from the territory that Jews could claim through divine promise. And the attack was directed specifically against the Palestinian symbols of the Arab nation. Yet no Arab leader responded to Arafat's appeals. Moreover, most Arab governments initially refused to provide haven for the PLO fighters. Algeria, Iraq, Jordan, and Tunisia provided limited hospitality. The Sudan, Syria, and the two Yemens also opened their doors. But in every case, the Palestinian guests have been isolated and carefully watched. Everyone uses them, but no one trusts them. As symbols of the Arab nation, they are inimical to the interests of an Arab state.

The Palestinians have reacted to their abandonment with dark but vague warnings that the traitors will be punished. But these pronouncements have stirred little reaction in the Arab world, perhaps because Arab masses seldom respond unless aroused by their leaders, and at this time no leader wants to use Arab nationalism to pillory his counterparts. Left to their own devices, most leaders will be inclined to back away from the concept of the Arab nation and concentrate instead on a subject that holds greater political promise, namely, the state and the benefits it can bring to its citizens. Indeed, the chiefs of Arab states are presently engaged in the difficult task of shifting public attention from nation to state. This pragmatism may be the brightest spot on the region's political horizon.

Considerable national sentiment still lurks in the background. In April 1983, for example, Hussein chose not to enter into U.S.-sponsored negotiations with Israel after the PLO refused to endorse the venture. For he did not yet feel capable of acting as a Jordanian. But Hussein and others like him must be careful; the emerging importance of Arab states has given considerable credence to the Israeli idea of a Palestinian state in Jordan. This slight adjustment in Arab political goals could obviate further references to a homeland for the Palestinians on the West Bank that would fulfill the aspirations of the Arab nation.

Beyond Jordan, however, much evidence suggests that individual Arab states are gaining an edge over the Arab nation. It took Arab leaders more than a year after the Israeli invasion of Lebanon, for example, to agree to hold a summit meeting—those gatherings where chiefs of state profess loyalty to the Arab nation's objectives. And when the designated time arrived, the summit conference did not take place. In addition, the Arab League—the main organizational expression of pan-Arab nationalism—has become almost moribund.

New forms of state-to-state relations are emerging as well. The Gulf Cooperation Council coordinates economic and security matters among states of the Arabian Peninsula while eschewing the emotional rhetoric of Arab unity. Egypt and the Sudan have developed similar cooperative relations. The Arab governments speak of integration—not unity. The joint Sudanese-Egyptian legislature resembles the European Parliament more than a sovereign law-making body. In North Africa increased down-to-earth cooperative efforts have been made by Algeria, Mauritania, and Tunisia, occasionally Morocco, and even Libya. Arab leaders now feel free to participate in joint enterprises without intoning pan-Arab national themes. Arab regionalism appears to be replacing Arab nationalism.

Even in the case of Muammar el-Qaddafi's Libya, state interests predominate. The Libyan leader has sought to devise new ways for achieving the traditional objectives of moral welfare. But he has intermingled them with the newer ideas of state-provided social welfare. Moreover, Qaddafi's Chadian adventure is a simple example of a state extending its power without reference to Arabism. The policies of Syria's

Assad share the same characteristics. He harbors the traditional Syrian fear of a Christian state emerging in Lebanon under American hegemony. Such a development would be antithetical to an old idea that has little to do with the Arab nation—Greater Syria. Arab leaders are taking a new tack. Instead of redefining the state to correspond to pan-Arab national objectives, they are revising their concept of the nation to accommodate the present state structure.

Curiously, by continually insisting on negotiations, it has been the United States that has focused attention on Arab national symbols. Just as Arab leaders have begun to question its value, the United States continues to nourish the old Arab nationalism. The negotiating process has largely rested on paradox and fallacy. Most Arabs consider the U.S.-Israeli relationship to be the source of Arab national torment. But far from ostracizing the United States, Arabs have given Washington's envoys virtually unlimited access to Arab councils because of their firm conviction that only the United States can push Israel closer to the Arab position on the Palestinian question.

By now it is apparent, however, that the United States cannot or will not exercise this influence—and that Washington has also failed to convince many Arabs to modify their views about Israel. America's insistence on dealing with Arabs and Israelis principally as a mediator has been unproductive. Yet American optimism keeps the Arab-Israeli dialogue alive. To be sure, this optimism helps keep the peace, at least in the short run, which alone justifies the mediator's posture.

But there are drawbacks as well. American diplomacy has helped limit the Arab-Israeli dialogue to a single topic—the Palestinians, and specifically, the issue of dislodging the Israelis from the West Bank. This is the purpose of the Arab nation. It can be the purpose of no state other than Jordan. Yet, up to this point, all Arabs have claimed it as a purpose.

These states have no reason not to claim this goal, for the American determination to mediate maintains the salience of the Palestinian issue regardless of the Palestinians' fortunes. In this respect the so-called Arab national extremists are indebted to the United States. Without the continuing life support provided by the mediation effort, Arafat would have difficulty occupying center stage as he did in March 1983 when he and Hussein discussed the possibility of negotiating with Israel. The U.S. refusal to recognize the PLO, however, helpfully detracts from this pan-Arab national theme.

For 10 years, the United States has failed to gain a West Bank agreement. The hyperactive posture adopted by successive administrations has only heightened the impression of American failure and damaged America's prestige worldwide. U.S. diplomacy also makes it more difficult for the Arabs to shed the national sentiments they have harbored for so long. Worse, the American posture feeds Arab hostility toward the United States even among those states that appear to be cooperating with U.S. efforts. Eventually, the single-minded determination to mediate could weaken the U.S. position in the Middle East.

Conventional wisdom holds that once headed down this road the United States has no choice but to continue. Other wisdom maintains that such peace efforts are a moral obligation. In addition, the careers of many U.S. foreign-policy makers are bound up in active Middle East diplomacy.

The mediation route, however, holds little promise for an Arab-Israeli peace. But if Arab national sentiment has rendered the direct road to peace impassable, more circuitous routes may exist. If Arabs and Israelis are not yet ready to set aside their differences, perhaps the United States should back off from the mediation effort. The United States would do well to contemplate a new approach before Arab leaders still dedicated to nationalism replace the present leadership, which is weary of national politics.

Support the New Regionalism

Certain new perceptions need to be encouraged in order to change the emphasis of U.S. Middle East diplomacy. The United States should treat the various Arab regions as discrete entities and convince them that it is working for a relationship rooted in pragmatism. The United States should view the notion of distinctly Arab countries as a cultural rather than a political concept. Finally, American officials should assure these states that Arab state concerns will receive serious attention and will benefit from cooperation with the United States, particularly in the area of security and defense. Recent history suggests that the United States should avoid overwhelming any of these states with its presence. Already the domineering American image has soured U.S. relations with Egypt. To the chagrin of some Pentagon enthusiasts, U.S. relations with Persian Gulf states have probably benefited from the Saudi tendency to hold outsiders at arm's length on defense matters.

While remaining attentive to the possibilities for a negotiated settlement, the United States could shift its focus toward enhancing the security of the friendliest Arab states. Both political and economic support could be provided the new regionalism, manifested in regional gatherings in the Persian Gulf, the Nile Valley, and the Maghreb (Morocco, Tunisia, and Algeria).

Washington can encourage the oil rich countries of the Gulf Cooperation Council to expand their security, trade, and technological cooperation—subjects already of vital interest to the United States. The council needs no economic support, but the United States can provide political support and military cooperation. U.S. relations with the Nile Valley countries will continue to hinge on defense and economic assistance designed to encourage however much integration the Sudan and Egypt desire. The Maghreb could use some economic support, but political and commercial assistance will make a far greater contribution to its cooperative efforts. In addition, the United States should promote an appropriate political dialogue between these regions and the non-Arab world.

The relationship between Egypt and other moderate Arab states requires particular attention, even if events soon permit Egypt to reenter the Arab world. After its peace with Israel, Egypt was ostracized by its Arab neighbors. Those that adhered to nationalist sentiment regarded the policies initiated by Sadat and perpetuated by President Hosni Mubarak as traitorous. Yet most Arabs have recognized that continuity in Arab politics is difficult without Egypt, which represents too much in the way of Arab power, intellect, and tradition to be ignored. Now a process of reconciliation seems well under way, a process that can greatly contribute to regional peace and stability if its spirit and logic spread to Saudi Arabia. Since 1973 Saudi oil and wealth along with Egypt's power have become a mainstay of Arab strength, but the Saudis have actively supported the campaign to keep Cairo isolated. Nevertheless, a Cairo-Riyadh axis would represent the greatest aggregation of power that can be created in the Arab world and could guide less secure Arab states toward a more moderate course.

Relations with the Levant cannot, of course, avoid the fallout from U.S. ties with Israel. In the case of Syria, both Damascus and Tel Aviv must accommodate their respective and sometimes conflicting interests in Lebanon. The United States should continue to address the Palestinian problem in a bilateral manner, returning to the sound strategy of treating it as an Israeli-Jordanian matter. It should ignore the warnings of those who constantly predict that U.S. relations with Israel are about to antagonize permanently the entire Arab world. Despite 30 years of frustration for all parties, the Arabs have not turned their backs on Washington. Peace may not be in the offing, but that is a matter for the governments of the Levant. The United States should not encourage the other Arab states to remain transfixed by the Levant or its problems. With a strong state system less vulnerable to outside interference and to the emotions of nationalism, the Arabs would be less inclined to think in terms of traditional objectives. Arab capabilities need not be permanently directed against Israel.

Israeli Hopes

In the Middle East the competition between the nation and the state is not confined to the Arab world. Israel is also experiencing a conflict in loyalties as it changes from an emotion-laden nation to a power-wielding state. Jews have never traditionally spoken in terms of an Israeli nation but rather of a Jewish nation embracing an entire people irrespective of Israel's physical boundaries. For Jews, as well as for Arabs, the nation and the state are distinct entities, and today, they are ideas in competition.

For decades, in ways similar to the Arab pattern, the Jewish nation had been succumbing to the Israeli state. But the 1982 invasion of Lebanon changed the situation. The attack, which was a state initiative, placed tremendous strains on the state's resources and on the ideals of nationhood and has prompted many Israelis to re-examine their country's position.

In response to the massacre at Sabra and Shatila, about 350,000 people filled the streets of Tel Aviv to express their horror. An official commission of inquiry into the massacre followed. In December 1982 at a meeting of the World Zionist Congress in Jerusalem, the majority supported a resolution urging Begin to relinquish occupied territory in return for peace and to limit Jewish settlements on the West Bank to sparsely populated sites.

The Lebanon invasion has also troubled many American Jews—who themselves are members of the Jewish nation. Rabbi Alexander Schindler, president of the Union of American Hebrew Congregations, has said that Jews have for too long been plugged into Israel as if it were a kidney machine—a scientific marvel that keeps them alive as Jews. While expressing deep love for Israel, Schindler has stated, "I want us to make Israel more truly Jewish, with a quality of life that reflects the most profound Jewish vision."

Similar sentiments have come from Edgar Bronfman, president of the World Jewish Congress. In a February 1983 exchange with Israeli Defense Minister Moshe Arens, then Israel's ambassador to Washington, Bronfman observed that given the peace treaty with Egypt, the destruction of the PLO's military capability, and the apparent superiority of the Israeli Defense Force, the security of the state can no longer be Israel's ultimate motivation. He insisted that Israel must reach a political accommodation with its neighbors.

With the passage of time and the American-sponsored agreement for the withdrawal of Israeli forces from Lebanese territory, criticism of Israel within the American Jewish community has abated. But the concern remains that the Likud government's obsession with security approaches a narrow militarism antithetical to the intellectual humanism with which Jews have always identified.

Involved here is a conflict between nation and state. The World Zionist Congress, in particular, is widely and properly seen as nothing less than a guardian of the Jewish nation. But its suggestions in December 1982 to urge Begin to limit Jewish settlements on the West Bank were judged to be in opposition to the will of the Israeli state. These proposals created such consternation that the chairman of the congress's meeting halted the proceedings before the resolution could be brought to a vote. Despite an effort to formulate a position that did not appear too critical of Israel's policies, the matter had to be dropped.

In striving to create an acceptable political environment, the Israelis have channeled all of their efforts through the state—unlike the Arabs, who heretofore have favored the nation for this purpose. From a security standpoint, the Israelis may have had little choice. The state can be an exceedingly efficient security device. Nevertheless, the Israelis are likely to experience the same disillusionment as the Arabs. For beneath their outward scorn for the Arabs, the Israelis truly yearn for their neighbors' acceptance. Proposals for open borders, commerce, tourism, and cultural exchange are in the forefront of every Israeli peace plan. This hope is reflected first in their relations with Egypt, now with Lebanon, and someday perhaps with Jordan. Security alone is never enough, for no people can retain their vitality in isolation.

The difficulty may be that although the Israelis rely on the state, the state is not an effective vehicle for achieving many Israeli goals. Tourism, cultural exchange, and commerce are unlikely to be produced by the present Middle East equation. For regional acceptance can only result from the good will between peoples—between nations. It cannot be produced by states. Yet the Israelis are so disdainful of Arab symbols that they could inadvertently drive Arab leaders to continue struggling for national goals that they otherwise might abandon—or at least redefine in nonpolitical terms. If a less virulent form of Arab nationalism that is tied to state interests could emerge, Arab and Israeli nationalisms could coexist. But such cooperation is impossible unless the Israelis become less compulsive about proving the legitimacy of their own national experience to the rest of the world.

The Israeli problem perhaps was best expressed by Meron Benvenisti, a former deputy mayor of Jerusalem, in February 1983. Commenting on the Palestinians, he contended, "We cannot stand a symmetry of claims . . . Israelis have a profound feeling that once they accept the symmetry that the other side is also a legitimate national movement, then their own feeling about their own right and legitimacy will be dimmed." The same agony torments many Arabs. They believe that to accept the other side's legitimacy one must, in effect, deny one's own. Relative truth comes hard in a part of the world where the tradition of premising national existence on divine pronouncement convinces Arabs and Israelis alike that their truths are absolute.

Current policies, whether American, Arab, or Israeli, will not lead to greater peace in the Middle East. The United States is dedicated to a negotiating stance over the West Bank that will never close the gap between the contesting parties. Instead, it can only fix Arab and Israeli attention on old and irreconcilable national aims. Changing the basis of U.S.-Israeli relations requires that one grand assumption be borne out—that the Lebanon experience exerts a truly sobering effect on Israeli views of the destiny of their state. Perhaps the Lebanon adventure has rubbed off a bit of the excess gloss on the surface of *Eretz Yisrael*—but without diminishing its beauty or its value for the Jewish nation. The result may be a conception of Israel's destiny prudently reflecting contemporary realities, one no longer frozen within biblical prescriptions or the horrors of the 1930s and 1940s. To insure that this transition does in fact take place, the United States must rely more on the American Jewish community. How much influence the nation should have in the affairs of the state is for Jews to decide. But the unusual relationship of the Jewish nation, and particularly of American Jews, to the Israeli state permits the U.S. government to work openly through the nation to achieve moderation in the state.

The current mood in Israel also offers an opportunity for the United States. But the cure is not the same as that prescribed for the Arabs. In contrast to the voices of the Arab nation and the earlier Israeli state, the voice of the Jewish nation has at times proved a restraining force. U.S. policy should try to exploit this influence. Effective pressure on the Israeli state can only come from the Jewish nation.

Regardless of American efforts and preferences, peace in the Middle East will only occur when Arabs and Israelis want it, and until now, each has concluded that peace is still too costly. The Arabs have feared the sacrifice of their national resolve, while the Israelis have feared the loss of state security. But these attitudes appear to be softening and the United States should encourage the change. Subtlety can be the mark of U.S. policy in the coming years.

9

Stress and Disintegration in the Arab World

Abdul-Monem Al-Mashat

The normal patterns of interaction in the Arab system are undergoing a fundamental change which poses a serious challenge to the integrative abilities of that system by threatening its ability to form consensus.

This political reality has stimulated sharp debate among Arab intellectuals and academicians. Some look upon this change with a mixture of indulgence, exhilaration and malice, but go too far when they argue that we are in fact witnessing the "end of pan-Arabism."[1] Others argue that "The Arab states' system is first and foremost a 'Pan' system," but their enthusiasm sometimes leads them to contradict themselves, as in the assertion that "explicit or transparent *raison d'etat* is *heresy*" in such a *state*-system.[2]

A third group tries to carefully scrutinize this process of change in order to ascertain its direction. They argue that the Arab states are moving away from the Arab system advocated by Nasser toward one which is not yet clearly defined. In other words, the Arab states are moving from a consensual into a disintegrative environment.[3]

This debate is not a new phenomenon in the Arab world, nor is it unique to the Arab system. Since the early years of this century, the conceptual question asked in the Arab world has been not about nationalism per se, but about the type of nationalism that exists in the Arab world. Is it Islamic nationalism, Arab nationalism, or a combination of both? Another important question concerns the contextualization of the concept. Is it cultural nationalism or social nationalism that unleashes the forces of social revolution? It is my belief that these two questions

Reprinted with permission from *Journal of Arab Affairs* 4, 1 (Spring 1985):29–45. Copyright 1985 by the Middle East Research Group, Inc.

are still the core of the debate. It would be naive to expect an early agreement on these questions. Nevertheless, it would be useful to acknowledge three characteristics of contemporary Arab reality.

First, the Arab World is not a homogeneous but a heterogeneous system. There is enormous diversity among the Arab states on four vital indicators; namely, wealth, population size, literacy and standard of living. For instance, Egypt, with the largest population (40 million), is considered the proletariat of the Arab world, while the three richest countries, Kuwait, Qatar and the United Arab Emirates, are under-populated (with a combined native population of 1.2 million). Nor does literacy necessarily accompany wealth. With the exception of Kuwait, the wealthiest countries (i.e., Saudi Arabia, Qatar and the Emirates) are among those with the lowest literacy rates. Many instances of disparity between the level of wealth and the standard of living can also be pointed out. If one were to add to these the discrepancies in the areas of institution-building, and the establishment of norms, and in the levels of social and political relations, one could argue that the advocates of a homogeneous and harmonious Arab system ought to address themselves to such issues.

Secondly, the articulation of Arab nationalism and the growth of the pan-Arab movement coincided with the struggle against the colonial powers and Arab demands for independence. In the present era, the principal struggle is at the intra- and inter-Arab levels. How can forces of Arab nationalism confront questions such as freedom, equity, equality and mutual understanding? These are questions that remain unanswered.

Thirdly, the military defeat of Egypt in 1967, and the oil wealth of Saudi Arabia, and the Gulf created a new atmosphere for the redistribution of power in the Arab world. Nasser's Egypt, which had been the advocate of Arab nationalism, was challenged by Saudi Arabia, which was advocating pan-Islamism. This was not only an ideological opposition, but a power struggle at the regional level. It would appear that there was a change in the balance of power, and the power was now distributed among several Arab states. The response of the region to this diffusion of power is another question which Arab nationalism must face.

Rather than join in the debate over Arab nationalism and whether it is a passing fad, an artifact or a substantial force, my task will be to examine whether or not the Arab system is in the process of disintegration, i.e., to determine the patterns of change in regional interactions and their motivations and consequences. To undertake this task, I will propose several assumptions.

First, Egypt will be the focal point for tracing and examining Arab interactions. As the most enthusiastic advocate of Arab nationalism and integration, Egypt was once the center of the Arab world, but it has now defected from the Arab system.

Secondly, I will refer to four extremely serious stresses which challenge the Arab system at the same time as they offer opportunities for integrative action. These stresses are the Palestinian-Israeli conflict, the exponential growth of population, the challenge of development, and the contradiction between statism and the sense of community among the Arabs. Three other conditions, i.e., dependency, the diffusion of power, and the role of outside forces, together with the aforementioned factors, will provide the framework for my discussion. In presenting and analyzing the disintegration process in the Arab world, I will utilize events from Edward Azar's Conflict and Peace Data Bank (COPDAB), which are categorized into types of interactions according to issue areas (symbolic, economic, military, cultural and scientific, human and environmental, and political).[4] And finally, I will use a theoretical model of disintegration coupled with my personal knowledge of the regime.

II

The idea of a disintegrative process is itself problematic. The model must be a dynamic interactive process or it is no process at all. It should account for various forms and conditions of stress in the regional system, including internal and external stresses.

The international interactions approach focuses primarily on the overt activities of nation-states as a means to describe, explain and predict interstate relations, whether cooperative or conflictive. This approach is significant, particularly when we know that nation-states behave to a certain extent as individuals do. They maintain a memory structure and a cognitive dictionary which they consult whenever they intend to send a message, i.e., actions or reactions toward other factors. In this sense, the interactions approach is helpful in understanding the reciprocal motivations of the behavior of states.

The international interactions approach, which depends on large data sets such as that of COPDAB, is useful in the study of aggregate macro-cross-national trends over time. It helps to discern crisis escalation processes and peaks of conflict or cooperation spirals, as well as points of breakdown in the system. This is because countries interact in highly routinized and patterned ways. Whenever such interactions reach the upper threshold (conflictive end) or the lower threshold (cooperative end) of the "Normal Relations Range," a crisis will be unfolding.

While the international interactions approach is generally employed in the analysis of the integrative process to determine the volume and intensity of interactions, it can also be usefully employed in the analysis of the disintegration process. In the model for disintegration proposed in this paper, two components will be studied mainly through the use of events data. Political interactions within the Arab system (consensus over issues of regional concern) and between outside forces and the central regional power will be studied over time to determine the type, direction and level of these processes.

Interactions between Egypt and the Arab system as a whole will be examined by issue areas.

Interactions between Egypt and the other major regional actors (i.e., Saudi Arabia, Syria, Iraq and the PLO) will be analyzed to see whether or not these interactions determine the total behavior pattern within the Arab system over time. What are the changes, if any, in these interactions, and how can one predict the future of the system from them?

Interactions between Egypt and three outside forces, i. e., Israel and the two superpowers, will be analyzed in terms of their impact on the patterns of interaction between Egypt and the rest of the Arab states (collectively or dyadically). The period from 1948 to 1977 will be divided into three ten-year intervals. Emphasis will be given to the year 1974, when two outside forces, i.e., the U.S. and Israel, were able to begin a new phase of trilateral interaction with Egypt which resulted in the bilateral peace treaty between Egypt and Israel and Egypt's defection from the Arab system.

III

Stress, as it affects international actors, generates events of such intensity as to disrupt patterned or routinized interstate behavior. The capacity of the system to cope with or manage internal and external stresses depends upon many things, including the role of leadership, popular perceptions, and the latent adaptive capabilities of the system itself. For instance, Nasser's non-cooptation policy vis-a-vis the great powers led him to confront various kinds of stresses and threats generated by these powers, particularly during the 1950's (e.g., the Allied Middle East Command, the Baghdad Pact). Through his charisma and popularity, he was able to rally popular Arab support for his proposed responses to the stresses confronting the Arab system. Perceptions of stress and the means of coping with them change with time, place and circumstances. What might be perceived as severe stress in one situation may seem less stressful in another situation. At the same time, cognitive structures of leaders and peoples play essential roles in determining the significance or irrelevance of certain stressful forces.

The sources of stress vary in international relations: some are internal, some are international, and others are a combination of both. Whatever the source, stress manifests itself either in conflictive or cooperative patterns of reactions. Generally, conflictive patterns of interactions supersede cooperative patterns. Such patterns may be susceptible to observation and investigation (i. e., overt conflictive behavior) or they may require a different research strategy (i.e., measures of structural victimization). If patterns of conflictive response to stresses, whether behavioral or structural, persist without resolution, they may very well develop into conflict processes characterized by duration, fluctuation, spillover, and the absence of a distinct termination. These conflicts, which can be internal as well as international, ethnic as well as interstate, have been termed "protracted social conflicts" to distinguish them from strategic conflicts.[5] When both behavioral and structural conflicts simultaneously create stresses in a system, one can predict disruption and perhaps fundamental discontinuities in patterns of interactions.

If the system under investigation is an integrative system, it can easily be speculated that such disruptions and discontinuities will lead to disintegration and fragmentation. Such stresses may originate within the confines of the system or in its external environment. In either case, the process of consensus formation will probably be superseded by dissonance which may bring the system to the verge of collapse.

IV

Egypt has played a pivotal role in the Arab system, particularly during the 1950's and 1960's. Egyptian-Arab relations have experienced periods of close cooperative interactions, i.e., 1956–57, 1963–64, 1966–67, 1970–73 and 1976. In the first ten-year period (1948–57), a consensus was formed regarding national independence and Arab sovereignty as a means of confronting foreign influence. This period witnessed the 1956 war, the first moves toward the Egyptian-Syrian experiment in unity, and Egypt's greatest cooperative interaction with conservative Saudi Arabia. Intensive interaction between Egypt and the Arabs must be understood in light of Egypt's international role in helping to establish the Third World non-alignment movement, and as part of her attempts to play a leading role in Arab politics.

The most serious debate took place on the issues of Arabism and integration during the second ten-year period (1958–67), particularly during 1963–64, the era of Arab summit diplomacy. However, the failure of the Egyptian-Syrian unity as well as the failure of Egypt even to defend her own territory in the 1967 war not only moderated Egypt's position in Arab politics, but also disillusioned her constituency in the

Arab system for years to come. Cooperative interaction with the Arabs between 1970 and 1973 was directed essentially toward the rescue of the newly emerging Palestinian political movement. It is important to note the increase of cooperative interactions between Egypt and Saudi Arabia in this direction since 1970. Egypt needed economic assistance, or more importantly, an open channel to the U.S., especially before 1974, and Saudi Arabia was capable of providing such assistance to an Arab country known for its anti-American attitude.

Overall, the Arabs showed a great deal of concern about issues of Arab interest. They interacted cooperatively with Egypt during the 1956 crisis, the 1967 war and the 1973 war. During these crises, the Arab system proved to be responsive and capable in terms of management. The highest level of cooperative interactions took place in 1976. Why? This was the first year after the second Sinai disengagement treaty with Israel (September 1975); it was also the second year of the civil war in Lebanon. Although Saudi Arabia was competing with Egypt over roles and regional status, it did not want to lose Egyptian capabilities. It therefore played a game of cooptation by supporting Egypt politically and economically. This policy did not last, however, after Egypt's decision to "go it alone" with Israel. In fact, there was almost a complete collapse in the Arab-Egyptian political sub-system.

In terms of conflictive interaction, Egypt was less conflictive toward the Arabs than vice versa. In 1957–58 the Arabs, particularly Saudi Arabia, played a severely antagonistic role toward Egypt, attempting to eliminate its radical policies in the Arab world.[6] In 1961 and 1963, there was conflict over Egyptian-Syrian unity and the Yemen question. This period witnessed the highest level of Saudi-Egyptian conflictive interactions. But the most serious conflictive interaction took place in 1977, after Sadat's visit to Israel. The role played by external forces and events within the region weakened the relationship between Egypt and the rest of the Arab States. And while the system had previously shown itself capable of managing all crisis situations, even overt military crises, it proved incapable of managing or containing this one. Since that time, consensus over regional issues has been lacking.

The U.S., the U.S.S.R. and Israel have been trying to penetrate the Arab system since the end of World War II. While the regional grievances against the first two are either minimal or indirect or, in very general terms, a part of the overall grievances of the developing nations against the developed nations, the Arab grievances against Israel are so deep-seated that if Israel continues to penetrate the Arab system without these problems being resolved, there will be serious repercussions on inter-Arab politics.

Although relations between Egypt and the U.S.S.R. and between Egypt and the U.S. can be characterized as unstable, there is a fundamental change in the direction of these relations. Egyptian cooperative interactions with the Soviets have deteriorated since 1972 and conflictive interactions are on the increase, while Egyptian cooperative interactions with the U.S. have been increasing, particularly since 1974, and conflictive interactions decreasing. This has been accompanied by Egypt's new economic and military dependence on the U.S. For example, imports from the U.S. in 1975 amounted to almost a billion dollars, a tenfold increase over 1952. The U.S. has also been perceived as the engineer of the peace process in the Middle East.

On the conflictive level, the year 1967 saw the most conflictive reciprocal interactions between Egypt and the U.S. Since 1974, however, the number of conflictive interactions has dropped dramatically. While this pattern was taking shape, the conflictive behavior pattern of relations between Egypt and the U.S.S.R. reached its peak in 1977, which also coincided with the peak of Egyptian-Arab conflictive interactions.

Egyptian-Israeli interactions have been conflictive for the most part. But they have taken a different direction since 1974, and particularly following the 1975 disengagement treaty. While conflictive interactions are decreasing, cooperative interactions are on the rise. Why is this the case?

As indicated in the first section of this paper, the diffusion of power in the Arab world is a fundamental challenge to Egyptian society. Egypt's moves toward Israel and the U.S. should be evaluated in light of this fact. It would appear that Egypt recognizes the diffusion of power and the change in the balance of power but is not willing to accept it. This fact, as well as the unwillingness of the newly emerging regional powers, particularly Saudi Arabia, to acknowledge Egypt's traditional role, have led Egypt to opt for a separate peace with Israel.

On the other hand, the dependence of the region on the West—and particularly the dependence of Egypt on the U.S.—for economic and military assistance has opened the way for non-regional solutions to its problems. At the same time, there have been fundamental changes in domestic attitudes toward this opening to the West, and these new conditions may also affect Egypt's role vis-à-vis Israel and the Arab states, not to mention the U.S.S.R.

Egypt's perception of viable external options has facilitated her decision to sever her political ties to the Arabs. Indeed, there has been a fundamental collapse of Arab interactions with Egypt, particularly on political, economic and military issues.

There are many sources of stress on the Arab system, the most serious of which are the Palestinian-Israeli conflict, exponential population growth, development needs and challenges, and nationalism versus pan-Arab or pan-Islamic identity. The way the system responds to these stresses is a function of relations between all its members as well as their relations with outside forces. Any unilateral option which disregards the concerns of regional partners will be devastating to the consensus-formation process. Because these relations are so intertwined and difficult to deal with in isolation, I will discuss two issues which demonstrate how the system has responded in the past and may be expected to respond in the future to these stresses: the conflict over identity and the failure of intrusive trilateralism in the Arab world.

V

The conflict over identity began, in my view, in the aftermath of Egypt's defeat in the 1967 war. The constituency for Arab nationalism lost confidence in the concept. Arab nationalism as an ideological force for political action in the Arab world had proven to be ineffective. At the same time, the emergence of Saudi wealth and Saudi will to share power and influence in the region offered a new challenge to Egypt's traditional role.

The waning of Arab nationalism as the basis for Arab identity, as well as the inability of Egypt to continue to champion the cause of Arab nationalism, encouraged the Saudis to cultivate a new identity orientation, that is to say, pan-Islamism.[7] From the Saudi point of view, pan-Islamism can provide the force of collectivity to meet the challenge of stresses in Arab politics. Through pan-Islamism, the Muslim masses can be mobilized to meet the Israeli challenge. The Saudis recognize that they do not have the solution to the conflict, but they can pressure the West to provide a solution. This view is based on two political realities. In the first place, their special friendship with the U.S. gives them the confidence to try the American option. Secondly, their past role in trying to eliminate Soviet influence in the area, e.g. in Egypt in 1972 and Somalia in 1977, gives them credibility in those Western circles that can be influential in resolving the Arab-Israeli conflict.

Furthermore, the challenge of underdevelopment in Arab and Muslim countries can be met by providing financial aid. These countries have only to accept the Saudi view of regional and international politics. The Saudis (as well as other oil-rich countries, particularly Libya and the Gulf states) opened their borders to poor Arab and Muslim workers. In this way the Saudis tried to prove that pan-Islamism is a fruitful identity orientation while Arab nationalism is not. It is their belief that the sense of national community in the Arab world does not and should not supersede the sense of belonging to the community of Islam.

This new identity has not worked out as expected, however. In fact, pan-Islamism has alienated some of the states in the region simply because it has not provided solutions to the problems facing the region. At the same time, different ethnic and religious minorities in the Arab world could not accept the dominance of one group over another, particularly in the political and economic areas. In fact, the emergence of "political Islamism," as sponsored by the Saudis, is one factor in the Lebanese civil war.

Furthermore, local identities and affiliations have already begun to flourish in the Arab world. This is true in North Africa, in Iraq, and particularly in Egypt. The search for group and national affiliation has become an important issue in Egyptian political and cultural life. After thirty years of "Arabism" and now "Islamism," cultural interactions between the Egyptians and the rest of the Arabs have decreased considerably. At the same time, discontent with the Saudi role, as well as the demoralizing effect of close contact with rich fellow Arabs, had already paved the way, socially even before politically, for "Egyptianism," "Egyptianness," or "Pharoaism."

Egypt's response to this discontent, i.e., her peace with Israel, went far beyond the expectations of most Middle East observers. It should be kept in mind, however, that this complete turnabout was in part a response to Arab and Saudi pressure.

Another important reason for the failure of pan-Islamism as a political force in the Arab world was the Iranian revolution. Just as Nasser's activism frightened the Saudis and other conservative Arabs, so did the Iranian revolution. Pan-Islamism was thought to be an instrument to be used in the inter-Arab power struggle, but it turned out to be an agitating force, a challenge to non-committed Muslim leaders to follow the path of Islam, to return to their origins and traditions and the glory of the past.

This new identity of "Islamism" not only generated inter-Arab cleavages, but it also introduced a new outside force. Iran entered the scene through Muslim activism and mere inspiration at first, and then, through its war with Iraq, it accelerated the process of dissension and disintegration among the Arab states. Pan-Islamism, which the Saudis had encouraged, was now making them vulnerable as well as widening the breach between the Arabs.

The failure of both pan-Arabism and pan-Islamism to integrate the Arab system is due to the failure of the advocates of both to link these two ideologies to the questions of democracy and development. The Arab nationalist movement produced oppressive practices during Nasser's era and afterwards. The concept of an "enlightened despot" was at best fallacious. Furthermore, neither pan-Arabism nor pan-Islamism have been able to meet the challenge of development, and both have resulted in severe dependency and intensified underdevelopment. In this sense, neither force has contributed to the process of integration. In fact, fragmentation has been one of the most salient features of the Arab world in recent years. The Gulf states are working for a Gulf system, Iraq is alone with Jordan, Syria with Libya, the North African states are looking to the North, not to the East, the PLO is shuttling between all these states while Egypt, as we shall see, is going ahead to create an alienated sub-system with Israel and the U.S.

VI

As previously indicated Egyptian-Israeli cooperative interactions have increased dramatically, particularly since 1976, while the number of conflictive interactions has dropped just as dramatically. Egyptian interactions with the U.S. have also been increasing, which suggests that a new sub-system is developing between Egypt and Israel under U.S. auspices.

Egypt and Israel are both developing a narcissistic character in dealing with each other and with the U.S. Furthermore, the sub-system which is being established between them is alienated from other regional actors as well as from the popular masses in both countries.

It should also be pointed out here that this sub-system is built on the idea of the dominance of the exchange system. According to Boulding's formulation, there are three types of systems, i.e., the threat system, the exchange system, and the integrative system.[8] The threat system between Egypt and Israel has been manipulated since the onset of the peace process, while the integrative system will not be viable between these two countries until their grievances and cultural differences and, more importantly, the Palestinian issue have been resolved. The only remaining area of cooperation is that of exchange. However, even in this area the prospects are very limited because both economies are dependent and small in size. The U.S., another outside force, is the only one that can pressure both countries, through intensive aid and economic and military cooperation, to coordinate their policies.

The ability of the U.S. to perform this role is limited not only by its willingness to create a new trilateralism, which is a risky undertaking in the Arab world, but also by Egyptian and Israeli willingness to accept the U.S. role. By and large, prospects for the success of this new trilateralism are very limited, because it does not address the stresses which face Egypt and Israel in the Arab environment.

VII

When utilized within a valid theoretical framework, the international interactions approach is a reliable device for describing, analyzing and predicting the processes of disintegration. By evaluating the intensity of interaction among the parts of a system and the trends of interaction between its members and the outside forces, it will be possible, as has been shown in this paper, to observe the ongoing disintegration processes.

Arab nationalism, as it is presently discussed by intellectual circles in the Arab world, is not as progressive and secular a force as that advocated by Syrian and Lebanese intellectuals during the 1920's and 1950's. On the contrary, it is a force used to serve local political interests and exaggerated self-perceptions, particularly on the part of the Egyptians. Such ethnic arrogance does not serve as an integrative force, but works in the direction of narrow ethnic concerns. Meanwhile, pan-Islamism has also shown its weakness as a unifying force.

Both Arab nationalists and pan-Islamists derive their legitimacy from the past and not from the future or from a continuum of past, present and future. This exaggerated identification, when confronted with its failure to produce any concrete achievements, generates alienation not only internally but also externally, i.e., from non-Arab and non-Islamic sources of knowledge and progress.[9]

Finally, the deterioration in all aspects of Egyptian-Arab interactions, the conflict over identity, and the new cooperative interactions between Egypt and Israel are all signs of disintegration in the Arab system, a process which may continue its destructive activity for many years to come. It will be difficult to heal the rifts in the Arab world in the near future, for they concern issues of security, development, identity and consensus, issues which the system has thus far proven incapable of managing.

Notes

1. Fouad Ajami, "The End of Pan-Arabism," *Foreign Affairs*, Winter 1978–79, pp. 355–372.

2. Walid Khalidi, "Thinking the Unthinkable: A Sovereign Palestinian State," *Foreign Affairs*, July 1978, pp. 695–714.

3. Mohamed Heikal, "Egyptian Foreign Policy," *Foreign Affairs*, July 1978, pp. 714–739.

4. Edward Azar, *The Codebook of the Conflict and Peace Data Bank* (COPDAB), 1980. For more information concerning the data set, its history, development and uses, write to Professor Edward Azar, Department of Political Science, University of North Carolina, Chapel Hill, North Carolina 27514. See also

Edward Azar, "Saudi Arabia's International Behavior: A Quantitative Analysis" (Paper delivered at the Symposium on State, Economy and Power in Saudi Arabia, University of Exeter, July 4–7, 1980).

5. Edward Azar, Ronald McLaurin and Paul Jureidini, "Protracted Conflict in the Middle East," *Journal of Palestine Studies*, Autumn 1978, pp. 41–60.

6. For this era, see Malcolm H. Kerr, *The Arab Cold War 1958–1964* (London: Oxford University Press, 1965).

7. The term "pan-Islamism" as it is used here refers to the utilization of Islam as a political force to achieve political ends. It does not refer to Islam as a religion, ideology and way of life which the devout may advocate.

8. Kenneth E. Boulding, *Conflict and Defense: A General Theory* (New York: Harper, 1963).

9. See Abdallah Laroui, *The Crisis of Arab Intellectuals* (Berkeley: University of California Press, 1976).

10

The October War and Arab Students' Self Conceptions

Paul D. Starr

The Arab-Israeli conflict of October 1973 had a great impact on the lives of millions. It brought about significant changes in world economic and political relationships and produced important repercussions in the internal affairs of the countries involved. The study presented here considers the consequences of the war at another level, the social psychological, and the effect it had upon a group of young Arabs in Lebanon and their perceptions of themselves.[1]

In Beirut, the outbreak of fighting on October 6 was viewed initially as just another in a series of sharp exchanges of fire across the lines. When it soon became evident that the armies of Egypt and Syria were engaged in full scale offensives on the Golan and Sinai fronts, the popular reaction in Beirut was one of complete surprise. Few had paid much attention to the recurrent pronouncements from Damascus and Cairo that the Israeli occupation could no longer go unchallenged and all could remember the crushing defeat of the Arabs in 1967. There was also initial rejection or skepticism regarding broadcasts from Cairo and Damascus reporting battlefield successes. As these stations had broadcast erroneous and propagandistic reports during the 1967 war, their accounts were given almost no credence until they were corroborated by the BBC and other foreign news sources, including Radio Israel, several hours after the initial attack (Rais and Nahas 1973; Hatim 1974; Rugh 1975). When it was clear that the Egyptian Army had indeed crossed the Suez Canal and that their antiaircraft systems had initially inflicted serious losses upon the Israelis, caution and surprise gave way

---

Reprinted with permission from *Middle East Journal* 32, 4 (Autumn 1978). Copyright 1984 by *Middle East Journal*.

to expressions of optimism among many and elation among others, most visibly adolescents and young adults.

Although Lebanon was not a combatant in the war, small scale fighting between Palestinian guerillas and Israeli forces was reported along the southern border area; fighting in the Mount Hermon region could be heard from several miles away, and Syrian and Israeli aircraft occasionally flew overhead. As in past Arab-Israeli conflicts, a security detail was assigned to prevent the molestation of Jews in Beirut's Jewish quarter, which at the time numbered about 4,000 persons.[2] During most of the first week the airport was closed, schools did not open, most businesses or offices were shut down or maintained by token staffs, car and bus traffic was reduced, and fewer people could be seen on the streets. These activities had almost returned to normal during daylight hours three weeks after the war began but, even though interest in political and military developments lessened somewhat, it continued to be intense. Most newspapers were sold out by midmorning, and small groups gathered around radios in coffee houses, neighborhood markets and barbershops to discuss the news and exchange gossip and rumors. Air raid sirens occasionally rang out but were virtually unheeded.

A day after the fighting started, student groups from Beirut's universities and secondary schools, many of them components of Lebanese political parties or Palestinian political organizations, collected funds for medical and relief supplies, donated blood and assisted with the evacuation and care of wounded from Syria. Volunteer medical teams were also organized and dispatched to the Syrian cities of Damascus and Homs.

Even though no classes were held, many students went to their universities to be with their friends and teachers and discuss ongoing events. In several encounters during the first few days of fighting, it was apparent that the war had a great emotional impact on many of the students and others with whom I spoke. The words of a Palestinian graduate student reflect a sentiment expressed by several during that time. While looking at part of an Israeli plane which had been downed by the Syrians and placed on display in Beirut, he said in a wavering voice, "You know, I used to believe everything that he (Moshe Dayan) said. I used to think we were no good; couldn't fight or anything. Now I'll never believe him . . . them . . . again. This is fantastic."

With sonic booms and low flying aircraft providing occasional disruptions, such conversations were quite different from the mundane and routine exchanges which occurred before the fighting. They had a greater emotional intensity and often dealt with topics of a more abstract nature. These conversations seldom emphasized individual problems or topics unique to the local situation and centered about the students' concern for friends and relatives in Syria, Jordan and southern Lebanon; conflicting news reports and rumors; the strategic positions of America and various Arab states, and, in some instances, questions of an existential or religious nature. For many of these young people the initial Arab success was a peak emotional experience.

Propagandistic accounts and rumors of Israeli soldiers refusing to fight and of pilots and tank crews being chained to their vehicles also circulated, and some Damascus and Beirut newspapers carried front page photos of charred Israeli bodies and equipment. After repeating the rumors that he had heard about, an Arab Christian from the Israeli-occupied West Bank of Jordan concluded, "It means that young people in Israel don't want to fight. They don't want war. They're like us. War is stupid . . . for nothing."

A few of the students with Palestinian backgrounds and Lebanese citizenship asserted their prior identity and emphasized at the time that they were "really Palestinian." There were also indications that during the first few days of the war some conventional barriers to communication had been suspended. For example, in several public places people of divergent backgrounds and statuses, many of whom had apparently never met before, openly shared newspapers and discussed events among themselves in a spontaneous and informal manner.

The war also affected the behavior patterns of Arabs living under Israeli occupation. The number of Arabs from occupied areas commuting to work in Israel, an estimated 85,000 persons, was reported to have fallen drastically, and by mid-December only about 25 per cent had returned. Although this was partially due to increased Israeli security measures, it was also the result of a loosely organized boycott. On the occupied West Bank, Arab schools were closed as a gesture of solidarity, resistance slogans were painted on walls, a number of demonstrations took place and petrol bomb attacks were reported (Graham 1973; Mortimer 1974).

While the passage of time, the subsequent reports of Israeli counter-attacks and the ceasefire dampened enthusiasm and discouraged those who thought that the Arabs would eventually succeed in a prolonged war of attrition, there were indications that the conflict may have produced a basic change in the attitudes of many Arabs, particularly among the young, regarding themselves and their "people."

By any measure, the Arabs' reactions in 1973 were quite different from those which followed the 1967 war. Within a few weeks after that conflict, there were massive, sometimes hysterical, demonstrations in many Arab cities and extensive political maneuvering by those in power to maintain control. In addition, several thousand people, Christians of various sects as well as Muslims, reportedly saw apparitions of the

Holy Virgin at the Coptic Orthodox Church in suburban Cairo and also above the dome of the Syrian Orthodox Cathedral in Beirut. Rumors were passed among Maronite Christians that the large hill-top statue of the "Holy Virgin of the Lebanon" at the village of Harissa had miraculously turned itself slightly at the time of the Arab defeat (Meindarus 1971). Similar reports of the intervention of the Holy Virgin in national crisis situations in the eastern Mediterranean have been traced back farther than the sixth century.

Phenomena such as these were not observed after the 1973 war, apparently because the Arabs were not shocked by a great defeat and did not have to cope with the immediate and, for some, intense frustration or sorrow over losing control of religious shrines in East Jerusalem. In contrast to their feelings of defeat in 1967, in 1973 the Arabs perceived their part in the conflict as relatively, if not clearly, successful. If Arabs are viewed as a group or "nation" which shares a common culture and heritage, regardless of specific political boundaries, we would anticipate, based on these observations and other similar accounts of their reactions, that a significant upsurge of national feeling, unity and pride could have resulted from the 1973 experience. As Durkheim (1951:352) noted in his classic study of suicide, greater cohesion may be brought about when a society is perceived to be confronted by a serious common external threat, such as warfare with another nation.

In contrast to the 1967 debacle, the much improved performance of their armies in 1973 seemed to give many Arabs a significant psychological boost. As indicated in the words of several editorialists, both in the Middle East and abroad, they no longer appeared destined for defeat and had demonstrated to themselves, the Israelis and others that they could perform with discipline in combat with what many, including a large proportion of Arabs, believed to be the invincible forces of the Israelis. This view was well expressed by Salāḥ al-dīn al-Biṭār, a former Syrian Prime Minister.

> The most prominent result of the war was the psychological victory attained by the Arabs. Prior to the war, the Arab sense of dishonor, shame and loss of self respect was overwhelming. The world seemed to be looking askance at the Arabs and a feeling of national humiliation prevailed.
>
> In this atmosphere the inveterate pessimists and defeatists within the Arab world were only too ready to reproach the Arabs' cowardice and submissiveness. It became common club and drawing room talk to say that the Arabs were only good at rhetoric, that the Arab soldier was incapable of fighting and coping with advanced weapons, that he fled the battlefield. . . .
>
> Then came the surprise, and along with it, the psychological shock. The Arab soldier fought and fought well; they distinguished themselves

in attack and defence and were able to cope with advanced weapons. ... The Arabs recovered their self confidence and their honour, wiped out the blow to their self respect and the disgrace that had befallen them in the June War (1974:36).

It was the growing Arab bitterness and intensification of their desire to restore the honor lost in 1967, according to the noted Israeli editorialist Zeev Schiff, that eventually overcame the "fear barrier," the Arabs' anxiety over another defeat, and to test successfully their own self esteem (1974; 74–77).

It is clear from the immediate popular reaction to the fighting in Beirut, Cairo and Damascus that the performance of the Arab forces was followed with enthusiasm and that the war may have had some impact on the Arabs' image as soldiers in particular and, to some extent, as a people in general. On the other hand, the psychological effects of the conflict may have been exaggerated. Living in a highly unstable political climate over several decades, many Arabs have become quite accustomed to coping with dramatic political changes. Although Lebanon was only peripherally involved in the war, this country provides a case in point. In the several years preceeding the war, Israeli hit and run attacks, conflicts between the Lebanese Army and Palestinian guerillas, and internal political disturbances had come to be taken in stride by many Lebanese residents. Whenever possible, they typically responded to such events by physically or mentally isolating themselves from the situation. Until the civil war of 1975–77 made such strategies more difficult to follow, most Lebanese commonly withdrew from their ordinary routines, stayed indoors or visited their home villages and returned to their everyday affairs as the circumstances improved, only temporarily inconvenienced by what had happened.

If the war did have some psychological effect on the Arabs, one might also expect its impact to vary with the individual's degree of involvement. Patriotic Egyptians, Syrians and Palestinians, as members of groups intensely involved in the fighting, would be expected to be more influenced by the war than those from non-combatant or less involved nations, such as Lebanon, Jordan, Kuwayt, Saudi Arabia and the Arab Amirates. Pan-Arabist sentiments, however, which are found to some extent in all of the non-combatant states, may have served to equalize such an influence.

What then were the consequences, if any, of the October War with respect to the ways in which the Arabs viewed themselves? Did the war, as some observers contend, significantly change Arab self perceptions or had such accounts exaggerated the impact of what was an intense but passing response to immediate events which left little lasting impact?

This study provides information about these questions by examining the impact of the war upon a select group of Arab youth, Arab students at the American University of Beirut, and the ways in which it affected their attitudes or images that they hold of themselves.

Self Conceptions: Some Theoretical Considerations

Through various processes, including interaction with significant others and communication with different social groups, individuals come to acquire attitudes about the nature of the world and of themselves as objects in it. Although there has been much emphasis upon socialization during childhood, the process is more appropriately seen as a continuing one in which a person undergoes certain changes, either gradually or in a more drastic way, as roles, group memberships and social environments change. Much conduct is influenced through those persons, groups or beliefs which the individual takes as his model or source of reference. The study of the development and change of identifications, as reviewed by Epstein (1973), has an extensive literature, much of which has been derived from the symbolic interactionist perspective reflected in works by Shibutani (1961) and Blumer (1969) and collections by Gordon and Gergen (1968) and Manis and Meltzer (1978).

Viewing the individual as an object within a dynamic environment, a person's self conception or identity is seen as developing through time in interaction with others coping with changing situations. Although hypothetically a person could have a wide variety of identities, the range is limited to the possibilities which exist within the world known to the individual and by his particular location within it. Some identities are more important to the individual and to his society than others and may require significantly more exposure and commitment. Other identities may be situationally based and may only become salient in particular contexts.

The categories and attributes which are used by a person to describe or indicate his self are commonly evaluative in nature and may refer to positive and negative characteristics. The self may also be defined in terms of the person's attitudes, either positive or negative, toward other individuals, groups, objects or ideas.

The "Who am I?" Method

Viewing the self in such a comprehensive and dynamic manner, there is a strong case for operationalizing the concept through a highly unstructured method which would allow a person spontaneously to express himself. Of the various ways in which social scientists have explored the self, through personality inventories, adjective checklists, depth interviews and projective tests, one method permits the respondent to express his beliefs about himself in any framework he feels appropriate, in terms of attitudes, group memberships, categories or adjectives.

The "Who am I?" method, also called the Twenty Statements Test in a longer version, has been employed effectively by several researchers in different cultural contexts, and is particularly well suited to cross cultural research. It consists simply of a sheet of paper on which the respondent is asked to give answers to the question "Who am I?" in a few minutes time.[3]

The specific directions for the form used in the present study were as follows:

WHO AM I?

Directions:
There are fifteen numbered blanks on the page below. Please write fifteen different answers to the simple questions "Who Am I? in the blanks, answering as if you were giving the answers to yourself, not to somebody else. Write the answers in the order that they occur to you. Don't worry about "logic" or "importance." Please do not take more than six or seven minutes for this part. Do not change or rewrite your answers once you have put them down.

The method usually elicits a wide variety of responses, some rather mundane and others which seem to reveal important inner thoughts of the respondent, as exemplified in the following answers (presented with the original capitalizations) obtained in April 1973.

A rather typical set of answers, which is very similar in form to responses commonly made by American undergraduates, are those of a 19-year-old biology student from Damascus.

I am:
1. a girl
2. a student
3. a member of my family
4. an Arab
5. a Muslim
6. a Syrian
7. intelligent
8. courteous
9. kind toward others
10. idealistic
11. nervous

    12. Single
    13. a science student
    14. sensitive
    15. (no response)

Some replied with answers related to political and social concerns, such as those which follow, which were written by an 18-year-old male Palestinian agricultural student.

I am:
    1. A PALESTINIAN
    2. able to see sufferings around me
    3. able to feel what others feel
    4. going to help those who suffer
    5. going to work very hard
    6. a poor person
    7. a revolutionary person
    8. a member of a political party
    9. living in Beirut
    10. for the Arab Nation
    11. a believer in human justice
    12. a student
    13. not a religious person
    14. tall
    15. tired

Also interesting were the responses of a 20-year-old male student of literature who did not specify his nationality on the back of the answer sheet, as requested, but wrote "ARAB" in large block letters.

I am:
    1. a man
    2. a student
    3. healthy
    4. a concerned being
    5. a believer
    6. a Searcher
    7. a curious human
    8. with a purpose
    9. a builder for my country
    10. one with responsibilities to develop my society
    11. a modern man but
    12. with traditional bounds
    13. belonging to a passing way of life

    14. learning to be myself
    15. a Lebanese

As can be seen, the data provided by the method are diffuse, highly unstructured and present a challenge to the researcher attempting to provide some interpretation of them.

Data Collection

The responses made, which have been briefly discussed previously (Starr 1975), were not originally collected for research purposes. The "Who am I?" form was administered as an instructional aid in courses given by the researcher in 1973 and 1974. The students were asked to complete the form and to indicate afterwards on the back of the sheet their age, sex, nationality, religion, language used at home and major field of study. The data were collected in late April 1973, October 23, 1973, 18 days after the war began, and on May 29, 1974, three days before the Syrian-Israeli disengagement agreement.

The responses of the second group impressionistically appeared more often to be politically oriented and related to the war than were those of the first group, as indicated in the answers of a 20-year-old Lebanese male economics student.

I am:
    1. for justice and peace
    2. against Israel's aggression
    3. with the Arab cause
    4. for my country
    5. a political person
    6. member of a group
    7. one who will persist
    8. honest
    9. kind
    10. for the people
    11. a student
    12. a nationalist
    13. fair to all
    14. a Christian
    15. (no response)

All three of the groups were very similar with regard to age, sex, religion, nationality and academic major.

The mean age of respondents was 19.4, SD = .96, and the mean number of responses was 12.3 with SD = 2.33. Only students from

Arab countries, 16 per cent of whom were ethnic Armenians with Syrian or Lebanese citizenship, were included in the study. The total group of respondents was composed of 66 per cent Lebanese, 14 per cent Palestinian, eight per cent Syrian, three per cent Egyptian and the remaining nine per cent from Jordan, Kuwayt, Saudi Arabia and other Arab states.[4] Males composed 69 per cent of the respondents and females 31 per cent.

Hypothesis

Although the psychological impact of warfare upon civilian society is frequently assumed to be ultimately disintegrative (Powell 1970), it is important to differentiate between the initial and longer term phases of such an experience. Based on informal interviews, observations and the accounts of observers in different parts of the Arab world, several hypotheses regarding the initial psychological effect of the war upon Arabs were inductively formulated.

If the war had a significant effect upon the self conceptions of Arab students, it was hypothesized that the change would produce:

1. more positive self descriptions;
2. less negative self descriptions;
3. increased identifications by individuals as "Arabs";
4. increased identification with one's respective nation state;
5. more descriptions of one's self in political terms, such as political affiliations, ideologies or attitudes;
6. greater reference to one's self in existential or religious terms, including statements regarding the purpose of life, assertions of religious belief or affiliation;
7. heightened perceptions of one's self in relation to one's antagonists;
8. more descriptions of one's self with reference to military activity, war or peace.

Coding

After reviewing the different methods used by other researchers to code such data, an eight category coding scheme was devised which would allow each of the hypotheses to be examined.

1. Positive Self Statement: included those who described themselves in positive terms, such as "intelligent, clever, attractive, considerate to others, hard-working, honest," etc.

2. Negative Self Statement: included self descriptions of a negative sort, such as "stupid, unkind, greedy, unattractive" etc.

3. Arab Identity: simply referred to those who identified themselves as "Arab, Arabic person" or "member of Arab society."

4. National Identification: included those who described themselves in terms of their nationality or citizenship, such as "Lebanese, Palestinian, Syrian, Egyptian" and others.

5. Political Being: categorized those who referred to themselves in terms of political affiliations, ideologies or concerns, such as "political man, anti–communist, socialist, member of political group, against tyranny, concerned with the state of my nation," etc.

6. Religious/Existential Being: referred to statements concerned with the meaning of life and religious attitudes and affiliations, such as "Christian, Sunni, Druze, a child in God's universe, wanting to know the meaning of life, an unbeliever" and others.

7. Anti-Israeli/Zionist/US Statement: included those statements in which the individual described himself as being against Israel, Zionism or Israel's chief ally, the United States. This category included such statements as "against Zionists, anti-Israeli, against US imperialism, a defender of actions against Israel," etc.

8. War/Peace Statement: referred to those who described themselves in relation to military operations, war or peace such as "one who is for peace, wishing for peace in my country, likes military equipment and guns, one who wants to defend my country, a future fighter pilot," and others.

Each respondent who made one or more statements which could be placed in one of these categories was counted once for each category, showing that our concern was with the number of individuals who described themselves in such ways rather than with the total number of responses each individual or group made. The total scores refer to the number of respondents who made statements which could be placed within each category. Each statement was coded only once, with the exception of a few compound designations, which were included in two categories, such as "I am an anti-communist Lebanese," which was coded as a political statement as well as a national identification. Two coders, working separately and unaware to which group each respondent belonged, coded all of the responses, achieving an intercoder reliability coefficient of more than .8.

Results

Two types of comparisons were made with the data. The first examined responses made by the students at the three different points in time. The second compared the responses of members of national groups which were most actively involved in the war, Syrians, Egyptians and

TABLE 10.1
Self Designations of Arab Students in Percents:
April 1973, October 1973, May 1974

				Differences		
	A—April'73	B—October'73	C—May'74	A–B	B–C	A–C
1. Positive self statement	45.2	55.2	46.	10.*	9.2*	.8
2. Negative self statement	20.2	19.	27.6	1.2	8.6*	7.4
3. Arab	24.2	28.2	14.9	4.0	13.3	9.3
4. National identification	50.	50.3	33.3	.3	17.*	16.7*
5. Political being	25.	37.4	32.3	12.4*	5.2	7.2
6. Religious/existential being	25.8	42.9	20.8	17.1*	22.1*	5.
7. Anti-Israel/Zionism/USA	4.	10.4	3.4	6.4*	7.*	.6
8. War/peace statement	1.6	8.6	0.	7.0*	8.6*	1.6
	N=124	N=163	N=87			

*Differences are statistically significant, see note 5.

Palestinians, in relation to those from less involved or non-combatant national groups, Lebanese, Jordanians, Saudi Arabians, Kuwaytis and other Arabs, at the three different points in time.

Statistical measures (Z-tests) were applied to determine if the differences indicated were beyond that normally expected by chance.[5]

As shown in Table 10.1, the data indicate that the immediate effect of the war was to bring about a significant increase in the proportion of those who expressed positive statements about themselves, those who saw themselves in political terms, religious or existential terms, as holding a negative attitude toward Zionism, Israel or the United States, and those who viewed themselves in relation to war or peace. Although not statistically significant, a greater proportion of the respondents also described themselves as Arabs and as belonging to a specific nation. There was also a slight decrease in the proportion of those who described themselves in negative terms. Of most interest is the fact that all the differences between pre-war and war-time designations are in the directions predicted.

Seven months later, however, the pattern of responses was much closer to those expressed at the first point in time. Seven months after the start of the war only one measure was significantly different from those elicited before the conflict. It shows a decrease in the proportion of respondents who identified themselves with regard to their nationality.

These data suggest that the self concepts of the Arab students participating in the study were affected by the war and were positively influenced by it. The effects of the conflict appear, however, to have been short lived and were substantially reduced with the passage of time. It may be that the psychological "rewards" derived from serious conflicts in the Middle East and other areas have been similarly exaggerated, are linked with immediate events, and are also rather short lived.

Unexpectedly, there was no pattern of a significant difference between respondents from combatant nations in comparison with those from noncombatant nations. Respondents affiliated with a combatant national group were apparently no less nor no more affected by the conflict than were those from nations that were less involved in the fighting. This indicates that the sentiments expressed seem little influenced by a respondent's association with a nation state.

The data do not provide support for the view that the Arabs experienced a substantial lasting change in self conceptions as a result of the war, or that the conflict affected the self images of those of combatant national groups more than it did respondents from countries indirectly involved.

Many appreciate the link between larger political events and the attitudes of those involved regarding themselves and others, but such dynamics are poorly understood and have been seldom systematically studied during actual political conflicts. The study provided here vividly reflects some of the intense feelings which have characterized the Arab-Israeli conflict and shows how they are influenced by ongoing events. Although such hostilities have a considerable history and are regarded by some as having their own pathological momentum, this study indicates that many of those involved do experience significant changes in their attitudes regarding themselves and others. It remains possible that dynamic alterations in self images and related attitudes may also occur in ways which reduce hostility toward members of other groups. In spite of the continuing violence in the Levant, it remains important to appreciate how people in several other contexts have been able, on a reciprocal basis, to overcome rapidly their traditions of mutual animosity. Although there is reason for pessimism, we should acknowledge the possibility that mutual beneficial redefinitions of oneself and others are possible even among the several "intransigent" groups involved in the Arab-Israeli conflict.

Notes

1. There is substantially more information available about the effects of the Arab-Israeli conflict upon Israelis than there is about Arab reactions. These include psychological analyses by Winnik, Moses and Ostrow (1973) and Moses and associates (1976), studies by other scholars (i.e. Davis, 1974) and contributions by journalists. The richest single source of data concerning reactions to the October War by Israelis and Jews in other countries is available from the Contemporary Jewry Oral History Collection at Hebrew University. The section of the collection dealing with the war is comprised of accounts by 69 persons of their immediate reactions to the conflict.

2. A sensitive portrayal of the reactions of Moroccan Arabs and Jews to the 1967 war and a description of the effect it had on their relationships has been

provided by Rosen (1968). The protective attitude on the part of some Moroccan Arabs toward Jewish families under such circumstances which is described by Rosen has also been observed in Lebanon.

3. Kuhn and McPartland (1954) obtained a coefficient of reproductability in their studies of over .90, based on 151 respondents, and a test-retest reliability of approximately +.85. Spitzer and Parker (1976) have also recently shown that, in comparison with three other instruments devised to study self concepts (Semantic Differentiation Scales, the Index of Adjustment and Values, and the Adjectives Checklist), respondents themselves regarded the Twenty Statements Test as the most genuine and accurate method of assessment.

4. Persons who stated their nationality as "Palestinian/Jordanian" or "Lebanese/Palestinian" were categorized as Palestinian. Those who listed their nationality as Jordanian only were categorized as such.

5. As it was predicted that the war would tend to increase the proportions of those who described themselves using positive terms, as Arabs, as members of national groups, as political beings, in religious or existential terms, in relationships hostile to Israel or her ally and in terms related to war or peace, while the proportion of those who described themselves in negative terms would decrease, one-tailed tests of statistical significance were employed in considering the differences in responses made before and during the war. Two-tailed tests of significance were applied to determine if there were significant changes in either direction with respect to self descriptions made during the war in comparison with those made seven months later. A Z of 1.65 or more is considered statistically significant ($p < .05$) for a one-tailed test and 1.96 or more for a two-tailed test.

References Cited

al-Bitar, S. 1974. "The implications of the October war for the Arab world." *Journal of Palestine Studies* 3:34–45.

Blumer, H. 1969. *Symbolic Interactionism.* Englewood Cliffs, N.J.: Prentice-Hall.

Davis, M. (ed.). 1974. *The Yom Kippur War: Israel and the Jewish People.* New York: Arno Press.

Durkheim, E. 1951. *Suicide.* (G. Simpson, ed.) Glencoe, Ill.: The Free Press.

Epstein, S. 1973. "The self-concept revisited." *American Psychologist:* 404–416.

Gordon, C., and K. J. Gergen (eds.). 1968. *The Self in Social Interaction,* vol. 1. New York: Wiley & Sons.

Graham, R. 1973. "A new mood of defiance." *The Financial Times* (London), Dec. 12, 1973.

Hatim, M. 1974. *Information and the Arab Cause.* London: Longmans.

Kuhn, M., and T. McPartland. 1954. "An empirical investigation of self-attitudes." *American Sociological Review* 19:68–79.

Manis, J. G., and B. N. Meltzer (eds.). 1978. *Symbolic Interaction: A Reader in Social Psychology* (Third Edition). Boston: Allyn and Bacon.

Meinardus. O.F.A. 1971. "A critical examination of collective hallucinations after the six days' war in the Middle East." *Ethnomedizin* 1, 2:191–208.

Mortimer, E. 1974. "Why the Arabs rallied to the cause of Palestine." *The Times* (London), Jan. 29, 1974.

Moses, R., and others. 1976. "A rear unit for the treatment of combat reactions in the wake of the Yom Kippur War." *Psychiatry* 39:153–162.

Powell, E. H. 1970. *The Design of Discord: Studies of Anomie.* New York: Oxford University Press.

Rais, R., and D. Nahas. 1973. *The October War.* Beirut: al-Nahar.

Rosen, L. 1968. "A Moroccan Jewish community during the Middle Eastern crisis." *The American Scholar* 37:435–451.

Rugh, W. A. 1975. "Arab media and politics during the October war." *The Middle East Journal* 29:310–328.

Schiff, Z. 1974. *October Earthquake: Yom Kippur 1973.* Tel Aviv: University Publishing Projects, Ltd.

Shibutani, T. 1961. *Society and Personality.* Englewood Cliffs, N.J.: Prentice-Hall.

Spitzer, S. P., and J. Parker. 1976. "Perceived validity and assessment of the self: a decade later." *The Sociological Quarterly* 17:236–246.

Starr, P. D. 1975. "How the Arabs see themselves after the war." *New Society* 31:186–7 (Jan. 23, 1975).

Winnik, H. Z., R. Moses and M. Ostrow (eds.). 1973. *Psychological Bases of War.* Jerusalem: Quadrangle Books and Jerusalem Academic Press.

Postscript

The World Beyond the Words

Fouad Ajami

The "word" is not well; it is hard to write. This is the verdict issued by two of the greatest contemporary Arab poets, Nizar Qabbani and Adonis. For a quarter-century now both men, both Syrian-born but living in Beirut, Qabbani (b. 1923) and Adonis (b. 1930) have enriched Arab letters with some of the most engaging poetry. Qabbani, the "lighter" of the two, with a relatively large audience, has been the romantic poet par excellence. His free verse broke with the stilted classical strictures of Arabic poetry and made poetry more accessible and less forbidding. Adonis has done this, and a little more. He has also been a great literary critic, and an essayist with brilliant ventures into the history of Arab thought and ideas, into the relationship between Arab politics and the literary metaphor. Both men have been able to express what was on the minds of others, to dig into psychological and emotional depths that eluded the Arab intelligentsia and analysts. Both have been pioneers of a generation trying to find its own voice, to speak in ways true and authentic to itself, to shake off the hold and the style of the past.

Now both tell us that something out there in the Arab reality eludes them, that there is a disquieting lack of fit between the words men utter and speak and the daily realities that men and women in the Arab world confront. I shall begin with Qabbani, for he provides a point of entry that explains some of the bewilderment and, at times, the stunned silence with which modern-day Arabs have been looking at their own society and its breakdown.

"I can't write," says Qabbani in a mid-1985 interview he gave to a Kuwaiti daily; "I don't write for I can't say something that equals the sorrow of this Arab nation; I can't open any of the countless dungeons in this large prison. The poet is made of blood and flesh; we can't make him speak when he loses his appetite for words, we can't ask him to entertain and enthrall when there is nothing in the Arab world that entertains or enthralls. When we were secondary-school children our history teacher used to call the Ottoman empire 'the sick man.' What is the history teacher to call these mini-empires of the Arab world being devoured by disease? What are we to call these mini-empires with broken doors and shattered windows and blown-away roofs? What can the writer say and write in this large Arab hospital?"

"I am not alone," says Qabbani, "living this existence that approximates being a form of house arrest. All others in the Arab world are under house arrest, in one way or another. People may go to restaurants, the movies or the beach; they may watch their video-machines; they may even go to Paris and London and Geneva and New York; but they are not free, because they carry their imprisonment and their exile within them. The moment they read an Arabic newspaper in Europe, they are again imprisoned." Poetry, he says, takes courage and celebrates the human soul. But in the Arab world today it is a time of political and intellectual drought.

Qabbani borrows the term of *jahiliyya* (pre-Islamic ignorance) to describe the Arab reality of today. Even that sordid time, he says, had a function for the poet: the poet was his tribe's "lawyer" and chronicler and singer. The new *jahiliyya* of today is darker than the old; it has annulled the role of the poet, because it wants men on their knees and it wants them to crawl. The "sultans of today" want loyalty and sycophants. They have emasculated the word. The "modern-day sultans" fear the word. This is because poetry and the word are "intrinsically" instruments of opposition. The enmity between the word and *al sulta* (authority) is inevitable: it is a classical enmity. Give me "a great country" and a great culture, he writes, and you will have great and enduring works of art. "Poetry is the child of history," he says; and in today's Arab world—a "large supermarket in which everything is for sale"— it is hard for the word to retain its purity, its power, and its truth.

Arab men and women everywhere are "false witnesses" to their own ordeal. They are not consulted in matters of war and peace; denied an elementary measure of freedom, they are left to suffer and stagnate. Qabbani, who lost his wife in one of Beirut's daily episodes of violence— a bombing of the Iraqi embassy in 1981—is asked about the city that had nurtured him and had been home for him. It is an "orphaned city," with broken wings, and why does he stay there? Beirut, he says, is a "ball of fire" that has "burned my hands but I still hold onto it," just like the child who puts in the palm of his hand "poisonous insects, who holds onto a scorpion without being afraid of being stung." The Beirut of the 1950s and 1960s—the city of his youth and poetry and escapades—is a "thing of the past," he concedes. You can't bring it back to life, as you can't bring back the old glories of Rome and of Athens. "History is a river that never flows backward; every city has its golden era, just like every woman has a period of youth and of enchantment. Just like youth slips away . . . we must have the courage to admit that the war in Lebanon has over-turned the old Lebanon. Some of us may dream of young Beirut, the playful city which enthralled millions of men, but we have to be realistic and think of the city before us. Nothing remains of old Beirut except the scent of it that blows from old notebooks. . . ."

The lament of the poet—the feeling that words are futile—had been foreshadowed in *Balqees* (his wife's name), a long poem written in grief after his wife's death in 1981:

Balqees, don't be absent from me,
After you, the sun doesn't shine on the shore.
I will say in my inquiry that the thief has come to wear a
    fighter's clothes,
I will say in my inquiry that the gifted leader is now an agent,
I will say that the tale of enlightenment is the most ludicrous
    joke ever told.
And that we are a tribe among tribes.
This is history . . . oh Balqees.
How do people distinguish between gardens and dunghills?

. . . . . .

Balqees, oh my beloved until the end,
The false prophets squat, they ride on the people, but there is no
    mission.
If they had brought us a star or an orange from sad Palestine,
If they had brought us from the coast of Gaza
A small stone . . . or an oyster,
If they had liberated an olive tree in the past quarter-century
Or brought back a lemon tree
And erased from history its shame,
Then I would thank those who killed you Balqees,
O darling until the end,
But they abandoned Palestine . . . in order to slaughter a gazelle.

What does poetry say in this era, Balqees?
What does poetry say in the cowardly era . . . ?
The Arab wold is crushed, repressed, its tongue cut . . .
We are crime personified. . . .

Balqees . . .
I beg your forgiveness.
Perhaps your life was the ransom of my own.
Indeed I know well
That the purpose of those who were entangled in murder was to
    kill my words!

Rest in God's care, oh beautiful one,
Poetry, after you, is impossible. . . .[1]

In Adonis's diagnosis, contained in a book of literary criticism *Al Shi'riyya Al-Arabiyya* (Arabic Poetics) (Beirut, 1985) we go beyond the grief of Qabbani. For here we have a sustained analysis that grapples with what Adonis calls the "dual siege" of the Arab writer, caught as he is today between Western thought on the one hand and the hold of the Islamic traditional past on the other. Adonis's is not the standard and often false concern that had bedevilled Arab thought since its encounter with the West about reconciling "tradition" and "modernity." We are beyond this here: If anything, what we have in this short and provocative book is an obituary to *asr al Nahada* (the age of the renaissance), or what Albert Hourani called the "Liberal Age."[2]

Stripped to its essentials, Adonis's argument is that the marriage between the kind of West and modernity that the Arabs imported and the kind of *turath* (tradition) that the dominant political and cultural order in the Arab world holds up for men and women to adhere to has produced a monstrous and arid world. We have a "vast desert of imports and consumption" that has created a false image of modernity, really a large swindle, a world donning outward trappings that have nothing to do with either the Arab world as it really is or the West. "Our contemporary modernity is a mirage." The poet and the writer who succumb to this kind of temptation are doomed from the start. Try as they do to emulate the style and literary forms of an alien civilization, they produce dead works, alienated works that turn the "experience and literary forms" of one civilization into replicas of an alien world. So long as the Arab world fails to understand that there is more to the spirit of the West—its curiosity, its search for knowledge, its daring before dogma—the modernity that comes in the West's image will be a "hired" form of modernity, brought to Arab lands through "trick" or "theft."

And then there is that second false option paralyzing Arab thought, offering to rescue it from the assault of the foreigner: the unquestioned adherence to the world of the ancestors. Indeed, and this is a theme that I myself explored in *The Arab Predicament* (1981), the authority of the ancestor increases as the cultural seduction of foreign models grows more intense, as the intrusion of foreign powers into the Arab world becomes more relentless.[3] Surely, says Adonis, "authenticity" and "fidelity" do not require a slavish imitation of the ways of the elders or an insistence in the face of reality that inherited ways have an answer to modern ailments. "Authenticity is not a specific point in the past; identity does not require a return to a particular position in our history." Fidelity is more about creativity; it is retaining that spirit that moved Arabic-Islamic civilization in its more creative eras; it is making sure that the "new" emerges out of the present, that there are no "false discontinuities" with the present, no contrived breakthroughs.

The opposition of "Muslim-Arab society" to the "European-American West" is not a "human or philosophic or poetic opposition," Adonis warns his readers. It is only a "political" opposition. "Our opposition to the West should not mean its total and generic rejection; it should only entail our rejection of its colonial-ideological formation. Thus when we reject its machines and technology, this should not mean that we reject the intellectual process that produced these machines; it only means that we oppose the way this technology is dumped on us, the way it turns us into mere consumers, the way it turns our country into a large flea-market."

Care must be exercised, says Adonis, lest this false dichotomy between an "Islamic-Arab East" and an "advanced European-American West" become a warrant for backwardness and retrogression in the Arab world. Strictly speaking, he says, there is no specific east or west. Each of these two worlds has many worlds within it. There are "many worlds" within that one Western world which are more backward than anything in the east; likewise there are "small worlds of creativity and progress" within the east. Like it or not, there is something of a "world civilization" emcompassing us all. Modernity is no longer a property of a given place or people or clime. It is hard to duck or find cover or avoid this world civilization. Arab-Islamic society has no such luxury today, and there is no use pretending it does.

Real modernity begins when that false choice between the contrived world of the foreigner and the equally contrived world of the ancestor is transcended. Modernity—real and living—would have a chance when the repressed yearnings of this large and silent Arab civilization are released, when men write new things, acquire daring in the face of taboos. Then the Arabic language, freed from the hold of the past, and the equally paralyzing attempts to emulate the more glamorous European-American world, will give expression to something living and decent. Hitherto Arab thought has been timid. Insecure and on the run, there is something in it that resembles an "awe of magic"—either the magic of the foreigner or the magic of the past. Authority (*al sulta*) has always paid homage to the magic of the ancestor, persecuted those who questioned it, while at the same time falling under the sway of foreign powers. (Those "blown-away roofs" of the Arab world alluded to by Qabbani.) This "dual dependence" on the West and on the past explains the silence and the confusion and the aridity of Arab thought.

"Something in the Arab world has died," I was told by Adonis during a recent visit he made to New York to attend the PEN meeting convened in that city, its theme the imagination of the writer and the imagination of the state. Adonis was then struggling with a hard decision: he was finally giving up on Beirut to settle in France. He had endured Beirut's carnage and Beirut's breakdown for more than a decade. This was the city that had long sustained him as a poet, an essayist, and as editor of two path-breaking literary journals, *Shi'r* and *Mawaqif*. He was reluctant to leave Beirut and to let go of his literary material. He knew the sad fate of exiled writers, their alienation from new surroundings, their nostalgia for an old country that grows more distant and more abstract with time. He was worried about his distance from the Arabic language; he worried what teaching in France and its demands would do to his creativity and schedule. But there was in this uniquely gifted and sturdy man a deep sense of sorrow and resignation. Like Qabbani, he spoke of the death of Arab civilization. There comes a time, he said, when a people can no longer give. Beirut's sectarianism had broken his heart. He had seen the wilting of that brief moment of flowering in the aftermath of 1967 in which he was a leading literary figure. He had seen how all the grand ideas and all the ideological assertions had ended in carnage and in the return of Lebanese and other Arabs in Lebanon to a primitive kind of tribalism. Adonis no longer recognizes the city he knew. And for a man who delighted in words, who must be reckoned one of the greatest living Arab poets, there was in him a distinct weariness, almost a reluctance to name and describe things.

*   *   *

From the very beginning, Arab nationalism was an affair of the heart and of words, an endeavor of the intellectuals, an idea flung in the face of an Arab political order that was always fragmented and torn by all sorts of conflicts. So by the time the written and spoken word wearies of itself, by the time the usual incantations are at clear variance with stark realities, it is hard even for the most devoted to persist.

Vast stretches of the Arab and Muslim world today are slaughter-grounds. Several of its cities are either ruined or in the grip of brittle and merciless dictatorships. There is, to borrow Victor Hugo's language in *Les Miserables*, a stand-off between "egoists" and "outcasts," or put more squarely, between privilege and wrath. The former is in the saddle but precariously so. The latter, claiming on its side Islam and authenticity, emboldened by the Iranian revolution, offers rage and anger, turns politics into the realm of God and Satan and martyrology. Hardly anything grows in the middle between the old privilege and the new wrath. The tradition of an Arab-Muslim middle class holding its world together, maintaining traditions of concern and toil, living within time-honored limits, has unravelled. The windfall society of the last decade—enormous wealth on one side generating enormous resentments on the other—has claimed so many time-honored truths and limits in its way.

What the confusion of the last decade has produced is a mighty storm. The nationalism of "proper manners," which accepted the cultural assumptions of the Western nation-state model, has given way to a more ferocious rebellion. We have given this storm an Islamic label; we have dubbed it Islamic fundamentalism. And depending on the place and the circumstances we have emphasized its sectarian dimensions, pointing out the revolt of a militant form of neo-Shiism. We have been right at times in the labels we applied, wrong in other circumstances. We would have been better off if we had emphasized the elements of wrath and resentment that have given this rebellion its intensity and ferocity. We have spent too much time speaking of Islam, and not enough of those familiar sentiments that have given revolts launched from the depths of society their power in other places and times. In *Les Miserables* there is the following discourse on revolution which could explain the frenzy of Lebanon, or of Iran, or the fury of other Islamic movements:

> Of what does a revolt consist? Of everything and nothing, a spring slowly released, a fire suddenly breaking out, force operating at random, a passing breeze. The breeze stirs heads that think and minds that dream, spirits that suffer, passions that smoulder, wrongs crying out to be righted, and carries them away. . . .
>
> A revolt is a sort of whirlwind in the social atmosphere which swiftly forms in certain temperatures, and rising and travelling as it spins, uproots, crushes, and demolishes, bearing with it great and sickly spirits alike, strong men and weaklings, the tree-trunk and the wisp of straw. Woe to those it carries away no less than to those it seeks to destroy.[4]

In much of the Fertile Crescent, this revolt now waves a Shia banner. The flag of Shiism has been unfurled. And the force behind this Shia thrust is a mix of Iran's push into the Arab realm and of deep accumulated resentments within Arab society itself. But the infatuation with analyzing Shiism should be checked. In a nutshell, this militant form of Shiism is the third successor to the defeated Arab nationalism of yesterday. The first inheritor was the Palestinian movement, which knew three or four years of ascendancy in the aftermath of 1967. It, too, the Palestinian movement, insisted that it had answers to wider Arab ailments. But in Jordan, then in Lebanon, that movement had lost its direction. Then came the moment of the dominant political order in the aftermath of the October War of 1973. The deep assumptions of that era (the petro-era) were thoroughly conservative ones: man was to be a consumer, the Arab world would be de-radicalized, and there would be something of a solution in that extravagant season for the Palestinian dilemma. But that era proved to be a very short one indeed. In 1979–80, the Iranian revolution served a warrant on that period of plunder and confusion. It was apt that the era of technique and finance spawned a rebellion of wrath and anger.

The petro-era had experimented with an impossible combination: It paid homage to the *turath* (the tradition) while throwing the doors of the Arab political-cultural order wide open to the American push into the region. It had tried to have it both ways and it ultimately failed.

The third, Shia, bid has not yet run its course. But there is no evidence that it can succeed where the other two successors to Pan-Arabism had failed. The third bid will fail because so far it has added no new skills to a civilization falling behind the rest of the world in technique and productive abilities. It will fail because Shiism is the embattled faith of a minority; hurling itself against the awesome limits of Muslim history today, it is unable to peddle to others its belief in virtue and zeal— and terror.

The Shia themes of solitude and martyrdom cannot carry the day. For the mainstream of Muslim (Sunni) society the Shia passion is easy to pass off as the pent-up resentments of an aggrieved sect. So while the Shia movement is not yet a spent force, it is hard to see it carrying Arab and Muslim society along. In its better moments, this Shia movement can put an end to the quietism and withdrawal of the Shia in Arab and Muslim history. But beyond that, we are face to face with the crisis of the Arab world: weakness abroad and tyranny at home.

All three attempts to reconstruct Arab political life since 1967—the Palestinian interlude, the petro-era, the Shia movement—had in them a curious messianic element. All three, despite differences in temperament and goals, believed in the possibility of a quick fix, that long-standing problems of historical competence could be exorcised in a hurry. It was the Palestinian belief that "guerrilla warfare," or a "war of national liberation," to use the language of the late 1960s, would deliver Arab society, with all its superstitions and all its weaknesses, its finicky, complacent classes and its vanquished ones, into some bright new world. But all that was delirium. The Arab world had given the Palestinian movements yarn because it had to in the immediate aftermath of 1967. And thus when the dominant political order of states bounced back three years or so after 1967, the Jordanian army shattered the Palestinian sanctuary and its illusions. A decade or so later, the Arab world, numbed by a dizzying decade which jumbled the permissible and the impermissible, which mixed tribalism and high finance and gave the Arab world the illusory sense of a new place in the sun, left the task of dealing with the troublesome Palestinians to Ariel Sharon. By then the petro-era, with its bet on stability, on the reason of the merchant, on the American connection, had come to a disastrous end.

In the third movement, the *Mahdi* (the messiah) appears in full force— no apology, no secular cover, no Western discourse. Khomeini, the great conjurer, offering redemption, serving like some pied piper for the downtrodden, for those awaiting and seeking revenge, may have been a new phenomenon, a Prophet of the outcasts. But for all the attempts to depict him as something wholly new and unprecedented, he shared with his more "secular" predecessors the same belief in a quick fix, the tendency to wish away historic problems, the belief that passions and stout lungs, and a pristine philosophy, could provide redemption and deliverance. With Khomeini, and what he came to represent in Arab and Muslim realms, the mask falls: here for everyone to see was the failure of yesterday's generation to take in the poor, to build anything beyond some vulnerable islands of affluence and prosperity and false Westernism.

The men and women bemoaning the end of that small American enclave in West Beirut, like those bemoaning the charms of Iran under the Shah, grieve only for easier and complacent times that they themselves enjoyed. The unwashed now clamor for their own place in Arab and Muslim life. Are yesterday's liberals and professionals as blameless as they now declare themselves in exile? The young urban poor in Arab and Muslim cities brandishing weapons and doing "embarrassing" things: they were spawned by the ways of yesterday's more comfortable "national movement." The unwashed may be headed for failure. But the last ones who are entitled to deny them the right to try are the "pampered" ones who had their day and their chance and built nothing more than a complacent political order with its mix of Western pretensions and Levantine cynicism. We can't take seriously those who bemoan what it was like for them "back then." They have the history they built—and now deserve.

The books and pamphlets of Arab nationalism were the product of an innocent era. To write an obituary to Arab nationalism is not to prophesy something pretty for the Arab world. Eight years ago, a naive author such as myself could write that the demise of Pan-Arabism would bring in its train a more "normal" state system. I was only partly right and in a banal sort of way. The kind of hell that was to befall the Arab world was far beyond my wildest dreams. Arabs were then still talking and writing. Since then, in Beirut and elsewhere, they have gone on to more deadly endeavors. If a writer had a magic wand, I would call back to life the pamphleteers and dreamers of those simpler years. I would have Qabbani write of Beirut's languid evenings and of his sexual conquests. And I would have Adonis back in the Beirut of his imagination and memory. . . .

Notes

1. The poem *Balqees* was translated to English by a gifted young scholar, a former student of mine, Ms. Lisa Buttenheim.

2. Albert Hourani, *Arabic Thought in the Liberal Age* (Oxford: Oxford University Press, 1970).

3. Fouad Ajami, *The Arab Predicament* (Cambridge: Cambridge University Press, 1981).

4. Victor Hugo, *Les Miserables*, vol. 2 (Penguin ed.), pp. 187–188.

Contributors

Fouad Ajami is a professor of political science at the School of Advanced International Studies, Johns Hopkins University, Washington, D.C.

William Brown is Mission Director for the U.S. Agency for International Development in the Sudan.

Elie Chalala is a Ph.D. candidate in political science at the University of California at Los Angeles.

James A. Bill is a professor of political science at the University of Texas, Austin.

Tawfic E. Farah is president of the Middle East Research Group, Inc., of Fresno, California, and editor of its publication, *Journal of Arab Affairs.*

Saad Eddin Ibrahim is a professor of sociology at the American University in Cairo, Egypt.

Abdul-Monem Al-Mashat is a professor of political science at Cairo University, Cairo, Egypt.

Hassan Nafaa is a professor of political science at Cairo University, Cairo, Egypt.

Stewart Reiser is a professor of political science at Northeastern University, Boston, Massachusetts.

Faisal Al-Salem is a professor of political science at Kuwait University.

Paul Starr is a professor in the Department of Sociology and Anthropology at Auburn University, Auburn, Alabama.

Index